Arctic Explorations

in

1853, 1854, 1855

Elisha Kent Kane

In two volumes

Volume I

Arno Press & The New York Times
New York * 1971

PHYSICIAN TRAVELERS

Editor
ROBERT M. GOLDWYN, M.D.

This book is reprinted from a copy in the
Francis A. Countway Library of Medicine

Library of Congress Catalog Card No. 74-115615
ISBN 0-405-01735-9
ISBN for complete set 0-405-01710-3

Manufactured in the United States of America, 1971

Physician Travelers

About the Author

ELISHA KENT KANE was thirty years old when he made his first Arctic expedition; four years later he was a national hero; two years after that, he was dead.

Born in 1820 into a prominent Philadelphia family, Kane later entered the University of Virginia, where he studied geology, natural history, and mathematics in preparation for a career in civil engineering. Recurring rheumatic fever with endocarditis forced him to leave school. He then decided upon medicine and obtained his degree from the University of Pennsylvania in 1842, graduating first in his class. Instead of establishing himself as a practitioner, he joined the Navy as an assistant-surgeon and traveled to China, Brazil, India, Ceylon, Egypt, Europe, and the Philippines.

In 1847, after a brief convalescence from malaria contracted in South America, Kane participated in the Mexican War and distinguished himself by saving the life of an enemy guerrilla, the son of one of the Mexican generals.

In 1850, an American Relief Expedition was formed to help search for the lost British Polar Expedition of 1845 commanded by Sir John Franklin. Kane volunteered and was made senior medical officer. After 15 months, only Franklin's abandoned winter quarters could be located. Kane returned to plan his own Arctic expedition and also wrote about the search for Franklin (*The U. S. Grinnell Expedition in Search of Sir John Franklin,* New York, 1854).

The events of the next two and a half years are well-documented and presented dramatically in Kane's *Arctic Explorations*. His major accomplishments consisted of having charted more than seven hundred miles of the North West Coast of Greenland and, perhaps more important, the development of practical methods of polar travel and survival which future explorers, such as Perry, were to use. Kane studied and adopted the ways of the Eskimo: he ate raw seal and walrus meat (antiscorbutic), wore furs, used dog sleds, and lived in igloos. His tenacity and accomplishments seem more remarkable in view of his constant struggle against a rheumatic heart.

After his return from the Arctic, Kane received many honors throughout the world. Pleased at the recognition but weakened by poor health, he went to Cuba to convalesce. Shortly after his arrival in Havana, he died at the age of thirty-six.

R. M. G.

ARCTIC EXPLORATIONS

IN THE YEARS 1853, '54, '55

BY

ELISHA KENT KANE, M. D., U. S. N.

VOL. I.

PHILADELPHIA

CHILDS AND PETERSON,

124 ARCH STREET.

1856.

J. Watt.

ELISHA KENT KANE, M. D., U. S. N.

ARCTIC
EXPLORATIONS:

The Second Grinnell Expedition

IN SEARCH OF

SIR JOHN FRANKLIN,

1853, '54, '55.

BY

ELISHA KENT KANE, M.D., U.S.N.

ILLUSTRATED BY UPWARDS OF THREE HUNDRED ENGRAVINGS,

From Sketches by the Author.

THE STEEL PLATES EXECUTED UNDER THE SUPERINTENDENCE OF J. M. BUTLER,
THE WOOD ENGRAVINGS BY VAN INGEN & SNYDER.

VOL. I.

PHILADELPHIA:
CHILDS & PETERSON, 124 ARCH STREET.
J. B. LIPPINCOTT & CO., 20 N. FOURTH ST.
BOSTON: PHILLIPS, SAMPSON & CO., 13 WINTER STREET.
NEW YORK: G. P. PUTNAM & CO., 321 BROADWAY.
CINCINNATI: APPLEGATE & CO., 48 MAIN STREET.
1856.

STEREOTYPED BY L. JOHNSON & CO.
PHILADELPHIA.
PRINTED BY J. B. LIPPINCOTT & CO.

PUBLISHERS' ADVERTISEMENT.

Having purchased the stereotype plates of the "FIRST GRINNELL EXPEDITION," by Dr. Kane, we have improved it by the addition of many new illustrations, together with a fine steel portrait of Sir John Franklin, and a sketch of his life, extracted from Allibone's forthcoming Dictionary of Literature and Authors.

We will hereafter issue the volume in a style to correspond with the present work.

CHILDS & PETERSON.

Philadelphia, September, 1856.

PREFACE.

THIS book is not a record of scientific investigations.

While engaged, under the orders of the Navy Department, in arranging and elaborating the results of the late expedition to the Arctic seas, I have availed myself of the permission of the Secretary to connect together the passages of my journal that could have interest for the general reader, and to publish them as a narrative of the adventures of my party. I have attempted very little else.

The engravings with which my very liberal publishers have illustrated it, will certainly add greatly to any value the text may possess. Although largely, and, in some cases exclusively, indebted for their interest to the artistic skill of Mr. Hamilton, they are, with scarcely an exception, from sketches made on the spot.

E. K. K.

PHILADELPHIA, *July* 4, 1856.

CONTENTS.

7

CHAPTER XIII.

PAGE

CHAPTER XIV.

CHAPTER XV.

CHAPTER XVI.

CHAPTER XVII.

CHAPTER XVIII.

CHAPTER XXIV.

CHAPTER XXV.

CHAPTER XXVI.

CHAPTER XXVII.

CHAPTER XXVIII.

CHAPTER XXIX.

12 CONTENTS.

GLOSSARY OF ARCTIC TERMS.

Bay-ice, ice of recent formation, so called because forming most readily in bays and sheltered spots.

Berg, (see Iceberg.)

Beset, so enclosed by floating ice as to be unable to navigate.

Bight, an indentation.

Blasting, breaking the ice by gunpowder introduced in canisters.

Blink, (see Ice-blink.)

Bore, to force through loose or recent ice by sails or steam.

Brash, ice broken up into small fragments.

Calf, detached masses from berg or glacier, rising suddenly to the surface.

Crow's nest, a look-out place attached to the top-gallant-masthead.

Dock, an opening in the ice, artificial or natural, offering protection.

Drift ice, detached ice in motion.

Field-ice, an extensive surface of floating ice.

Fiord, an abrupt opening in the coast-line, admitting the sea.

Fire-hole, a well dug in the ice as a safeguard in case of fire.

Floe, a detached portion of a field.

Glacier, a mass of ice derived from the atmosphere, sometimes abutting upon the sea.

Hummocks, ridges of broken ice formed by collision of fields.

Ice-anchor, a hook or grapnel adapted to take hold upon ice.

13

Ice-belt, a continued margin of ice, which in high northern latitudes adheres to the coast above the ordinary level of the sea.

Iceberg, a large floating mass of ice detached from a glacier.

Ice-blink, a peculiar appearance of the atmosphere over distant ice.

Ice-chisel, a long chisel for cutting holes in ice.

Ice-face, the abutting face of the ice-belt.

Ice-foot, the Danish name for the limited ice-belt of the more southern coast.

Ice-hook, a small ice-anchor.

Ice-raft, ice, whether field, floe, or detached belt, transporting foreign matter.

Ice-table, a flat surface of ice.

Land-ice, floes or fields adhering to the coast or included between headlands.

Lane or *lead*, a navigable opening in the ice.

Nip, the condition of a vessel pressed upon by the ice on both sides

Old ice, ice of more than a season's growth.

Pack, a large area of floating ices driven together more or less closely

Polynia, a Russian term for an open-water space.

Rue-raddy, a shoulder-belt to drag by.

Tide-hole, a well sunk in the ice for the purpose of observing tides.

Tracking, towing along a margin of ice.

Water-sky, a peculiar appearance of the sky over open water.

Young ice, ice formed before the setting in of winter; recent ice.

ARCTIC EXPLORATIONS.

CHAPTER I.

ORGANIZATION—PLAN OF OPERATIONS—COMPLEMENT—EQUIPMENT
—ST. JOHN'S.

In the month of December, 1852, I had the honor
of receiving special orders from the Secretary of the
Navy, to "conduct an expedition to the Arctic seas in
search of Sir John Franklin."

I had been engaged, under Lieutenant De Haven, in
the Grinnell Expedition, which sailed from the United
States in 1850 on the same errand; and I had occupied myself for some months after our return in maturing the scheme of a renewed effort to rescue the
missing party, or at least to resolve the mystery of its
fate. Mr. Grinnell, with a liberality altogether characteristic, had placed the Advance, in which I sailed
before, at my disposal for the cruise; and Mr. Peabody, of London, the generous representative of many
American sympathies, had proffered his aid largely
toward her outfit. The Geographical Society of New
York, the Smithsonian Institution, the American Phi-

losophical Society,—I name them in the order in
which they announced their contributions,—and a
number of scientific associations and friends of science
besides, had come forward to help me; and by their
aid I managed to secure a better outfit for purposes
of observation than would otherwise have been possible to a party so limited in numbers and absorbed
in other objects.

Ten of our little party belonged to the United
States Navy, and were attached to my command by
orders from the Department; the others were shipped
by me for the cruise, and at salaries entirely dispro-
portioned to their services: all were volunteers. We
did not sail under the rules that govern our national
ships; but we had our own regulations, well considered and announced beforehand, and rigidly adhered
to afterward through all the vicissitudes of the expedition. These included—first, absolute subordination
to the officer in command or his delegate; second,
abstinence from all intoxicating liquors, except when
dispensed by special order; third, the habitual disuse
of profane language. We had no other laws.

I had developed our plan of search in a paper
read before the Geographical Society. It was based
upon the probable extension of the land-masses of
Greenland to the Far North,—a fact at that time not
verified by travel, but sustained by the analogies of
physical geography. Greenland, though looked upon
as a congeries of islands connected by interior glaciers,
was still to be regarded as a peninsula whose forma-

tion recognised the same general laws as other peninsulas having a southern trend.

From the alternating altitudes of its mountain-ranges, continued without depression throughout a meridional line of nearly eleven hundred miles, I inferred that this chain must extend very far to the north, and that Greenland might not improbably approach nearer the Pole than any other known land.

Believing, then, in such an extension of this peninsula, and feeling that the search for Sir John Franklin would be best promoted by a course that might lead most directly to the open sea of which I had inferred the existence, and that the approximation of the meridians would make access to the West as easy from Northern Greenland as from Wellington Channel, and access to the East far more easy,—feeling, too, that the highest protruding headland would be most likely to afford some traces of the lost party,—I named, as the inducements in favor of my scheme,—

1. Terra firma as the basis of our operations, obviating the capricious character of ice-travel.

2. A due northern line, which, throwing aside the influences of terrestrial radiation, would lead soonest to the open sea, should such exist.

3. The benefit of the fan-like abutment of land, on the north face of Greenland, to check the ice in the course of its southern or equatorial drift, thus obviating the great drawback of Parry in his attempts to reach the Pole by the Spitzbergen Sea.

4. Animal life to sustain travelling parties.

5. The co-operation of the Esquimaux; settlements of these people having been found as high as Whale Sound, and probably extending still farther along the coast.

We were to pass up Baffin s Bay therefore to its most northern attainable point; and thence, pressing on toward the Pole as far as boats or sledges could carry us, examine the coast-lines for vestiges of the lost party.

All hands counted, we were seventeen at the time of sailing. Another joined us a few days afterward; so that the party under my command, as it reached the coast of Greenland, consisted of

HENRY BROOKS, First Officer.   ISAAC I. HAYES, M.D., Surgeon.
JOHN WALL WILSON,   AUGUST SONTAG, Astronomer.
JAMES McGARY,   AMOS BONSALL,
GEORGE RILEY,   GEORGE STEPHENSON,
WILLIAM MORTON,   GEORGE WHIPPLE,
CHRISTIAN OHLSEN,   WILLIAM GODFREY.
HENRY GOODFELLOW,   JOHN BLAKE,
              JEFFERSON BAKER,
              PETER SCHUBERT,
              THOMAS HICKEY.

Two of these, Brooks and Morton, had been my associates in the first expedition; gallant and trustworthy men, both of them, as ever shared the fortunes or claimed the gratitude of a commander.

The Advance had been thoroughly tried in many encounters with the Arctic ice. She was carefully inspected, and needed very little to make her all a seaman could wish. She was a hermaphrodite brig of one hundred and forty-four tons, intended originally for carrying heavy castings from an iron-foundry, but strengthened afterward with great skill and at large expense. She was a good sailer, and easily managed. We had five boats; one of them a metallic life-boat, the gift of the maker, Mr. Francis.

Our equipment was simple. It consisted of little else than a quantity of rough boards, to serve for housing over the vessel in winter, some tents of India-rubber and canvas, of the simplest description, and several carefully-built sledges, some of them on a model furnished me by the kindness of the British Admiralty, others of my own devising.

Our store of provisions was chosen with little regard to luxury. We took with us some two thousand pounds of well-made pemmican, a parcel of Borden's meat-biscuit, some packages of an exsiccated potato, resembling Edwards's, some pickled cabbage, and a liberal quantity of American dried fruits and vegetables; besides these, we had the salt beef and pork of the navy ration, hard biscuit, and flour. A very moderate supply of liquors, with the ordinary *et ceteras* of an Arctic cruiser, made up the diet-list. I hoped to procure some fresh provisions in addition before reaching the upper coast of Greenland; and I carried some barrels of malt, with a compact apparatus for brewing.

We had a moderate wardrobe of woollens, a full

supply of knives, needles, and other articles for barter, a large, well-chosen library, and a valuable set of instruments for scientific observations.

We left New York on the 30th of May, 1853, escorted by several noble steamers; and, passing slowly on to the Narrows amid salutes and cheers of farewell, cast our brig off from the steam-tug and put to sea.

It took us eighteen days to reach St. John's, Newfoundland. The Governor, Mr. Hamilton, a brother of the Secretary of the Admiralty, received us with a hearty English welcome; and all the officials, indeed all the inhabitants, vied with each other in efforts to advance our views. I purchased here a stock of fresh beef, which, after removing the bones and tendons, we compressed into rolls by wrapping it closely with twine, according to the nautical process of *marling*, and hung it up in the rigging.

After two days we left this thriving and hospitable city; and, with a noble team of Newfoundland dogs on board, the gift of Governor Hamilton, headed our brig for the coast of Greenland.

We reached Baffin's Bay without incident. We took deep-sea-soundings as we approached its axis, and found a reliable depth of nineteen hundred fathoms: an interesting result, as it shows that the ridge which is known to extend between Ireland and Newfoundland in the bed of the Atlantic is depressed as it passes farther to the north. A few days more found us off the coast of Greenland, making our way toward Fiskernaes.

FISKERNAES.

CHAPTER II.

FISKERNAES—THE FISHERY—MR. LASSEN—HANS CRISTIAN—
LICHTENFELS—SUKKERTOPPEN.

We entered the harbor of Fiskernaes on the 1st of
July, amid the clamor of its entire population, assembled on the rocks to greet us. This place has an en-
viable reputation for climate and health. Except perhaps Holsteinberg, it is the dryest station upon the
coast; and the springs, which well through the mosses,
frequently remain unfrozen throughout the year.[1]

The sites of the different Greenland colonies seem
to have been chosen with reference to their trading
resources. The southern posts around Julianshaab and

21

Fredericstahl supply the Danish market with the valued
furs of the saddle-back seal; Sukkertoppen and Holsteinberg with reindeer-skins; Disco and the northern
districts with the seal and other oils. The little settlement of Fiskernaes rejoices in its codfish, as well as
the other staples of the upper coast. It is situated on
Fisher's Fiord, some eight miles from the open bay,
and is approached by an island-studded channel of
moderate draught.

OOMIAK, OR WOMEN'S BOAT, FISHING—FISKERNAES

We saw the codfish here in all the stages of preparation for the table and the market; the stockfish, dried
in the open air, without salt; crapefish, salted and
pressed; fresh-fish, a *lucus a non lucendo*, as salt as a
Mediterranean anchovy: we laid in supplies of all of
them. The exemption of Fiskernaes from the continued fogs, and its free exposure to the winds as they
draw up the fiord, make it a very favorable place for
drying cod. The backbone is cut out, with the exception of about four inches near the tail; the body expanded and simply hung upon a frame: the head, a

luxury neglected with us, is carefully dried in a separate piece.

Seal and shark oils are the next in importance among the staples of Fiskernaes.[2] The *spec* or blubber is purchased from the natives with the usual articles of exchange, generally coffee and tobacco, and rudely *tried out* by exposure in vats or hot expression in iron boilers. None of the nicer processes which economy and despatch have introduced at St. John's seem to have reached this out-of-the-way coast. Even the cod-livers are given to the dogs, or thrown into the general vat.

We found Mr. Lassen, the superintending official of the Danish Company, a hearty, single-minded man, fond of his wife, his children, and his pipe. The visit of our brig was, of course, an incident to be marked in the simple annals of his colony; and, even before I had shown him my official letter from the Court of Denmark, he had most hospitably proffered every thing for our accommodation. We became his guests, and interchanged presents with him before our departure; this last transaction enabling me to say, with confidence, that the inner fiords produce noble salmon-trout, and that the reindeer-tongue, a recognised delicacy in the old and new Arctic continents, is justly appreciated at Fiskernaes.

Feeling that our dogs would require fresh provisions, which could hardly be spared from our supplies on shipboard, I availed myself of Mr. Lassen's influence to obtain an Esquimaux hunter for our party. He

recommended to me one Hans Cristian, a boy of nineteen, as an expert with the kayak and javelin; and
after Hans had given me a touch of his quality by
spearing a bird on the wing, I engaged him. He was
fat, good-natured, and, except under the excitements
of the hunt, as stolid and unimpressible as one of our
own Indians. He stipulated that, in addition to his

PORTRAIT OF HANS.

very moderate wages, I should leave a couple of barrels
of bread and fifty-two pounds of pork with his mother;
and I became munificent in his eyes when I added the
gift of a rifle and a new kayak. We found him very
useful; our dogs required his services as a caterer, and
our own table was more than once dependent on his
energies.

J. Hamilton.

Engraved at J M Butler's establishment 84 Chestnut St.

A W Graham.

FISKENAES FROM THE GOVERNORS HOUSE,

SOUTH GREENLAND

(From a sketch by Dr. Kane.)

No one can know so well as an Arctic voyager the value of foresight. My conscience has often called for the exercise of it, but my habits make it an effort. I can hardly claim to be provident, either by impulse or education. Yet, for some of the deficiencies of our outfit I ought not, perhaps, to hold myself responsible. Our stock of fresh meats was too small, and we had no preserved vegetables: but my personal means were limited; and I could not press more severely than a strict necessity exacted upon the unquestioning liberality of my friends.

While we were beating out of the fiord of Fiskernaes, I had an opportunity of visiting Lichtenfels, the ancient seat of the Greenland congregations, and one of the three Moravian settlements. I had read much of the history of its founders; and it was with feelings almost of devotion, that I drew near the scene their labors had consecrated.[3]

As we rowed into the shadow of its rock-embayed cove, every thing was so desolate and still, that we might have fancied ourselves outside the world of life; even the dogs—those querulous, never-sleeping sentinels of the rest of the coast—gave no signal of our approach. Presently, a sudden turn around a projecting cliff brought into view a quaint old Silesian mansion, bristling with irregularly-disposed chimneys, its black overhanging roof studded with dormer windows and crowned with an antique belfry.

We were met, as we landed, by a couple of grave ancient men in sable jackets and close velvet skull-

caps, such as Vandyke or Rembrandt himself might
have painted, who gave us a quiet but kindly welcome.
All inside of the mansion-house—the furniture, the
matron, even the children—had the same time-sobered
look. The sanded floor was dried by one of those huge

MORAVIAN SETTLEMENT OF LICHTENFELS.

white-tiled stoves, which have been known for genera-
tions in the north of Europe; and the stiff-backed
chairs were evidently coeval with the first days of the
settlement. The heavy-built table in the middle of
the room was soon covered with its simple offerings of
hospitality; and we sat around to talk of the lands we
had come from and the changing wonders of the times.

We learned that the house dated back as far as the days of Matthew Stach; built, no doubt, with the beams that floated so providentially to the shore some twenty-five years after the first landing of Egedé; and that it had been the home of the brethren who now greeted us, one for twenty-nine and the other twenty-seven years. The "Congregation Hall" was within the building, cheerless now with its empty benches; a couple of French horns, all that I could associate with the gladsome piety of the Moravians, hung on each side the altar. Two dwelling-rooms, three chambers, and a kitchen, all under the same roof, made up the one structure of Lichtenfels.

Its kind-hearted inmates were not without intelligence and education. In spite of the formal cut of their dress, and something of the stiffness that belongs to a protracted solitary life, it was impossible not to recognise, in their demeanor and course of thought, the liberal spirit that has always characterized their church. Two of their "children," they said, had "gone to God" last year with the scurvy; yet they hesitated at receiving a scanty supply of potatoes as a present from our store.

We lingered along the coast for the next nine days, baffled by calms and light adverse winds; and it was only on the 10th of July that we reached the settlement of Sukkertoppen.

The Sukkertop, or Sugar-loaf, a noted landmark, is a wild isolated peak, rising some 3000 feet from the sea. The little colony which nestles at its base occupies a rocky gorge, so narrow and broken that a stairway connects the detached groups of huts, and the tide, as it rises, converts a part of the groundplot into a temporary island.

Of all the Danish settlements on this coast, it struck me as the most picturesque. The rugged cliffs seemed to blend with the grotesque structures about their base. The trim red and white painted frame mansion, which, in virtue of its green blinds and flagstaff, asserted the

APPROACH TO SUKKERTOPPEN.

gubernatorial dignity at Fiskernaes, was here a lowly, dingy compound of tarred roof and heavy gables. The dwellings of the natives, the natives themselves, and the wild packs of dogs that crowded the beach, were all in keeping. It was after twelve at night when we came into port; and the peculiar light of the Arctic summer at this hour,—which reminds one of the effect of an eclipse, so unlike our orthodox twilight,—bathed every thing in gray but the northern background—an Alpine chain standing out against a blazing crimson sky.

Sukkertoppen is a principal depôt for reindeer-skins;

and the natives were at this season engaged in their summer hunt, collecting them. Four thousand had already been sent to Denmark, and more were on hand. I bought a stock of superior quality for fifty cents a piece. These furs are valuable for their lightness and warmth. They form the ordinary upper clothing of both sexes;[4]the seal being used only for pantaloons and for waterproof dresses. I purchased also all that I could get of the crimped seal-skin boots or moccasins, an admirable article of walking gear, much more secure against the wet than any made by sewing. I would have added to my stock of fish; but the cod had not yet reached this part of the coast, and would not for some weeks.

Bidding good-bye to the governor, whose hospitality we had shared liberally, we put to sea on Saturday, the 10th, beating to the northward and westward in the teeth of a heavy gale.

CHAPTER III.

COAST OF GREENLAND — SWARTE-HUK — LAST DANISH OUTPOSTS — MELVILLE BAY — IN THE ICE — BEARS — BERGS — ANCHOR TO A BERG — MIDNIGHT SUNSHINE.

THE lower and middle coast of Greenland has been visited by so many voyagers, and its points of interest have been so often described, that I need not dwell upon them. From the time we left Sukkertoppen, we had the usual delays from fogs and adverse currents, and did not reach the neighborhood of Wilcox Point, which defines Melville Bay, until the 27th of July.

On the 16th we passed the promontory of Swarte-huk, and were welcomed the next day at Proven by my old friend Christiansen, the superintendent, and found his family much as I left them three years before. Frederick, his son, had married a native woman, and added a summer tent, a half-breed boy, and a Danish rifle to his stock of valuables. My former patient, Anna, had united fortunes with a fat-faced Esquimaux, and was the mother of a chubby little girl. Madame Christiansen, who counted all these and so many others as her happy progeny, was hearty

and warm-hearted as ever. She led the household in
sewing up my skins into various serviceable garments;
and I had the satisfaction, before I left, of completing
my stock of furs for our sledge parties.

While our brig passed, half sailing, half drifting, up
the coast, I left her under the charge of Mr. Brooks,

SWARTE-HUK—BLACK HEAD.

and set out in the whale-boat to make my purchases of
dogs among the natives. Gathering them as we went
along from the different settlements, we reached Upernavik, the resting-place of the Grinnell Expedition in
1851 after its winter drift, and for a couple of days
shared, as we were sure to do, the generous hospitality
of Governor Flaischer.

Still coasting along, we passed in succession the Esquimaux settlement of Kingatok, the Kettle,—a mountain-top so named from the resemblances of its profile,—and finally Yotlik, the farthest point of colonization; beyond which, save the sparse headlands of the charts, the coast may be regarded as unknown. Then, inclining more directly toward the north, we ran close to the Baffin Islands,—clogged with ice when I saw them three years before, now entirely clear,—sighted the landmark which is known as the Horse's Head, and, passing the Duck Islands, where the Advance grounded in 1851, bore away for Wilcox Point.[5]

We stood lazily along the coast, with alternations of perfect calm and off-shore breezes, generally from the south or east; but on the morning of the 27th of July, as we neared the entrance of Melville Bay, one of those heavy ice-fogs, which I have described in my former narrative as characteristic of this region, settled around us. We could hardly see across the decks, and yet were sensible of the action of currents carrying us we knew not where. By the time the sun had scattered the mist, Wilcox Point was to the south of us; and our little brig, now fairly in the bay, stood a fair chance of drifting over toward the Devil's Thumb, which then bore east of north. The bergs which infest this region, and which have earned for it among the whalers the title of the "Bergy Hole," showed themselves all around us: we had come in among them in the fog.

It was a whole day's work, towing with both boats; but toward evening we had succeeded in crawling off shore, and were doubly rewarded for our labor with a wind. I had observed with surprise, while we were floating near the coast, that the land ice was already broken and decayed; and I was aware, from what I had read, as well as what I had learned from whalers and observed myself of the peculiarities of this navigation, that the in-shore track was in consequence beset with difficulty and delays. I made up my mind at once. I would stand to the westward until arrested by the pack, and endeavor to *double* Melville Bay by an outside passage. A chronicle of this transit, condensed from my log-book, will have interest for navigators :—

"July 28, Thursday, 6 A.M.—Made the offsetting streams of the pack, and bore up to the northward and eastward; heading for Cape York in tolerably free water.

"July 29, Friday, 9½ A.M.—Made loose ice, and very rotten; the tables nearly destroyed, and much broken by wave action: water-sky to the northward. Entered this ice, intending to work to the northward and eastward, above or about Sabine Islands, in search of the northeastern land-ice. The breeze freshened off shore, breaking up and sending out the floes, the leads rapidly closing. Fearing a besetment, I determined to fasten to an iceberg; and after eight hours of very heavy labor, warping, heaving, and planting ice-anchors, succeeded in effecting it.

"We had hardly a breathing spell, before we were startled by a set of loud crackling sounds above us; and small fragments of ice not larger than a walnut began to dot the water like the first drops of a summer shower. The indications were too plain: we had barely time to cast off before the face of the berg fell in ruins, crashing like near artillery.

FASTENED TO AN ICEBERG.

"Our position in the mean time had been critical, gale blowing off the shore, and the floes closing and scudding rapidly. We lost some three hundred and sixty fathoms of whale line, which were caught in the floes and had to be cut away to release us from the drift. It was a hard night for boatwork, particularly with those of the party who were taking their first lessons in floe navigation.

"July 30, Saturday.—Again moored alongside of an iceberg. The wind off shore, but hauling to the southward, with much free water.

"12 M.—The fog too dense to see more than a quarter of a mile ahead; occasional glimpses through it show no practicable leads. Land to the northeast very rugged: I do not recognise its marks. Two lively bears seen about 2 A. M. The 'Red Boat,' with Petersen and Hayes, got one; I took one of the quarter-boats, and shot the other.

"Holding on for clearer weather.

"July 31, Sunday.—Our open water beginning to fill up very fast with loose ice from the south, went around the edges of the lake in my gig, to hunt for a more favorable spot for the brig; and, after five hours' hard heaving, we succeeded in changing our fasts to another berg, quite near the free water. In our present position, the first change must, I think, liberate us. In one hour after we reached it, the place we left was consolidated into pack. We now lie attached to a low and safe iceberg, only two miles from the open sea, which is rapidly widening toward us under the influence of the southerly winds.

"We had a rough time in working to our present quarters, in what the whalers term an open hole. We drove into a couple of bergs, carried away our jib-boom and shrouds, and destroyed one of our quarter-boats.

"August 1, Monday.—Beset thoroughly with drifting ice, small rotten floe-pieces. But for our berg, we would now be carried to the south; as it is, we drift with it to the north and east.

"2 A. M.—The continued pressure against our berg has begun to affect it; and, like the great floe all around us,

MELVILLE BAY.

it has taken up its line of march toward the south. At the risk of being entangled, I ordered a light line to be carried out to a much larger berg, and, after four hours' labor, made fast to it securely. This berg is a moving breakwater, and of gigantic proportions: it keeps its course steadily toward the north, while the loose ice drifts by on each side, leaving a wake of black water for a mile behind us.

"Our position last night, by midnight altitude of the sun, gave us 75° 27'; to-day at noon, with a more reliable horizon, we made 75° 37'; showing that, in spite of all embarrassments, we still move to the north. We are, however, nearer than I could wish to the land,—a blank wall of glacier.

"About 10 P. M. the immediate danger was past; and, espying a lead to the northeast, we got under weigh, and pushed over in spite of the drifting trash. The men worked with a will, and we bored through the floes in excellent style."

On our road we were favored with a gorgeous spectacle, which hardly any excitement of peril could have made us overlook. The midnight sun came out over the northern crest of the great berg, our late "fast friend," kindling variously-colored fires on every part of its surface, and making the ice around us one great resplendency of gemwork, blazing carbuncles, and rubies and molten gold.

CHAPTER IV.

BORING THE FLOES — SUCCESSFUL PASSAGE THROUGH MELVILLE
BAY — ICE NAVIGATION — PASSAGE OF THE MIDDLE PACK — THE
NORTH WATER.

OUR brig went crunching through all this jewelry;
and, after a tortuous progress of five miles, arrested
here and there by tongues which required the saw and
ice-chisels, fitted herself neatly between two floes. Here
she rested till toward morning, when the leads opened
again, and I was able, from the crow's-nest, to pick our
way to a larger pool some distance ahead. In this we
beat backward and forward, like China fish seeking
an outlet from a glass jar, till the fog caught us again;
and so the day ended.

"August 3, Wednesday.—The day did not promise
well; but as the wind was blowing in feeble airs from
the north-northwest, I thought it might move the ice,
and sent out the boats for a tow. But, after they had
had a couple of hours of unprofitable work, the breeze
freshened, and the floes opened enough to allow us to
beat through them. Every thing now depended upon
practical ice knowledge; and, as I was not willing to

trust any one else in selecting the leads for our course, I have spent the whole day with McGary at mast-head,—a somewhat confined and unfavorable preparation for a journal entry.

"I am much encouraged, however; this off-shore wind is favoring our escape. The icebergs too have assisted us to hold our own against the rapid passage of the broken ice to the south; and since the larger floes have opened into leads, we have nothing to do but to follow

THE NORTH WATER.

them carefully and boldly. As for the ice-necks, and prongs, and rafts, and tongues, the capstan and windlass have done a great deal to work us through them; but a great deal more, a brave headway and our little brig's hard head of oak.

"Midnight.—We are clear of the bay and its myriads of discouragements. The North Water, our highway to Smith's Sound, is fairly ahead.

"It is only eight days ago that we made Wilcox

Point, and seven since we fairly left the inside track of the whalers, and made our push for the west. I did so, not without full consideration of the chances. Let me set down what my views were and are."

The indentation known as Melville Bay is protected by its northern and northeastern coast from the great ice and current drifts which follow the axis of Baffin's Bay. The interior of the country which bounds upon it is the seat of extensive glaciers, which are constantly shedding off icebergs of the largest dimensions. The greater bulk of these is below the water-line, and the depth to which they sink when floating subjects them to the action of the deeper sea currents, while their broad surface above the water is of course acted on by the wind. It happens, therefore, that they are found not unfrequently moving in different directions from the floes around them, and preventing them for a time from freezing into a united mass. Still, in the late winter, when the cold has thoroughly set in, Melville Bay becomes a continuous field of ice, from Cape York to the Devil's Thumb.

On the return of milder weather, the same causes renew their action; and that portion of the ice which is protected from the outside drift, and entangled among the icebergs that crowd the bay, remains permanent long after that which is outside is in motion. Step by step, as the year advances, its outer edge breaks off; yet its inner curve frequently remains unbroken through the entire summer. This is the "fast ice" of the whalers, so important to their progress in the earlier

portions of the season; for, however it may be encroached upon by storms or currents, they can generally find room to *track* their vessels along its solid
margin; or if the outside ice, yielding to off-shore
winds, happens to recede, the interval of water between the fast and the drift allows them not unfrequently to use their sails.

It is therefore one of the whalers' canons of navigation, which they hold to most rigidly, to follow the
shore. But it is obvious that this applies only to the
early periods of the Arctic season, when the land ice of
the inner bay is comparatively unbroken, as in May or
June, or part of July, varying of course with the circumstances. Indeed, the bay is seldom traversed except in these months, the northwest fisheries of Pond's
Bay, and the rest, ceasing to be of value afterward.
Later in the summer, the inner ice breaks up into large
floes, moving with wind and tide, that embarrass the
navigator, misleading him into the notion that he is
attached to his "fast," when in reality he is accompanying the movements of an immense floating ice-
field.

I have been surprised sometimes that our national
ships of discovery and search have not been more
generally impressed by these views. Whether the
season has been mild or severe, the ice fast and solid,
or broken and in drift, they have followed in August
the same course which the whalers do in June, running their vessels into the curve of the bay in search
of the fast ice which had disappeared a month before,

and involving themselves in a labyrinth of floes. It
was thus the Advance was caught in her second season, under Captain De Haven; while the Prince Albert,
leaving us, worked a successful passage to the west.
So too the North Star, in 1849, was carried to the
northward, and hopelessly entangled there. Indeed, it
is the common story of the disasters and delays that
we read of in the navigation of these regions.

Now I felt sure, from the known openness of the
season of 1852 and the probable mildness of the following winter, that we could scarcely hope to make
use of the land ice for tracking, or to avail ourselves
of leads along its margin by canvas. And this opinion
was confirmed by the broken and rotten appearance
of the floes during our coastwise drift at the Duck
Islands. I therefore deserted the inside track of the
whalers, and stood to the westward, until we made the
first streams of the middle pack; and then, skirting
the pack to the northward, headed in slowly for the
middle portion of the bay above Sabine Islands. My
object was to double, as it were, the loose and drifting
ice that had stood in my way, and, reaching Cape
York, as nearly as might be, trust for the remainder
of my passage to warping and tracking by the heavy
floes. We succeeded, not without some laborious
boring and serious risks of entanglement among the
broken icefields. But we managed, in every instance,
to combat this last form of difficulty by attaching our
vessel to large icebergs, which enabled us to hold our
own, however swiftly the surface floes were pressing

by us to the south. Four days of this scarcely varied yet exciting navigation brought us to the extended fields of the pack, and a fortunate northwester opened a passage for us through them. We are now in the North Water. [6]

CHAPTER V.

My diary continues:—

"We passed the 'Crimson Cliffs' of Sir John Ross in
the forenoon of August 5th. The patches of red snow,
from which they derive their name, could be seen
clearly at the distance of ten miles from the coast. It
had a fine deep rose hue, not at all like the brown
stain which I noticed when I was here before. All the
gorges and ravines in which the snows had lodged were
deeply tinted with it. I had no difficulty now in justi-
fying the somewhat poetical nomenclature which Sir
John Franklin applied to this locality; for if the snowy
surface were more diffused, as it is no doubt earlier in
the season, crimson would be the prevailing color.

"Late at night we passed Conical Rock, the most
insulated and conspicuous landmark of this coast; and,
still later, Wolstenholme and Saunder's Islands, and
Oomenak, the place of the 'North Star's' winter-quar-

ters:—an admirable day's run; and so ends the 5th of August. We are standing along, with studding-sails set, and open water before us, fast nearing our scene of labor. We have already got to work sewing up blanket bags and preparing sledges for our campaignings on the ice."

We reached Hakluyt Island in the course of the next day. I have only this wood-cut to give an idea of its

HAKLUYT POINT, FROM NORTH-NORTHWEST.

northern face. The tall spire, probably of gneiss, rises six hundred feet above the water-level, and is a valuable landmark for very many miles around. We were destined to become familiar with it before leaving this region. Both it and Northumberland, to the southeast of it, afforded studies of color that would have rewarded an artist. The red snow was diversified with large surfaces of beautifully-green mosses and alopecurus,[7]and where the sandstone was bare, it threw in a rich shade of brown.

The coast to the north of Cape Atholl is of broken greenstone, in terraces. Nearing Hakluyt Island, the truncated and pyramidal shapes of these rocks may still be recognised in the interior; but the coast presents a coarse red sandstone, which continues well characterized as far as Cape Saumarez. The nearly horizontal strata of the sandstone thus exhibited contrast conspicuously with the snow which gathers upon their exposed ledges. In fact, the parallelism and distinctness of the lines of white and black would have dissatisfied a lover of the picturesque. Porphyritic rocks, however, occasionally broke their too great uniformity; occasionally, too, the red snow showed its colors; and at intervals of very few miles—indeed, wherever the disrupted masses offered a passage-way—glaciers were seen descending toward the water's edge. All the back country appeared one great rolling distance of glacier.

"August 6, Saturday.—Cape Alexander and Cape Isabella, the headlands of Smith's Sound, are now in sight; and, in addition to these indications of our progress toward the field of search, a marked swell has set in after a short blow from the northward, just such as might be looked for from the action of the wind upon an open water-space beyond.

"Whatever it may have been when Captain Inglefield saw it a year ago, the aspect of this coast is now most uninviting.[8] As we look far off to the west, the snow comes down with heavy uniformity to the water's edge, and the patches of land seem as rare as the summer's snow on the hills about Sukkertoppen and Fiskernaes. On the right we have an array of cliffs, whose frowning grandeur might dignify the entrance to the proudest of southern seas. I should say they

CAPE ALEXANDER.

would average from four to five hundred yards in height, with some of their precipices eight hundred feet at a single steep. They have been until now the Arctic pillars of Hercules; and they look down on us as if they challenged our right to pass. Even the sailors are impressed, as we move under their dark shadow. One

of the officers said to our look-out, that the gulls and
eider that dot the water about us were as enlivening as
the white sails of the Mediterranean. 'Yes, sir,' he rejoined, with sincere gravity; 'yes, sir, in proportion to
their size.'"

"August 7, Sunday.—We have left Cape Alexander

HARTSTENE BAY—LEAVING CAPE ALEXANDER.

to the south; and Littleton Island is before us, hiding
Cape Hatherton, the latest of Captain Inglefield's posi-
tively-determined headlands. We are fairly inside of
Smith's Sound.

"On our left is a capacious bay; and deep in its northeastern recesses we can see a glacier issuing from a fiord."

We knew this bay familiarly afterward, as the residence of a body of Esquimaux with whom we had many associations; but we little dreamt then that it would bear the name of a gallant friend, who found there the first traces of our escape. A small cluster of rocks, hidden at times by the sea, gave evidence of the violent tidal action about them.

"As we neared the west end of Littleton Island, after breakfast this morning, I ascended to the crow's-nest, and saw to my sorrow the ominous blink of ice ahead.[9] The wind has been freshening for a couple of days from the northward, and if it continues it will bring down the floes on us.

"My mind has been made up from the first that we are to force our way to the north as far as the elements will let us; and I feel the importance therefore of securing a place of retreat, that in case of disaster we may not be altogether at large. Besides, we have now reached one of the points, at which, if any one is to follow us, he might look for some trace to guide him."

I determined to leave a cairn on Littleton Island, and to deposit a boat with a supply of stores in some convenient place near it. One of our whale-boats had been crushed in Melville Bay, and Francis's metallic life-boat was the only one I could spare. Its length did not exceed twenty feet, and our crew of twenty could hardly stow themselves in it with even a few days' rations; but it was air-chambered and buoyant.

Selecting from our stock of provisions and field equipage such portions as we might by good luck be able to dispense with, and adding with reluctant liberality some blankets and a few yards of India-rubber cloth, we set out in search of a spot for our first depôt. It was essential that it should be upon the mainland; for the rapid tides might so wear away the ice as to make an island inaccessible to a foot-party; and yet it was desirable that, while secure against the action of sea and ice, it should be approachable by boats. We found such a place after some pretty cold rowing. It was off the northeast cape of Littleton, and bore S.S.E. from Cape Hatherton, which loomed in the distance above the fog. Here we buried our life-boat with her little cargo. We placed along her gunwale the heaviest rocks we could handle, and, filling up the interstices with smaller stones and sods of andromeda and moss, poured sand and water among the layers. This, frozen at once into a solid mass, might be hard enough, we hoped, to resist the claws of the polar bear.

We found to our surprise that we were not the first human beings who had sought a shelter in this desolate spot. A few ruined walls here and there showed that it had once been the seat of a rude settlement; and in the little knoll which we cleared away to cover in our storehouse of valuables, we found the mortal remains of their former inhabitants.

Nothing can be imagined more sad and homeless than these memorials of extinct life. Hardly a vestige of growth was traceable on the bare ice-rubbed rocks; and the huts resembled so much the broken

fragments that surrounded them, that at first sight it
was hard to distinguish one from the other. Walrus
bones lay about in all directions, showing that this
animal had furnished the staple of subsistence. There
were some remains too of the fox and the narwhal;
but I found no signs of the seal or reindeer.

ESQUIMAUX RUINED HUTS—LIFE-BOAT COVE.

These Esquimaux have no mother earth to receive
their dead; but they seat them as in the attitude of
repose, the knees drawn close to the body, and enclose
them in a sack of skins. The implements of the living
man are then grouped around him; they are covered
with a rude dome of stones, and a cairn is piled above.
This simple cenotaph will remain intact for generation
after generation. The Esquimaux never disturb a
grave.

From one of the graves I took several perforated

and rudely-fashioned pieces of walrus ivory, evidently
parts of sledge and lance gear. But wood must have
been even more scarce with them than with the
natives of Baffin's Bay north of the Melville glacier.

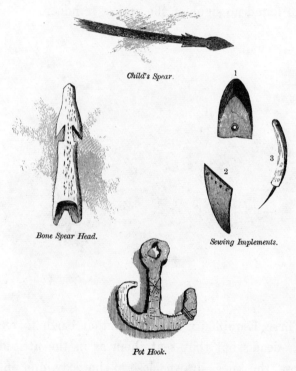

Child's Spear.

Bone Spear Head.

Sewing Implements.

Pot Hook.

ESQUIMAUX IMPLEMENTS, FROM GRAVES.

We found, for instance, a child's toy spear, which,
though elaborately tipped with ivory, had its wooden
handle pieced out of four separate bits, all carefully
patched and bound with skin. No piece was more
than six inches in length or half an inch in thickness.

We found other traces of Esquimaux, both on Littleton Island and in Shoal-Water Cove, near it. They consisted of huts, graves, places of deposit for meat, and rocks arranged as foxtraps. These were evidently very ancient; but they were so well preserved, that it was impossible to say how long they had been abandoned, whether for fifty or a hundred years before.

Our stores deposited, it was our next office to erect a beacon and intrust to it our tidings. We chose for this purpose the Western Cape of Littleton Island, as more conspicuous than Cape Hatherton; built our cairn; wedged a staff into the crevices of the rocks; and, spreading the American flag, hailed its folds with three cheers as they expanded in the cold midnight breeze. These important duties performed,—the more lightly, let me say, for this little flicker of enthusiasm, —we rejoined the brig early in the morning of the 7th, and forced on again toward the north, beating against wind and tide.

CHAPTER VI.

"AUGUST 8, Monday.—I had seen the ominous blink ahead of us from the Flagstaff Point of Littleton Island; and before two hours were over, we closed with ice to the westward. It was in the form of a pack, very heavy, and several seasons old; but we stood on, boring the loose stream-ice, until we had passed some forty miles beyond Cape Life-boat Cove. Here it became impossible to force our way farther; and, a dense fog gathering round us, we were carried helplessly to the eastward. We should have been forced upon the Greenland coast; but an eddy close in shore released us for a few moments from the direct pressure, and we were fortunate enough to get out a whale-line to the rocks and warp into a protecting niche.

"In the evening I ventured out again with the change of tide, but it was only to renew a profitless conflict. The flood, encountering the southward movement of

54

the floes, drove them in upon the shore, and with such rapidity and force as to carry the smaller bergs along with them. We were too happy, when, after a manful struggle of some hours, we found ourselves once more out of their range.

"Our new position was rather nearer to the south than the one we had left. It was in a beautiful cove.

REFUGE HARBOR.

landlocked from east to west, and accessible only from the north. Here we moored our vessel securely by hawsers to the rocks, and a whale-line carried out to the narrow entrance. At McGary's suggestion, I called it 'Fog Inlet;' but we afterward remembered it more thankfully as REFUGE HARBOR. [10]

"August 9, Tuesday.—It may be noted among our little miseries that we have more than fifty dogs on

board, the majority of whom might rather be characterized as 'ravening wolves.' To feed this family,
upon whose strength our progress and success depend,
is really a difficult matter. The absence of shore or
land ice to the south in Baffin's Bay has prevented
our rifles from contributing any material aid to our
commissariat. Our two bears lasted the cormorants
but eight days; and to feed them upon the meagre
allowance of two pounds of raw flesh every other day
is an almost impossible necessity. Only yesterday
they were ready to eat the caboose up, for I would
not give them pemmican. Corn meal or beans, which
Penny's dogs fed on, they disdain to touch; and salt
junk would kill them.

"Accordingly, I started out this morning to hunt
walrus, with which the Sound is teeming. We saw at
least fifty of these dusky monsters, and approached
many groups within twenty paces. But our rifle-balls
reverberated from their hides like cork pellets from a
pop-gun target, and we could not get within harpoon
distance of one. Later in the day, however, Ohlsen,
climbing a neighboring hill to scan the horizon and
see if the ice had slackened, found the dead carcass of
a narwhal or sea-unicorn: a happy discovery, which
has secured for us at least six hundred pounds of good
fetid wholesome flesh. The length of the narwhal was
fourteen feet, and his process, or 'horn,' from the tip
to its bony encasement, four feet—hardly half the size
of the noble specimen I presented to the Academy of
Natural Sciences after my last cruise.[11] We built a fire

on the rocks, and melted down his blubber: he will yield readily two barrels of oil.

"While we were engaged getting our narwhal on board, the wind hauled round to the southwest, and the ice began to travel back rapidly to the north. This looks as if the resistance to the northward was not very permanent: there must be either great areas

ICE-HILLS ON THE COAST ABOVE REFUGE HARBOR.

of relaxed ice or open-water leads along the shore. But the choking up of the floes on our eastern side still prevents an attempt at progress. This ice is the heaviest I have seen; and its accumulation on the coast produces barricades, more like bergs than hummocks. One of these rose perpendicularly more than sixty feet. Except the 'ice-hills' of Admiral Wrangell,

on the coast of Arctic Asia, nothing of ice-upheaval
has ever been described equal to this.[12]

"Still, anxious beyond measure to get the vessel released, I forced a boat through the drift to a point
about a mile north of us, from which I could overlook
the sound. There was nothing to be seen but a melan-
choly extent of impacted drift, stretching northward
as far as the eye could reach. I erected a small beacon-
cairn on the point; and, as I had neither paper, pencil,
nor pennant, I burnt a K. with powder on the rock,
and scratching O.K. with a pointed bullet on my cap-
lining, hoisted it as the representative of a flag."*

With the small hours of Wednesday morning came
a breeze from the southwest, which was followed by
such an apparent relaxation of the floes at the slack-
water of flood-tide that I resolved to attempt an escape
from our little basin. We soon warped to a narrow
cul-de-sac between the main pack on one side and the
rocks on the other, and after a little trouble made ourselves fast to a berg.

There was a small indentation ahead, which I had
noticed on my boat reconnoissance; and, as the breeze
seemed to be freshening, I thought we might venture
for it. But the floes were too strong for us: our eight-
inch hawser parted like a whip-cord. There was no

---

* It was our custom, in obedience to a general order, to build cairns
and leave notices at every eligible point. One of these, rudely marked,
much as I have described this one, was found by Captain Hartstene,
and, strange to say, was the only direct memorial of my whereabouts
communicated from some hundred of beacons.

time for hesitation. I crowded sail and bored into the drift, leaving Mr. Sontag and three men upon the ice : we did not reclaim them till, after some hours of adventure, we brought up under the lee of a grounded berg.

I pass without notice our successive efforts to work the vessel to seaward through the floes. Each had its somewhat varied incidents, but all ended in failure to make progress. We found ourselves at the end of the day's struggles close to the same imperfectly-defined headland which I have marked on the chart as Cape Cornelius Grinnell, yet separated from it by a barrier of ice, and with our anchors planted in a berg.

In one of the attempts which I made with my boat to detect some pathway or outlet for the brig, I came upon a long rocky ledge, with a sloping terrace on its southern face, strangely green with sedges and poppies. I had learned to refer these unusual traces of vegetation to the fertilizing action of the refuse which gathers about the habitations of men. Yet I was startled, as I walked round its narrow and dreary limits, to find an Esquimaux hut, so perfect in its preservation that a few hours' labor would have rendered it habitable. There were bones of the walrus, fox, and seal, scattered round it in small quantities; a dead dog was found close by, with the flesh still on his bones; and, a little farther off, a bear-skin garment that retained its fur. In fact, for a deserted homestead, the scene had so little of the air of desolation about it that it cheered my good fellows perceptibly.

The scenery beyond, upon the main shore, might

ESQUIMAUX HUT.

have impressed men whose thoughts were not otherwise absorbed. An opening through the cliffs of trap
rock disclosed a valley slope and distant rolling hills,—
in fine contrast with the black precipices in front,—
and a stream that came tumbling through the gorge:
we could hear its pastoral music even on board the
brig, when the ice clamor intermitted.

The water around was so shoal that at three hundred yards from the shore we had but twelve-feet
soundings at low tide. Great rocks, well worn and
rounded, that must have been floated out by the ice at
some former period, rose above the water at a half
mile's distance, and the inner drift had fastened itself
about them in fantastic shapes. The bergs, too, were
aground well out to seaward; and the cape ahead was
completely packed with the ice which they hemmed

in. Tied up as we were to our own berg, we were for the time in safety, though making no progress; but to cast loose and tear out into the pack was to risk progress in the wrong direction.

"August 12, Friday.—After careful consideration, I have determined to try for a further northing, by fol

PREPARING TO ENTER THE SHALLOWS—BEDEVILLED REACH—
FORCE BAY.

lowing the coast-line. At certain stages of the tides— generally from three-quarters flood to the commencement of the ebb—the ice evidently relaxes enough to give a partial opening close along the land. The strength of our vessel we have tested pretty thoroughly: if she will bear the frequent groundings that we must look for, I am persuaded we may seek these openings, and warp along them from one lump of

grounded ice to another. The water is too shoal for
ice masses to float in that are heavy enough to make
a nip very dangerous. I am preparing the little brig
for this novel navigation, clearing her decks, securing
things below with extra lashings, and getting out
spars, to serve in case of necessity as shores to keep
her on an even keel.

CAPE CORNELIUS GRINNELL.

"August 13, Saturday.—As long as we remain entangled in the wretched shallows of this bight, the long
precipitous cape ahead may prevent the north wind
from clearing us; and the nearness of the cliffs will
probably give us squalls and flaws. Careful angular
distances taken between the shore and the chain of
bergs to seaward show that these latter do not budge
with either wind or tide. It looks as if we were to

have a change of weather. Is it worth another attempt
to warp out and see if we cannot double these bergs to
seaward? I have no great time to spare: the young
ice forms rapidly in quiet spots during the entire
twenty-four hours.

"August 14, Sunday.—The change of weather yesterday tempted us to forsake our shelter and try another
tussle with the ice. We met it as soon as we ventured
out; and the day closed with a northerly progress, by
hard warping, of about three-quarters of a mile. The
men were well tired; but the weather looked so
threatening, that I had them up again at three o'clock
this morning. My immediate aim is to attain a low
rocky island which we see close into the shore, about
a mile ahead of us.

"These low shallows are evidently caused by the
rocks and foreign materials discharged from the great
valley. It is impossible to pass inside of them, for the
huge boulders run close to the shore.[13] Yet there is no
such thing as doubling them outside, without leaving
the holding-ground of the coast and thrusting ourselves into the drifting chaos of the pack. If we can
only reach the little islet ahead of us, make a lee of
its rocky crests, and hold on there until the winds give
us fairer prospects!

"Midnight.—We did reach it; and just in time. At
11·30 P.M. our first whale-line was made fast to the
rocks. Ten minutes later, the breeze freshened, and
so directly in our teeth that we could not have gained
our mooring-ground. It is blowing a gale now, and

the ice driving to the northward before it; but we
can rely upon our hawsers. All behind us is now
solid pack.

"August 15, Monday.—We are still fast, and, from
the grinding of the ice against the southern cape, the
wind is doubtlessly blowing a strong gale from the
southward. Once, early this morning, the wind shifted
by a momentary flaw, and came from the northward,
throwing our brig with slack hawser upon the rocks.
Though she bumped heavily she started nothing, till
we got out a stern-line to a grounded iceberg.

"August 16, Tuesday.—Fast still; the wind dying
out and the ice outside closing steadily. And here,
for all I can see, we must hang on for the winter, unless Providence shall send a smart ice-shattering breeze,
to open a road for us to the northward.

"More bother with these wretched dogs! worse than
a street of Constantinople emptied upon our decks;
the unruly, thieving, wild-beast pack! Not a bear's
paw, or an Esquimaux cranium, or basket of mosses,
or any specimen whatever, can leave your hands for a
moment without their making a rush at it, and, after
a yelping scramble, swallowing it at a gulp. I have
seen them attempt a whole feather bed; and here, this
very morning, one of my Karsuk brutes has eaten up
two entire birds'-nests which I had just before gathered
from the rocks; feathers, filth, pebbles, and moss,—a
peckful at the least. One was a perfect specimen of
the nest of the tridactyl, the other of the big burgomaster.

"When we reach a floe, or berg, or temporary harbor, they start out in a body, neither voice nor lash restraining them, and scamper off like a drove of hogs in an Illinois oak-opening. Two of our largest left themselves behind at Fog Inlet, and we had to send off a boat party to-day to their rescue. It cost a pull through ice and water of about eight miles before they found the recreants, fat and saucy, beside the carcass of the dead narwhal. After more than an hour spent in attempts to catch them, one was tied and brought on board; but the other suicidal scamp had to be left to his fate." [14]

DEGRADED BERG.

CHAPTER VII.

"August 16, Tuesday.—The formation of the young
ice seems to be retarded by the clouds: its greatest
nightly freezing has been three-quarters of an inch.
But I have no doubt, if we had continued till now in
our little Refuge Harbor, the winter would have closed
around us, without a single resource or chance for
escape. Where we are now, I cannot help thinking
our embargo must be temporary. Ahead of us to the
northeast is the projecting headland, which terminates
the long shallow curve of Bedevilled Reach. This
serves as a lee to the northerly drift, and forms a
bight into which the south winds force the ice. The
heavy floes and bergs that are aground outside of us
have encroached upon the lighter ice of the reach, and
choke its outlet to the sea. But a wind off shore
would start this whole pack, and leave us free. Meanwhile, for our comfort, a strong breeze is setting in

66

from the southward, and the probabilities are that it
will freshen to a gale.

"August 17, Wednesday.—This morning I pushed
out into the drift, with the useful little specimen of
naval architecture, which I call 'Eric the Red,' but
which the crew have named, less poetically, the 'Red

THE RED BOAT FORCED ON AN ICEBERG.

Boat.' We succeeded in forcing her on to one of the
largest bergs of the chain ahead, and I climbed it, in
the hope of seeing something like a lead outside, which
might be reached by boring. But there was nothing
of the sort. The ice looked as if perhaps an off-shore
wind might spread it; but, save a few meagre pools,

which from our lofty eminence looked like the merest ink-spots on a table-cloth, not a mark of water could be seen.   I could see our eastern or Greenland coast extending on, headland after headland, no less than five of them in number, until they faded into the mysterious North.   Every thing else, Ice!

"Up to this time we have had but two reliable observations to determine our geographical position since entering Smith's Sound.   These, however, were carefully made on shore by theodolite and artificial horizons; and, if our five chronometers, rated but two weeks ago at Upernavik, are to be depended upon, there can be no correspondence between my own and the Admiralty charts north of latitude 78° 18'.   Not only do I remove the general coast-line some two degrees in longitude to the eastward, but its trend is altered sixty degrees of angular measurement.   No landmarks of my predecessor, Captain Inglefield, are recognisable.[15]

"In the afternoon came a gale from the southward. We had some rough rubbing from the floe-pieces, with three heavy hawsers out to the rocks of our little ice-breaker; but we held on.   Toward midnight, our six-inch line, the smallest of the three, parted; but the other two held bravely.   Feeling what good service this island has done us, what a Godsend it was to reach her, and how gallantly her broken rocks have protected us from the rolling masses of ice that grind by her, we have agreed to remember this anchorage as 'Godsend Ledge.'

"The walrus are very numerous, approaching within twenty feet of us, shaking their grim wet fronts, and mowing with their tusks the sea-ripples.

"August 19, Friday.—The sky looks sinister: a sort of scowl overhangs the blink under the great brow of clouds to the southward. The dovekies seem to distrust the weather, for they have forsaken the channel; but the walrus curvet around us in crowds. I have always heard that the close approach to land of these sphinx-faced monsters portends a storm. I was anxious to find a better shelter, and warped yesterday well down to the south end of the ledge; but I could not venture into the floes outside, without risking the loss of my dearly-earned ground. It may prove a hard gale; but we must wait it out patiently.

"August 20, Saturday, 3½ P. M.—By Saturday morning it blew a perfect hurricane. We had seen it coming, and were ready with three good hawsers out ahead, and all things snug on board.

"Still it came on heavier and heavier, and the ice began to drive more wildly than I thought I had ever seen it. I had just turned in to warm and dry myself during a momentary lull, and was stretching myself out in my bunk, when I heard the sharp twanging snap of a cord. Our six-inch hawser had parted, and we were swinging by the two others; the gale roaring like a lion to the southward.

"Half a minute more, and 'twang, twang!' came a second report. I knew it was the whale-line by the shrillness of the ring. Our noble ten-inch manilla still held on. I was hurrying my last sock into its seal-skin boot, when McGary came waddling down the companion-ladders:—'Captain Kane, she won't hold much longer: it's blowing the devil himself, and I am afraid to surge.'

"The manilla cable was proving its excellence when I reached the deck; and the crew, as they gathered

PARTING HAWSERS OFF GODSEND LEDGE.

round me, were loud in its praises. We could hear its deep Eolian chant, swelling through all the rattle of the running-gear and moaning of the shrouds. It was the death-song! The strands gave way, with the noise of a shotted gun; and, in the smoke that followed their recoil, we were dragged out by the wild ice, at its mercy.

J. Hamilton.

Engraved at J M Butler's establishment 84 Chestnut St.

G Ulman.

PARTING HAWSERS OFF GODSEND LEDGE.

(From a sketch by Dr Kane.)

"We steadied and did some petty warping, and got the brig a good bed in the rushing drift; but it all came to nothing. We then tried to beat back through the narrow ice-clogged water-way, that was driving, a quarter of a mile wide, between the shore and the pack. It cost us two hours of hard labor, I thought skilfully bestowed; but at the end of that time, we were at least four miles off, opposite the great valley in the centre of Bedevilled Reach.[16] Ahead of us, farther to the north, we could see the strait growing still narrower, and the heavy ice-tables grinding up, and clogging it between the shore-cliffs on one side and the ledge on the other. There was but one thing left for us;—to keep in some sort the command of the helm, by going freely where we must otherwise be driven. We allowed her to scud under a reefed foretopsail; all hands watching the enemy, as we closed, in silence.

"At seven in the morning, we were close upon the piling masses. We dropped our heaviest anchor with the desperate hope of winding the brig; but there was no withstanding the ice-torrent that followed us. We had only time to fasten a spar as a buoy to the chain, and let her slip. So went our best bower!

"Down we went upon the gale again, helplessly scraping along a lee of ice seldom less than thirty feet thick; one floe, measured by a line as we tried to fasten to it, more than forty. I had seen such ice only once before, and never in such rapid motion. One up-turned mass rose above our gunwale, smashing in our bulwarks, and depositing half a ton of ice in a lump

upon our decks.   Our stanch little brig bore herself
through all this wild adventure as if she had a
charmed life.

"But a new enemy came in sight ahead.   Directly in
our way, just beyond the line of floe-ice against which
we were alternately sliding and thumping, was a group
of bergs.   We had no power to avoid them; and the
only question was, whether we were to be dashed in
pieces against them, or whether they might not offer
us some providential nook of refuge from the storm.
But, as we neared them, we perceived that they were
at some distance from the floe-edge, and separated from
it by an interval of open water.   Our hopes rose, as the
gale drove us toward this passage, and into it; and we
were ready to exult, when, from some unexplained
cause,—probably an eddy of the wind against the lofty
ice-walls,—we lost our headway.   Almost at the same
moment, we saw that the bergs were not at rest; that
with a momentum of their own they were bearing
down upon the other ice, and that it must be our fate
to be crushed between the two.

"Just then, a broad sconce-piece or low water-washed
berg came driving up from the southward.   The thought
flashed upon me of one of our escapes in Melville Bay;
and as the sconce moved rapidly close alongside us,
McGary managed to plant an anchor on its slope and
hold on to it by a whale-line.   It was an anxious moment.   Our noble tow-horse, whiter than the pale horse
that seemed to be pursuing us, hauled us bravely on;
the spray dashing over his windward flanks, and his

forehead ploughing up the lesser ice as if in scorn. The bergs encroached upon us as we advanced: our channel narrowed to a width of perhaps forty feet: we braced the yards to clear the impending ice-walls.

".... We passed clear; but it was a close shave,—so close that our port quarter-boat would have been crushed if we had not taken it in from the davits,—and found ourselves under the lee of a berg, in a comparatively open lead. Never did heart-tried men acknowledge with more gratitude their merciful deliverance from a wretched death. ...

"The day had already its full share of trials; but there were more to come. A flaw drove us from our shelter, and the gale soon carried us beyond the end of the lead. We were again in the ice, sometimes escaping its onset by warping, sometimes forced to rely on the strength and buoyancy of the brig to stand its pressure, sometimes scudding wildly through the half-open drift. Our jib-boom was snapped off in the cap; we carried away our barricade stanchions, and were forced to leave our little Eric, with three brave fellows and their warps, out upon the floes behind us.

"A little pool of open water received us at last. It was just beyond a lofty cape that rose up like a wall, and under an iceberg that anchored itself between us and the gale. And here, close

UNDER THE CLIFFS.

under the frowning shore of Greenland, ten miles nearer the Pole than our holding-ground of the morning, the men have turned in to rest.

"I was afraid to join them; for the gale was unbroken, and the floes kept pressing heavily upon our berg,—at one time so heavily as to sway it on its vertical axis toward the shore, and make its pinnacle overhang our vessel. My poor fellows had but a precarious sleep before our little harbor was broken up. They hardly reached the deck, when we were driven astern, our rudder splintered, and the pintles torn from their boltings.

"Now began the nippings. The first shock took us on our port-quarter; the brig bearing it well, and, after a moment of the old-fashioned suspense, rising by jerks handsomely. The next was from a veteran floe, tongued and honeycombed, but floating in a single table over twenty feet in thickness. Of course, no wood or iron could stand this; but the shoreward face of our iceberg happened to present an inclined plane, descending deep into the water; and up this the brig was driven, as if some great steam screw-power was forcing her into a dry dock.

"At one time I expected to see her carried bodily up its face and tumbled over on her side. But one of those mysterious relaxations, which I have elsewhere called the pulses of the ice, lowered us quite gradually down again into the rubbish, and we were forced out of the line of pressure toward the shore. Here we succeeded in carrying out a warp, and making fast.

We grounded as the tide fell; and would have heeled over to seaward, but for a mass of detached land-ice that grounded alongside of us, and, although it stove our bulwarks as we rolled over it, shored us up."

I could hardly get to my bunk, as I went down into our littered cabin on the Sunday morning after our hard-working vigil of thirty-six hours. Bags of

SHORED UP.

clothing, food, tents, India-rubber blankets, and the hundred little personal matters which every man likes to save in a time of trouble, were scattered around in places where the owners thought they might have them at hand. The pemmican had been on deck, the boats equipped, and every thing of real importance ready for a march, many hours before.

During the whole of the scenes I have been trying

to describe, I could not help being struck by the composed and manly demeanor of my comrades. The turmoil of ice under a heavy sea often conveys the impression of danger when the reality is absent; but in this fearful passage, the parting of our hawsers, the loss of our anchors, the abrupt crushing of our stoven bulwarks, and the actual deposit of ice upon our decks, would have tried the nerves of the most experienced icemen. All—officers and men—worked alike. Upon each occasion of collision with the ice which formed our lee-coast, efforts were made to carry out lines; and some narrow escapes were incurred, by the zeal of the parties leading them into positions of danger. Mr. Bonsall avoided being crushed by leaping to a floating fragment; and no less than four of our men at one time were carried down by the drift, and could only be recovered by a relief party after the gale had subsided.

As our brig, borne on by the ice, commenced her ascent of the berg, the suspense was oppressive. The immense blocks piled against her, range upon range, pressing themselves under her keel and throwing her over upon her side, till, urged by the successive accumulations, she rose slowly and as if with convulsive efforts along the sloping wall. Still there was no relaxation of the impelling force. Shock after shock, jarring her to her very centre, she continued to mount steadily on her precarious cradle. But for the groaning of her timbers and the heavy sough of the floes, we might have heard a pin drop. And then, as she settled

J. Hamilton.

A.W. Graham.

Engraved at J M Butler's establishment 84 Chestnut St.

THE NIP OFF CAPE CORNELIUS GRINNELL, FORCE BAY.

(From a sketch by Dr Kane.)

down into her old position, quietly taking her place among the broken rubbish, there was a deep-breathing silence, as though all were waiting for some signal before the clamor of congratulation and comment could burst forth.[17]

THE RESCUE.

CHAPTER VIII.

IT was not until the 22d that the storm abated, and our absent men were once more gathered back into their mess. During the interval of forced inaction, the little brig was fast to the ice-belt which lined the bottom of the cliffs, and all hands rested; but as soon as it was over, we took advantage of the flood-tide to pass our tow-lines to the ice-beach, and, harnessing ourselves in like mules on a canal, made a good three miles by tracking along the coast.

"August 22, Monday.—Under this coast, at the base of a frowning precipice, we are now working toward a large bay which runs well in, facing at its opening to the north and west. I should save time if I could cross from headland to headland; but I am obliged to follow the tortuous land-belt, without whose aid we would go adrift in the pack again.

"The trend of our line of operations to-day is almost
78

due east. We are already protected from the south,
but fearfully exposed to a northerly gale. Of this
there are fortunately no indications.

"August 23, Tuesday.—We tracked along the ice-
belt for about one mile, when the tide fell, and the
brig grounded, heeling over until she reached her bearings. She rose again at 10 P. M., and the crew turned
out upon the ice-belt.

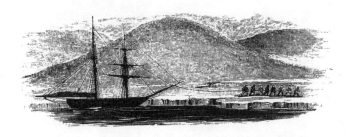

TRACKING ALONG THE ICE-BELT.

"The decided inclination to the eastward which the
shore shows here is important as a geographical feature; but it has made our progress to the actual north
much less than our wearily-earned miles should count
for us. Our latitude, determined by the sun's lower
culmination, if such a term can be applied to his midnight depression, gives 78° 41'. We are farther north,
therefore, than any of our predecessors, except Parry
on his Spitzbergen foot-tramp. There are those with
whom, no matter how insuperable the obstacle, failure
involves disgrace: we are safe at least from their
censure.

"Last night I sent out Messrs. Wilson, Petersen, and Bonsall, to inspect a harbor which seems to lie between a small island and a valley that forms the inner slope of our bay. They report recent traces of deer, and bring back the skull of a musk ox.

SYLVIA HEADLAND—INSPECTING A HARBOR.

"Hitherto this animal has never been seen east of Melville Island. But his being here does not surprise me. The migratory passages of the reindeer, who is even less Arctic in his range than the musk ox, led me to expect it. The fact points to some probable land connection between Greenland and America, or an ap

proach sufficiently close to allow these animals to migrate between the two.

"The head is that of a male, well-marked, but old;
the teeth deficient, but the horns very perfect. These
last measure two feet three inches across from tip to
tip, and are each one foot ten inches in length measured to the medium line of the forehead, up to which
they are continued in the characteristic boss or pro-

THE ICE-BELT.

tuberance. Our winter may be greatly cheered by
their beef, should they revisit this solitude. [18]

"We have collected thus far no less than twenty-
two species of flowering plants on the shores of this
bay. Scanty as this starved flora may seem to the
botanists of more favored zones, it was not without
surprise and interest that I recognised among its thoroughly Arctic types many plants which had before

been considered as indigenous only to more southern latitudes.[19]

"The thermometer gave twenty-five degrees last night, and the young ice formed without intermission : it is nearly two inches alongside the brig. I am loth to recognise these signs of the advancing cold. Our latitude to-day gives us 78° 37′, taken from a station some three miles inside the indentation to the south.

"August 24, Wednesday.—We have kept at it, tracking along, grounding at low water, but working like horses when the tides allowed us to move. We are now almost at the bottom of this indentation. Opposite us, on the shore, is a remarkable terrace, which rises in a succession of steps until it is lost in the low rocks of the back country. The ice around us is broken, but heavy, and so compacted that we can barely penetrate it. It has snowed hard since 10 P.M. of yesterday, and the sludge fills up the interstices of the floes. Nothing but a strong south wind can give us further progress to the north.

"August 25, Thursday.—The snow of yesterday has surrounded us with a pasty sludge; but the young ice continues to be our most formidable opponent. The mean temperatures of the 22d and 23d were 27° and 30° Fahrenheit. I do not like being caught by winter before attaining a higher northern latitude than this, but it appears almost inevitable. Favored as we have been by the mildness of the summer and by the abrading action of the tides, there are indications around us which point to an early winter.

We are sufficiently surrounded by ice to make our chances of escape next year uncertain, and yet not as far as I could wish for our spring journeys by the sledge.

"August 26, Friday.—My officers and crew are stanch and firm men; but the depressing influences of want of rest, the rapid advance of winter, and, above all, our slow progress, make them sympathize but little with this continued effort to force a way to the north. One of them, an excellent member of the party, volunteered an expression of opinion this morning in favor of returning to the south and giving up the attempt to winter."

It is unjust for a commander to measure his subordinates in such exigencies by his own standard. The interest which they feel in an undertaking is of a different nature from his own. With him there are always personal motives, apart from official duty, to stimulate effort. He receives, if successful, too large a share of the credit, and he justly bears all the odium of failure.

An apprehension—I hope a charitable one—of this fact leads me to consider the opinions of my officers with much respect. I called them together at once, in a formal council, and listened to their views in full. With but one exception, Mr. Henry Brooks, they were convinced that a further progress to the north was impossible, and were in favor of returning southward to winter.

Not being able conscientiously to take the same view,

I explained to them the importance of securing a position which might expedite our sledge journeys in the future; and, after assuring them that such a position could only be attained by continuing our efforts, announced my intention of warping toward the northern headland of the bay. "Once there, I shall be able to determine from actual inspection the best point for set-

CAPE THOMAS LEIPER.

ting out on the operations of the spring; and at the nearest possible shelter to that point I will put the brig into winter harbor." My comrades received this decision in a manner that was most gratifying, and entered zealously upon the hard and cheerless duty it involved.

The warping began again, each man, myself included, taking his turn at the capstan. The ice seemed less heavy as we penetrated into the recess of the bay;

our track-lines and shoulder-belts replaced the warps. Hot coffee was served out; and, in the midst of cheering songs, our little brig moved off briskly.

Our success, however, was not complete. At the very period of high-water she took the ground, while close under the walls of the ice-foot. It would have been madness to attempt shoring her up. I could only fasten heavy tackle to the rocks which lined the base of the cliffs, and trust to the noble little craft's unassisted strength.

"August 27, Saturday.—We failed, in spite of our efforts, to get the brig off with last night's tide; and, as our night-tides are generally the highest, I have some apprehensions as to her liberation.

"We have landed every thing we could get up on the rocks, put out all our boats and filled them with ponderables alongside, sunk our rudder astern, and lowered our remaining heavy anchor into one of our quarter-boats. Heavy hawsers are out to a grounded lump of berg-ice, ready for instant heaving.

"Last night she heeled over again so abruptly that we were all tumbled out of our berths. At the same time, the cabin stove with a full charge of glowing anthracite was thrown down. The deck blazed smartly for a while; but, by sacrificing Mr. Sontag's heavy pilot-cloth coat to the public good, I choked it down till water could be passed from above to extinguish it. It was fortunate we had water near at hand, for the powder was not far off.

"3 P.M.—The ground-ice is forced in upon our stern,

splintering our rudder, and drawing again the bolts of the pintle-casings.

"5 P.M.—She floats again, and our track-lines are manned. The men work with a will, and the brig moves along bravely.

AGROUND NEAR THE ICE-FOOT.

"10 P.M.—Aground again; and the men, after a hot supper, have turned in to take a spell of sleep. The brig has a hard time of it with the rocks. She has been high and dry for each of the two last tides, and within three days has grounded no less than five times. I feel that this is hazardous navigation, but am convinced it is my duty to keep on. Except the loss of a portion of our false keel, we have sustained no real injury. The brig is still water-tight; and her broken rudder and one shattered spar can be easily repaired.

"August 28, Sunday.—By a complication of purchases, jumpers, and shores, we started the brig at 4·10; and, Mr. Ohlsen having temporarily secured the rudder, I determined to enter the floe and trust to the calm of the morning for a chance of penetrating to the northern land-ice ahead.

"This land-ice is very old, and my hope is to get through the loose trash that surrounds it by springing, and then find a fast that may serve our tracking-lines. I am already well on my way, and, in spite of the ominous nods of my officers, have a fair prospect of reaching it. Here it is that splicing the main-brace is of service !(20)

"I took the boat this morning with Mr. McGary, and sounded along outside the land-floe. I am satisfied the passage is practicable, and, by the aid of tide, wind, and springs, have advanced into the trash some two hundred yards.

"We have reached the floe, and find it as I hoped; the only drawback to tracking being the excessive tides, which expose us to grounding at low-water."

We had now a breathing spell, and I could find time to look out again upon the future. The broken and distorted area around us gave little promise of successful sledge-travel. But all this might change its aspect under the action of a single gale, and it was by no means certain that the ice-fields farther north would

have the same rugged and dispiriting character.   Besides, the ice-belt was still before us, broken sometimes
and difficult to traverse, but practicable for a party
on foot, apparently for miles ahead; and I felt sure
that a resolute boat's crew might push and track
their way for some distance along it.   I resolved to
make   the   trial,   and   to   judge   what   ought   to   be

THE FORLORN HOPE.

our wintering ground from a personal inspection of
the coast.

I had been quietly preparing for such an expedition
for some time.   Our best and lightest whale-boat had
been fitted with a canvas cover, that gave it all the
comfort of a tent.   We had a supply of pemmican ready
packed in small cases, and a sledge taken to pieces was
stowed away under the thwarts.   In the morning of

the 29th, Mr. Brooks, McGary, and myself, walked fourteen miles along the marginal ice: it was heavy and complicated with drift, but there was nothing about it to make me change my purpose.

My boat crew consisted of seven, all of them volunteers and reliable:—Brooks, Bonsall, McGary, Sontag, Riley, Blake, and Morton. We had buffalo-robes for our sleeping-gear, and a single extra day suit was put on board as common property. Each man carried his

THE FORLORN HOPE, EQUIPPED.

girdle full of woollen socks, so as to dry them by the warmth of his body, and a tin cup, with a sheath-knife, at the belt: a soup-pot and lamp for the mess completed our outfit.

In less than three hours from my first order, the "Forlorn Hope" was ready for her work, covered with tin to prevent her being cut through by the bay-ice; and at half-past three in the afternoon she was freighted, launched, and on her way.

I placed Mr. Ohlsen in command of the Advance, and Dr. Hayes in charge of her log: Mr. Ohlsen with orders to haul the brig to the southward and eastward into a safe berth, and there to await my return.

Many a warm shake of the hand from the crew we left showed me that our good-bye was not a mere formality.   Three hearty cheers from all hands followed us,—a God-speed as we pushed off.

BROKEN RUDDER.

CHAPTER IX.

THE DEPÔT JOURNEY — THE ICE-BELT — CROSSING MINTURN RIVER — SKELETON MUSK OX — CROSSING THE GLACIER — PORTAGE OF INSTRUMENTS — EXCESSIVE BURDEN — MARY MINTURN RIVER — FORDING THE RIVER — THACKERAY HEADLAND — CAPE JOHN W FRANCIS — RETURN TO THE BRIG — THE WINTER HARBOR.

In the first portions of our journey, we found a narrow but obstructed passage between the ice-belt and the outside pack. It was but a few yards in width, and the young ice upon it was nearly thick enough to bear our weight. By breaking it up we were able with effort to make about seven miles a day.

After such work, wet, cold, and hungry, the night's rest was very welcome. A couple of stanchions were rigged fore and aft, a sail tightly spread over the canvas cover of our boat, the cooking-lamp lit, and the buffalo-robes spread out. Dry socks replaced the wet; hot tea and pemmican followed; and very soon we forgot the discomforts of the day, the smokers musing over their pipes, and the sleepers snoring in dreamless forgetfulness.

We had been out something less than twenty-four

hours when we came to the end of our boating. In front and on one side was the pack, and on the other a wall some ten feet above our heads, the impracticable ice-belt. By waiting for high tide, and taking advantage of a chasm which a water-stream had worn in the ice, we managed to haul up our boat on its surface; but it was apparent that we must leave her there. She was stowed away snugly under the shelter of a large hummock; and we pushed forward in our sledge, laden with a few articles of absolute necessity.

Here, for the first time, we were made aware of a remarkable feature of our travel. We were on a table or shelf of ice, which clung to the base of the rocks overlooking the sea, but itself overhung by steep and lofty cliffs. Pure and beautiful as this icy highway was, huge angular blocks, some many tons in weight, were scattered over its surface; and long tongues of worn-down rock occasionally issued from the sides of the cliffs, and extended across our course. The cliffs measured one thousand and ten feet to the crest of the plateau above them.*

We pushed forward on this ice-table shelf as rapidly as the obstacles would permit, though embarrassed a good deal by the frequent watercourses, which created

* The cliffs were of tabular magnesian limestone, with interlaid and inferior sandstones. Their height, measured to the crest of the plateau, was nine hundred and fifty feet—a fair mean of the profile of the coast. The height of the talus of debris, where it united with the face of the cliff, was five hundred and ninety feet, and its angle of inclination between 38° and 45°

Engraved at J. M. Butler's establishment 84 Chestnut St.

"CROSSING THE ICE BELT AT COFFEE GORGE."

(From a sketch by Dr Kane.)

large gorges in our path, winding occasionally, and generally steep-sided. We had to pass our sledge carefully down such interruptions, and bear it upon our shoulders, wading, of course, through water of an extremely low temperature. Our night halts were upon knolls of snow under the rocks. At one of these, the tide overflowed our tent, and forced us to save our buffalo sleeping-gear by holding it up until the water subsided. This exercise, as it turned out, was more of a trial to our patience than to our health. The circulation was assisted perhaps by a perception of the ludicrous. Eight Yankee Caryatides, up to their knees in water, and an entablature sustaining such of their household gods as could not bear immersion![21]

On the 1st of September, still following the ice-belt, we found that we were entering the recesses of another bay but little smaller than that in which we had left our brig. The limestone walls ceased to overhang us; we reached a low fiord, and a glacier blocked our way across it. A succession of terraces, rising with symmetrical regularity, lost themselves in long parallel lines in the distance. They were of limestone shingle, and wet with the percolation of the melted ice of the glacier. Where the last of these terraced faces abutted upon the sea, it blended with the ice-foot, so as to make a frozen compound of rock and ice. Here, lying in a pasty silt, I found the skeleton of a musk ox. The head was united to the atlas; but the bones of the spine were separated about two inches apart, and conveyed the idea of a displacement produced rather by the sliding of the bed beneath, than by a force from without. The paste, frozen so as to resemble limestone rock, had filled the costal cavity, and the ribs were beautifully polished. It was to the eye an imbedded fossil, ready for the museum of the collector.

THE CLIFFS OF GLACIER BAY.

I am minute in detailing these appearances, for they connect themselves in my mind with the fossils of the Eischoltz cliffs and the Siberian alluvions. I was startled at the facility with which the silicious limestone, under the alternate energies of frost and thaw, had been incorporated with the organic remains. It had already begun to alter the structure of the bones, and in several instances the vertebræ were entirely enveloped in travertin.

The table-lands and ravines round about this coast abound in such remains. Their numbers and the manner in which they are scattered imply that the animals made their migrations in droves, as is the case with

CROSSING THE GLACIER.

the reindeer now. Within the area of a few acres we found seven skeletons and numerous skulls: these all occupied the snow-streams or gullies that led to a gorge opening on the ice-belt, and might thus be gathered in time to one spot by the simple action of the watershed.[22]

To cross this glacier gave us much trouble. Its sides were steep, and a slip at any time might have sent us

into the water below. Our shoes were smooth, unfortunately; but, by using cords, and lying at full length
upon the ice, we got over without accident. On the
other side of the glacier we had a portage of about
three miles; the sledge being unladen and the baggage
carried on our backs. To Mr. Brooks, admitted with
singular unanimity to be the strongest man of our
party, was voted our theodolite, about sixty pounds of
well-polished mechanism, in an angular mahogany box.
Our dip-circle, equally far from being an honorary
tribute, fell to the lot of a party of volunteers, who
bore it by turns.

During this inland crossing, I had fine opportunities
of making sections of the terraces. We ascertained the
mean elevation of the face of the coast to be one thousand three hundred feet. On regaining the seaboard,
the same frowning cliffs and rock-covered ice-belt
that we had left greeted us.

After an absence of five days, we found by observation that we were but forty miles from the brig. Besides our small daily progress, we had lost much by the
tortuous windings of the coast. The ice outside did
not invite a change of plan in that direction; but I
determined to leave the sledge and proceed over land
on foot. With the exception of our instruments, we
carried no weight but pemmican and one buffalo-robe.
The weather, as yet not far below the freezing-point,
did not make a tent essential to the bivouac; and,
with this light equipment, we could travel readily two
miles to one with our entire outfit. On the 4th of

September we made twenty-four miles with comparative ease, and were refreshed by a comfortable sleep
after the toils of the day.*

The only drawback to this new method of advance
was the inability to carry a sufficient quantity of food.
Each man at starting had a fixed allowance of pemmican, which, with his other load, made an average
weight of thirty-five pounds. It proved excessive: the
Canadian voyageurs will carry much more, and for an
almost indefinite period; but we found—and we had
good walkers in our party—that a very few pounds
overweight broke us down.

Our progress on the 5th was arrested by another bay
much larger than any we had seen since entering
Smith's Straits. It was a noble sheet of water, perfectly open, and thus in strange contrast to the ice outside. The cause of this at the time inexplicable phenomenon was found in a roaring and tumultuous river,
which, issuing from a fiord at the inner sweep of the
bay, rolled with the violence of a snow-torrent over a
broken bed of rocks. This river, the largest probably
yet known in North Greenland, was about three-quarters of a mile wide at its mouth, and admitted the tides
for about three miles;[23] when its bed rapidly ascended,

---

* This halt was under the lee of a large boulder of greenstone, mea-
suring fourteen feet in its long diameter. It had the rude blocking
out of a cube, but was rounded at the edges. The country for fourteen
miles around was of the low-bottom series; the nearest greenstone must
have been many miles remote. Boulders of syenite were numerous;
their line of deposit nearly due north and south.

and could be traced by the configuration of the hills as
far as a large inner fiord. I called it Mary Minturn
River, after the sister of Mrs. Henry Grinnell. Its
course was afterward pursued to an interior glacier,
from the base of which it was found to issue in nume-

MARY MINTURN RIVER

rous streams, that united into a single trunk about forty
miles above its mouth. By the banks of this stream
we encamped, lulled by the unusual music of running
waters.

Here, protected from the frost by the infiltration of
the melted snows, and fostered by the reverberation of

solar heat from the rocks, we met a flower-growth, which, though drearily Arctic in its type, was rich in variety and coloring. Amid festuca and other tufted grasses twinkled the purple lychnis and the white star of the chickweed; and not without its pleasing associations I recognised a solitary hesperis,—the Arctic representative of the wallflowers of home.[24]

We forded our way across this river in the morning, carrying our pemmican as well as we could out of water, but submitting ourselves to a succession of plunge-baths as often as we trusted our weight on the ice-capped stones above the surface. The average depth was not over our hips; but the crossing cost us so much labor that we were willing to halt half a day to rest.

Some seven miles farther on, a large cape projects into this bay, and divides it into two indentations, each of them the seat of minor watercourses, fed by the glaciers. From the numerous tracks found in the mossbeds, they would seem to be the resort of deer. Our meridian observations by theodolite gave the latitude of but 78° 52′: the magnetic dip was 84° 49′.

It was plain that the coast of Greenland here faced toward the north. The axis of both these bays and the general direction of the watercourses pointed to the same conclusion. Our longitude was 78° 41′ W.

Leaving four of my party to recruit at this station, I started the next morning, with three volunteers, to cross the ice to the northeastern headland, and thus save the almost impossible circuit by the shores of the bay.

This ice was new, and far from safe: its margin along
the open water made by Minturn River required both
care and tact in passing over it.   We left the heavy
theodolite behind us; and, indeed, carried nothing except a pocket-sextant, my Fraunhöfer, a walking-pole,
and three days' allowance of raw pemmican.

We reached the headland after sixteen miles of

THACKERAY HEADLAND.

walk, and found the ice-foot in good condition, evidently better fitted for sledge-travel than it was to the
south.   This point I named Cape William Makepeace
Thackeray.   Our party knew it as Chimney Rock.   It
was the last station on the coast of Greenland, determined by intersecting bearings of theodolite, from
known positions to the south.   About eight miles be-

yond it is a large headland, the highest visible from the late position of our brig, shutting out all points farther north. It is indicated on my chart as Cape Francis Hawks. We found the table-lands were twelve hundred feet high by actual measurement, and interior plateaus were seen of an estimated height of eighteen hundred.

I determined to seek some high headland beyond the cape, and make it my final point of reconnoissance.

I shall never forget the sight, when, after a hard day's walk, I looked out from an altitude of eleven hundred feet upon an expanse extending beyond the eightieth parallel of latitude. Far off on my left was the western shore of the Sound, losing itself in distance toward the north. To my right, a rolling primary country led on to a low dusky wall-like ridge, which I afterward recognised as the Great Glacier of Humboldt; and still beyond this, reaching northward from the north-northeast, was the land which now bears the name of Washington: its most projecting headland, Cape Andrew Jackson, bore fourteen degrees by sextant from the farthest hill, Cape John Barrow, on the opposite side. The great area between was a solid sea of ice. Close along its shore, almost looking down upon it from the crest of our lofty station, we could see the long lines of hummocks dividing the floes like the trenches of a beleaguered city.[25] Farther out, a stream of icebergs, increasing in numbers as they receded, showed an almost impenetrable barrier; since I could not doubt that among their recesses the ice was so crushed as to be impassable by the sledge.

Nevertheless, beyond these again, the ice seemed less obstructed. Distance is very deceptive upon the ice, subduing its salient features, and reducing even lofty bergs to the appearance of a smooth and attractive plain. But, aided by my Fraunhöfer telescope, I could see that traversable areas were still attainable. Slowly, and almost with a sigh, I laid the glass down and made up my mind for a winter search.

I had seen no place combining so many of the requisites of a good winter harbor as the bay in which we left the Advance. Near its southwestern corner the wide streams and the watercourses on the shore promised the earliest chances of liberation in the coming summer. It was secure against the moving ice : lofty headlands walled it in beautifully to seaward, enclosing an anchorage with a moderate depth of water; yet it was open to the meridian sunlight, and guarded from winds, eddies, and drift. The space enclosed was only occupied by a few rocky islets and our brig. We soon came in sight of her on our return march, as she lay at anchor in its southern sweep, with her masts cutting sharply against the white glacier (C); and, hurrying on through a gale, were taken on board without accident.

My comrades gathered anxiously around me, waiting for the news. I told them in few words of the results of our journey, and why I had determined upon remaining, and gave at once the order to warp in be-

J. Hamilton.

Engraved at J.M.Butler's establishment 84 Chestnut St.

R Hinshelwood

THE LOOK OUT FROM CAPE GEORGE RUSSELL.

(From a sketch by Dr Kane.)

tween the islands. We found seven-fathom soundings and a perfect shelter from the outside ice; and thus laid our little brig in the harbor, which we were fated never to leave together,—a long resting-place to her indeed, for the same ice is around her still.

WINTER HARBOR.

"The same ice is around her still."

RENSSELAER HARBOR.

CHAPTER X.

APPROACHING WINTER — STORING PROVISIONS — BUTLER STORE-
HOUSE — SUNDAY AT REST — BUILDING OBSERVATORY — TRAIN-
ING THE DOGS — THE LITTLE WILLIE — THE ROAD — THE FAITH
— SLEDGING — RECONNOISSANCE — DEPÔT PARTY.

THE winter was now approaching rapidly. The
thermometer had fallen by the 10th of September to
14°, and the young ice had cemented the floes so that
we could walk and sledge round the brig. About sixty
paces north of us an iceberg had been caught, and was

104

frozen in: it was our neighbor while we remained in Rensselaer Harbor. The rocky islets around us were fringed with hummocks; and, as the tide fell, their sides were coated with opaque crystals of bright white. The birds had gone. The sea-swallows, which abounded when we first reached here, and even the young burgomasters that lingered after them, had all taken their departure for the south. Except the snow-birds, these are the last to migrate of all the Arctic birds.

"September 10, Saturday.—We have plenty of responsible work before us. The long 'night in which no man can work' is close at hand: in another month we shall lose the sun. Astronomically, he should disappear on the 24th of October if our horizon were free; but it is obstructed by a mountain ridge, and, making all allowance for refraction, we cannot count on seeing him after the 10th.

"First and foremost, we have to unstow the hold, and deposit its contents in the storehouse on Butler Island. Brooks and a party are now briskly engaged in this double labor, running loaded boats along a canal that has to be recut every morning.

"Next comes the catering for winter diet. We have little or no game as yet in Smith's Sound; and, though the traces of deer that we have observed may be followed by the animals themselves, I cannot calculate upon them as a resource. I am without the hermetically-sealed meats of our last voyage; and the use of salt meat in circumstances like ours is never safe. A fresh-water pond, which fortunately remains open at

Medary, gives me a chance for some further experiments in freshening this portion of our stock. Steaks of salt junk, artistically cut, are strung on lines like a countrywoman's dried apples, and soaked in festoons under the ice. The salmon-trout and salt codfish which we bought at Fiskernaes are placed in barrels, perforated to permit a constant circulation of fresh water through them. Our pickled cabbage is similarly treated, after a little potash has been used to neutralize the acid. All these are submitted to twelve hours of alternate soaking and freezing, the crust of ice being removed from them before each immersion. This is the steward's province, and a most important one it is.

"Every one else is well employed; McGary arranging and Bonsall making the inventory of our stores; Ohlsen and Petersen building our deck-house; while I am devising the plan of an architectural interior, which is to combine, of course, the utmost ventilation, room, dryness, warmth, general accommodation, comfort,—in a word, all the appliances of health.

"We have made a comfortable dog-house on Butler Island; but though our Esquimaux *canaille* are within scent of our cheeses there, one of which they ate yesterday for lunch, they cannot be persuaded to sleep away from the vessel. They prefer the bare snow, where they can couch within the sound of our voices, to a warm kennel upon the rocks. Strange that this dog-distinguishing trait of affection for man should show itself in an animal so imperfectly reclaimed from

a savage state that he can hardly be caught when
wanted!

"September 11, Sunday.—To-day came to us the first
quiet Sunday of harbor life. We changed our log re-
gistration from sea-time to the familiar home series that
begins at midnight. It is not only that the season has

BUTLER'S ISLAND STOREHOUSE.

given us once more a local habitation; but there is
something in the return of varying day and night
that makes it grateful to reinstate this domestic obser-
vance. The long staring day, which has clung to us
for more than two months, to the exclusion of the
stars, has begun to intermit its brightness. Even Al-
debaran, the red eye of the Bull, flared out into familiar recollection as early as ten o'clock; and the hea-

vens, though still somewhat reddened by the gaudy
tints of midnight, gave us Capella and Arcturus, and
even that lesser light of home memories, the Polar
Star. Stretching my neck to look uncomfortably at
this indication of our extreme northernness, it was hard
to realize that he was not directly overhead: and it
made me sigh, as I measured the few degrees of distance that separated our zenith from the Pole over
which he hung.

"We had our accustomed morning and evening
prayers; and the day went by, full of sober thought,
and, I trust, wise resolve.

"September 12, Monday.—Still going on with Saturday's operations, amid the thousand discomforts of
house-cleaning and moving combined. I dodged them
for an hour this morning, to fix with Mr. Sontag upon
a site for our observatory; and the men are already
at work hauling the stone for it over the ice on sledges.
It is to occupy a rocky islet, about a hundred yards
off, that I have named after a little spot that I long to
see again, 'FERN ROCK.' This is to be for me the
centre of familiar localities. As the classic Mivins
breakfasted lightly on a cigar and took it out in sleep,
so I have dined on salt pork and made my dessert of
home dreams.

"September 13, Tuesday.—Besides preparing our
winter quarters, I am engaged in the preliminary arrangements for my provision-depôts along the Greenland coast. Mr. Kennedy is, I believe, the only one
of my predecessors who has used October and Novem-

ber for Arctic field-work; but I deem it important to our movements during the winter and spring, that the depôts in advance should be made before the darkness sets in. I purpose arranging three of them at intervals,—pushing them as far forward as I can,—to contain in all some twelve hundred pounds of provision, of which eight hundred will be pemmican."

My plans of future search were directly dependent upon the success of these operations of the fall. With a chain of provision-depôts along the coast of Greenland, I could readily extend my travel by dogs. These noble animals formed the basis of my future plans: the only drawback to their efficiency as a means of travel was their inability to carry the heavy loads of provender essential for their support. A badly-fed or heavily-loaded dog is useless for a long journey; but with relays of provisions I could start empty, and fill up at our final station.

My dogs were both Esquimaux and Newfoundlanders. Of these last I had ten: they were to be carefully broken, to travel by voice without the whip, and were expected to be very useful for heavy draught, as their tractability would allow the driver to regulate their pace. I was already training them in a light sledge, to drive, unlike the Esquimaux, two abreast, with a regular harness, a breast-collar of flat leather, and a pair of traces. Six of them made a powerful travelling-team; and four could carry me and my instruments, for short journeys around the brig, with great ease.

The sledge I used for them was built, with the care of cabinet-work, of American hickory thoroughly seasoned. The curvature of the runners was determined experimentally:[26] they were shod with annealed steel, and fastened by copper rivets which could be renewed at pleasure. Except this, no metal entered into its construction. All its parts were held together by sealskin lashings, so that it yielded to inequalities of surface and to sudden shock. The three paramount con-

LITTLE WILLIE, AND NEWFOUNDLANDERS.

siderations of lightness, strength, and diminished friction, were well combined in it. This beautiful, and, as we afterward found, efficient and enduring sledge was named the "Little Willie."

The Esquimaux dogs were reserved for the great tug of the actual journeys of search. They were now in the semi-savage condition which marks their close approach to the wolf; and according to Mr. Petersen, under whose care they were placed, were totally useless for journeys over such ice as was now before us. A hard experience had not then opened my eyes to the inestimable value of these dogs: I had yet to learn their power and speed, their patient, enduring fortitude, their sagacity in tracking these icy morasses, among which they had been born and bred.

I determined to hold back my more distant provision parties as long as the continued daylight would permit; making the Newfoundland dogs establish the depôts within sixty miles of the brig. My previous journey had shown me that the ice-belt, clogged with the foreign matters dislodged from the cliffs, would not at this season of the year answer for operations with the sledge, and that the ice of the great pack outside was even more unfit, on account of its want of continuity. It was now so consolidated by advancing cold as to have stopped its drift to the south; but the large floes or fields which formed it were imperfectly cemented together, and would break into hummocks under the action of winds or even of the tides. It was made still more impassable by the numerous bergs* which kept ploughing with irresistible momentum through the ice-tables, and rearing up barricades that defied the passage of a sledge.

It was desirable, therefore, that our depôt parties should not enter upon their work until they could avail themselves of the young ice. This now occupied a belt, about one hundred yards in mean breadth,

---

* The general drift of these great masses was to the south,—a plain indication of deep sea-currents in that direction, and a convincing proof, to me, of a discharge from some northern water.

close to the shore, and, but for the fluctuations of the
tides, would already be a practicable road. For the
present, however, a gale of wind or a spring tide
might easily drive the outer floes upon it, and thus
destroy its integrity.

The party appointed to establish this depôt was
furnished with a sledge, the admirable model of which
I obtained through the British Admiralty. The only
liberty that I ventured to take with this model—
which had been previously tested by the adventurous
journeys of McClintock in Lancaster Sound—was to
lessen the height, and somewhat increase the breadth
of the runner; both of which, I think, were improve-
ments, giving increased strength, and preventing
too deep a descent into the snow. I named her the
"Faith." Her length was thirteen feet, and breadth
four. She could readily carry fourteen hundred pounds
of mixed stores.

This noble old sledge, which is now endeared to me
by every pleasant association, bore the brunt of the
heaviest parties, and came back, after
the descent of the coast, comparatively sound. The men were attached to her in such a way as to
make the line of draught or traction
as near as possible in the axis of the
weight. Each man had his own
shoulder-belt, or "rue-raddy," as we
used to call it, and his own track-
line, which for want of horse-hair

THE RUE-RADDY

was made of Manilla rope: it traversed freely by a
ring on a loop or bridle, that extended from runner
to runner in front of the sledge. These track-ropes
varied in length, so as to keep the members of the
party from interfering with each other by walking
abreast. The longest was three fathoms, eighteen
feet, in length; the shortest, directly fastened to the
sledge runner, as a means of guiding or suddenly arresting and turning the vehicle.

The cargo for this journey, without including the

SLEDGE DRAWN BY NINE MEN.

provisions of the party, was almost exclusively pemmican. Some of this was put up in cylinders of
tinned iron with conical terminations, so as to resist
the assaults of the white bear; but the larger quantity was in strong wooden cases or kegs, well hooped
with iron, holding about seventy pounds each. Sur-
mounting this load was a light India-rubber boat,
made quite portable by a frame of basket willow,
which I hoped to launch on reaching open water.[27]

The personal equipment of the men was a buffalo-
robe for the party to lie upon, and a bag of Mackinaw

blanket for each man to crawl into at night. India-
rubber cloth was to be the protection from the snow
beneath. The tent was of canvas, made after the
plan of our English predecessors. We afterward
learned to modify and reduce our travelling gear,
and found that in direct proportion to its simplicity
and our apparent privation of articles of supposed
necessity were our actual comfort and practical efficiency. Step by step, as long as our Arctic service
continued, we went on reducing our sledging outfit,
until at last we came to the Esquimaux ultimatum
of simplicity,—raw meat and a fur bag.

While our arrangements for the winter were still in
progress, I sent out Mr. Wilson and Dr. Hayes, accompanied by our Esquimaux, Hans, to learn something of
the interior features of the country, and the promise it
afforded of resources from the hunt. They returned on
the 16th of September, after a hard travel, made with
excellent judgment and abundant zeal. They penetrated into the interior about ninety miles, when their
progress was arrested by a glacier, four hundred feet
high, and extending to the north and west as far as
the eye could reach. This magnificent body of interior ice formed on its summit a complete plateau,—a
mer de glace, abutting upon a broken plain of syenite.[28]
They found no large lakes. They saw a few reindeer
at a distance, and numerous hares and rabbits, but no
ptarmigan.

"September 20, Tuesday.—I was unwilling to delay
my depôt party any longer. They left the brig,

McGary, and Bonsall, with five men, at half-past one to-day. We gave them three cheers, and I accompanied them with my dogs as a farewell escort for some miles.

"Our crew proper is now reduced to three men; but all the officers, the doctor among the rest, are hard at work upon the observatory and its arrangements."

CHAPTER XI.

THE island on which we placed our observatory was some fifty paces long by perhaps forty broad, and about thirty feet above the water-line. Here we raised four walls of granite blocks, cementing them together with moss and water and the never-failing aid of frost. On these was laid a substantial wooden roof, perforated at the meridian and prime vertical. For pedestals we had a conglomerate of gravel and ice, well rammed down while liquid in our iron-hooped pemmican-casks, and as free from all vibration as the rock they rested on. Here we mounted our transit and theodolite.

The magnetic observatory adjoining, had rather more of the affectation of comfort. It was of stone, ten feet square, with a wooden floor as well as roof, a copper fire-grate, and stands of the same Arctic breccia as those in its neighbor. No iron was used in its construction. Here were our magnetometer and dip instruments.

116

Our tide-register was on board the vessel, a simple pulley-gauge, arranged with a wheel and index, and dependent on her rise and fall for its rotation.[29]

BRIG IN HARBOR.

Our meteorological observatory was upon the open ice-field, one hundred and forty yards from the ship. It was a wooden structure, latticed and pierced with auger-holes on all sides, so as to allow the air to pass freely, and firmly luted to its frozen base. To guard against the fine and almost impalpable drift, which insinuates itself everywhere, and which would interfere with the observation of minute and sudden changes of temperature, I placed a series of screens at right angles to each other, so as to surround the inner chamber.

The thermometers were suspended within the central chamber: a pane of glass permitted the light of our lanterns to reach them from a distance, and a lens and eye-glass were so fixed as to allow us to observe the instruments without coming inside the screens. Their sensibility was such that when standing at 40° and 50° below zero, the mere approach of the observer caused a perceptible rise of the column. One of them, a three-feet spirit standard by Taliabue, graduated to 70° minus, was of sufficiently extended register to be read by rapid inspection to tenths of a degree. The influence of winds I did not wish absolutely to neutralize; but I endeavored to make the exposure to them so uniform as to give a relative result for every quarter of the compass. We were well supplied with thermometers of all varieties.[30]

I had devised a wind-gauge to be observed by a tell-tale below deck; but we found that the condensing moisture so froze around it as to clog its motion.

"September 30, Friday.—We have been terribly annoyed by rats. Some days ago, we made a brave effort to smoke them out with the vilest imaginable

compound of vapors,—brimstone, burnt leather, and
arsenic,—and spent a cold night in a deck-bivouac
to give the experiment fair play. But they survived
the fumigation. We now determined to dose them
with carbonic acid gas. Dr. Hayes burnt a quantity
of charcoal; and we shut down the hatches, after
pasting up every fissure that communicated aft and
starting three stoves on the skin of the forepeak.

"As the gas was generated with extreme rapidity in
the confined area below, great caution had to be exer-
cised. Our French cook, good Pierre Schubert,—who
to a considerable share of bull-headed intrepidity unites
a commendable portion of professional zeal,—stole below, without my knowledge or consent, to season a
soup. Morton fortunately saw him staggering in the
dark; and, reaching him with great difficulty as he
fell, both were hauled up in the end,—Morton, his
strength almost gone, the cook perfectly insensible.

"The next disaster was of a graver sort. I record
it with emotions of mingled awe and thankfulness.
We have narrowly escaped being burnt out of house
and home. I had given orders that the fires, lit under
my own eye, should be regularly inspected; but I
learned that Pierre's misadventure had made the
watch pretermit for a time opening the hatches. As
I lowered a lantern, which was extinguished instantly,
a suspicious odor reached me, as of burning wood. I
descended at once. Reaching the deck of the forecastle, my first glance toward the fires showed me that
all was safe there; and, though the quantity of smoke

still surprised me, I was disposed to attribute it to the recent kindling. But at this moment, while passing on my return near the door of the bulkhead, which leads to the carpenter's room, the gas began to affect me. My lantern went out as if quenched by water; and, as I ran by the bulkhead door, I saw the deck near it a mass of glowing fire for some three feet in diameter. I could not tell how much farther it extended; for I became quite insensible at the foot of the ladder, and would have sunk had not Mr. Brooks seen my condition and hauled me out.

"When I came to myself, which happily was very soon, I confided my fearful secret to the four men around me, Brooks, Ohlsen, Blake, and Stevenson. It was all-important to avoid confusion: we shut the doors of the galley, so as to confine the rest of the crew and officers aft; and then passed up water from the fire-hole alongside. It was done very noiselessly. Ohlsen and myself went down to the burning deck; Brooks handed us in the buckets; and in less than ten minutes we were in safety. It was interesting to observe the effect of steam upon the noxious gas. Both Ohlsen and myself were greatly oppressed until the first bucket was poured on; but as I did this, directly over the burning coal, raising clouds of steam, we at once experienced relief: the fine aqueous particles seemed to absorb the carbonic acid instantly. We found the fire had originated in the remains of a barrel of charcoal, which had been left in the carpenter's room, ten feet from the stoves, and with a bulkhead separating it from them.   How it had been ignited it was impossible to know.   Our safety was due to the dense charge of carbonic acid gas which surrounded the fire, and the exclusion of atmospheric air.   When the hatches were opened, the flame burst out with energy.   Our fire-hole was invaluable; and I rejoiced that in the midst of our heavy duties, this essential of an Arctic winter harbor had not been neglected.   The ice around the brig was already fourteen inches thick.

"October 1, Saturday.—Upon inspecting the scene of yesterday's operations, we found twenty-eight well-fed rats of all varieties of age.   The cook, though unable to do duty, is better: I can hear him chanting his Béranger through the blankets in his bunk, happy over his holiday, happy to be happy at every thing. I had a larger dose of carbonic acid even than he, and am suffering considerably with palpitations and vertigo.   If the sentimental asphyxia of Parisian charcoal resembles in its advent that of the Arctic zone, it must be, I think, a poor way of dying.

" October 3, Monday.—On shore to the southeast, above the first terrace, Mr. Petersen found unmistakeable signs of a sledge-passage.   The tracks were deeply impressed, but certainly more than one season old.   This adds to our hope that the natives, whose ancient traces we saw on the point south of Godsend Ledge, may return this winter.

"October 5, Wednesday.—I walked this afternoon to another group of Esquimaux huts, about three miles

from the brig. They are four in number, long deserted, but, to an eye unpractised in Arctic antiquarian
inductions, in as good preservation as a last year's
tenement at home. The most astonishing feature is
the presence of some little out-huts, or, as I first
thought them, dog-kennels. These are about four
feet by three in ground-plan. and some three feet

THE ESQUIMAUX HUTS.

high; no larger than the pologs of the Tchuschi
In shape they resemble a rude dome; and the stones
of which they are composed are of excessive size, and
evidently selected for smoothness. They were, without exception, of waterwashed limestone. They are
heavily sodded with turf, and a narrow slab of clay-
slate serves as a door. No doubt they are human
habitations,—retiring-chambers, into which, away from
the crowded families of the hut, one or even two Esquimaux have burrowed for sleep,—chilly dormitories in
the winter of this high latitude.[31]

  "A circumstance that happened to-day is of serious

concern to us. Our sluts have been adding to our stock. We have now on hand four reserved puppies of peculiar promise; six have been ignominiously drowned, two devoted to a pair of mittens for Dr. Kane, and seven eaten by their mammas. Yesterday, the mother of one batch, a pair of fine white pups, showed peculiar symptoms. We recalled the fact that for days past she had avoided water, or had drunk with spasm and evident aversion; but hydrophobia, which is unknown north of 70°, never occurred to us. The animal was noticed this morning walking up and down the deck with a staggering gait, her head depressed and her mouth frothing and tumid. Finally she snapped at Petersen, and fell foaming and biting at his feet. He reluctantly pronounced it hydrophobia, and advised me to shoot her. The advice was well-timed: I had hardly cleared the deck before she snapped at Hans, the Esquimaux, and recommenced her walking trot. It was quite an anxious moment to me; for my Newfoundlanders were around the housing, and the hatches open. We shot her, of course.

"October 6, Thursday.—The hares are less numerous than they were. They seek the coast when the snows fall in the interior, and the late southeast wind has probably favored their going back. These animals are not equal in size either to the European hare or their brethren of the North American continent. The latter, according to Seamann, weigh upon an average fourteen pounds. A large male, the largest seen by us in

Smith's Sound, weighed but nine; and our average so far does not exceed seven and a half. They measure generally less by some inches in length than those noticed by Dr. Richardson. Mr. Petersen is quite successful in shooting these hares: we have a stock of fourteen now on hand.

"We have been building stone traps on the hills for the foxes, whose traces we see there in abundance, and have determined to organize a regular hunt as soon as they give us the chance.

"October 8, Saturday.—I have been practising with my dog-sledge and an Esquimaux team till my arms ache. To drive such an equipage a certain proficiency with the whip is indispensable, which, like all proficiency, must be worked for. In fact, the weapon has an exercise of its own, quite peculiar, and as hard to learn as single-stick or broadsword.

"The whip is six yards long, and the handle but sixteen inches,—a short lever, of course, to throw out such a length of seal-hide. Learn to do it, however, with a masterly sweep, or else make up your mind to forego driving sledge; for the dogs are guided solely by the lash, and you must be able not only to hit any particular dog out of a team of twelve, but to accompany the feat also with a resounding crack. After this, you find that to get your lash back involves another difficulty; for it is apt to entangle itself among the dogs and lines, or to fasten itself cunningly round bits of ice, so as to drag you head over heels into the snow.

"The secret by which this complicated set of requirements is fulfilled consists in properly describing an arc from the shoulder, with a stiff elbow, giving the jerk to the whip-handle from the hand and wrist alone. The lash trails behind as you travel, and when thrown forward is allowed to extend itself without an effort to bring it back. You wait patiently after giving the projectile impulse until it unwinds its slow length, reaches the end of its tether, and cracks to tell you that it is at its journey's end. Such a crack on the ear or forefoot of an unfortunate dog is signalized by a howl quite unmistakeable in its import.

"The mere labor of using this whip is such that the Esquimaux travel in couples, one sledge after the other. The hinder dogs follow mechanically, and thus require no whip; and the drivers change about so as to rest each other.

"I have amused myself, if not my dogs, for some days past with this formidable accessory of Arctic travel. I have not quite got the knack of it yet, though I might venture a trial of cracking against the postillion college of Lonjumeau.

"October 9, Sunday.—Mr. Petersen shot a hare yesterday. They are very scarce now, for he travelled some five hours without seeing another. He makes the important report of musk ox tracks on the recent snow. Dr. Richardson says that these are scarcely distinguishable from the reindeer's except by the practised eye: he characterizes them as larger, but not wider. The tracks that Petersen saw had an interesting confirmation of their being those of the musk ox, for they were

accompanied by a second set of footprints, evidently belonging to a young one of the same species, and about
as large as a middle-sized reindeer's. Both impressions
also were marked as if by hair growing from the pastern
joint, for behind the hoof was a line brushed in the
snow.[(32)]

"To-day Hans brought in another hare he had shot.
He saw seven reindeer in a large valley off Bedevilled
Reach, and wounded one of them. This looks pro-
mising for our winter commissariat.

"October 10, Monday.—Our depôt party has been
out twenty days, and it is time they were back: their
provisions must have run very low, for I enjoined
them to leave every pound at the depôt they could
spare. I am going out with supplies to look after them.
I take four of our best Newfoundlanders, now well
broken, in our lightest sledge; and Blake will accompany me with his skates. We have not hands enough
to equip a sledge party, and the ice is too unsound for
us to attempt to ride with a large team. The thermometer is still four degrees above zero."

CHAPTER XII.

I FOUND little or no trouble in crossing the ice until we passed beyond the northeast headland, which I have named Cape William Wood. But, on emerging into the channel, we found that the spring tides had broken up the great area around us, and that the passage of the sledge was interrupted by fissures, which were beginning to break in every direction through the young ice.

My first effort was of course to reach the land; but it was unfortunately low tide, and the ice-belt rose up before me like a wall. The pack was becoming more and more unsafe, and I was extremely anxious to gain an asylum on shore; for, though it was easy to find a temporary refuge by retreating to the old floes which studded the more recent ice, I knew that in doing so we should risk being carried down by the drift.

The dogs began to flag; but we had to press them :—

127

we were only two men; and, in the event of the animals failing to leap any of the rapidly-multiplying
fissures, we could hardly expect to extricate our laden
sledge.   Three times in less than three hours my shaft
or hinder dogs went in; and John and myself, who had
been. trotting alongside the sledge for sixteen miles,
were nearly as tired as they were. This state of
things could not last; and I therefore made for the old
ice to seaward.

We were nearing it rapidly, when the dogs failed in
leaping a chasm that was somewhat wider than the
others, and the whole concern came down in the water.
I cut the lines instantly, and, with the aid of my companion, hauled the poor animals out. We owed the
preservation of the sledge to their admirable docility
and perseverance. The tin cooking-apparatus and the
air confined in the India-rubber coverings kept it afloat
till we could succeed in fastening a couple of seal-skin
cords to the cross-pieces at the front and back. By
these John and myself were able to give it an uncertain
support from the two edges of the opening, till the dogs,
after many fruitless struggles, carried it forward at last
upon the ice.

Although the thermometer was below zero, and in
our wet state we ran a considerable risk of freezing,
the urgency of our position left no room for thoughts
of cold. We started at a run, men and dogs, for the
solid ice; and by the time we had gained it we were
steaming in the cold atmosphere like a couple of
Nootka Sound vapor-baths.

We rested on the floe. We could not raise our tent, for it had frozen as hard as a shingle. But our buffalo-robe bags gave us protection; and, though we were too wet inside to be absolutely comfortable, we managed to

ICE-BELT OF OCTOBER.

get something like sleep before it was light enough for us to move on again.

The journey was continued in the same way; but we found to our great gratification that the cracks closed with the change of the tide, and at high-water we succeeded in gaining the ice-belt under the cliffs. This belt had changed very much since my journey in

September. The tides and frosts together had coated it with ice as smooth as satin, and this glossy covering made it an excellent road. The cliffs discharged fewer fragments in our path, and the rocks of our last journey's experience were now fringed with icicles. I saw with great pleasure that this ice-belt would serve as a highway for our future operations.

The nights which followed were not so bad as one would suppose from the saturated condition of our equipment. Evaporation is not so inappreciable in this Arctic region as some theorists imagine. By alternately exposing the tent and furs to the air, and beating the ice out of them, we dried them enough to permit sleep. The dogs slept in the tent with us, giving it warmth as well as fragrance. What perfumes of nature are lost at home upon our ungrateful senses! How we relished the companionship!

We had averaged twenty miles a day since leaving the brig, and were within a short march of the cape which I have named William Wood, when a broad chasm brought us to a halt. It was in vain that we worked out to seaward, or dived into the shoreward recesses of the bay: the ice everywhere presented the same impassable fissures. We had no alternative but to retrace our steps and seek among the bergs some place of security. We found a camp for the night on the old floe-ices to the westward, gaining them some time after the darkness had closed in.

On the morning of the 15th, about two hours before the late sunrise, as I was preparing to climb a berg from which I might have a sight of the road ahead, I perceived far off upon the white snow a dark object, which not only moved, but altered its shape strangely,—now expanding into a long black line, now waving, now gathering itself up into a compact mass. It was the returning sledge party. They had seen our black tent of Kedar, and ferried across to seek it.

They were most welcome; for their absence, in the

CAMP ON THE FLOES.

fearfully open state of the ice, had filled me with apprehensions. We could not distinguish each other as we drew near in the twilight; and my first good news of them was when I heard that they were singing. On they came, and at last I was able to count their voices, one by one. Thank God, seven! Poor John Blake was so breathless with gratulation, that I could not get him to blow his signal-horn. We gave them, instead, the good old Anglo-Saxon greeting, "three cheers!" and in a few minutes were among them.

They had made a creditable journey, and were, on the whole, in good condition. They had no injuries worth talking about, although not a man had escaped some touches of the frost. Bonsall was minus a big toe-nail, and plus a scar upon the nose. McGary had attempted, as Tom Hickey told us, to *pluck* a fox, it being so frozen as to defy skinning by his knife; and his fingers had been tolerably frost-bitten in the operation. "They're very horny, sir, are my fingers," said McGary, who was worn down to a mere shadow of his former rotundity; "very horny, and they water up like bladders." The rest had suffered in their feet; but, like good fellows, postponed limping until they reached the ship.

Within the last three days they had marched fifty-four miles, or eighteen a day. Their sledge being empty, and the young ice north of Cape Bancroft smooth as a mirror, they had travelled, the day before we met them, nearly twenty-five miles. A very remarkable pace for men who had been twenty-eight days in the field.

My supplies of hot food, coffee, and marled beef soup, which I had brought with me, were very opportune. They had almost exhausted their bread; and, being unwilling to encroach on the depôt stores, had gone without fuel in order to save alcohol. Leaving orders to place my own sledge stores in *cache,* I returned to the brig, ahead of the party, with my dog-sledge, carrying Mr. Bonsall with me.

On this return I had much less difficulty with the

NEWFOUNDLAND DOG TEAM.

ice-cracks; my team of Newfoundlanders leaping them
in almost every instance, and the impulse of our
sledge carrying it across.   On one occasion, while we
were making these flying leaps, poor Bonsall was
tossed out, and came very near being carried under
by the rapid tide.   He fortunately caught the runner
of the sledge as he fell, and I succeeded, by whipping
up the dogs, in hauling him out.   He was, of course,
wet to the skin; but we were only twenty miles from
the brig, and he sustained no serious injury from his
immersion.

I return to my journal.

"The spar-deck—or, as we call it from its wooden covering, the 'House'—is steaming with the buffalo-robes, tents, boots, socks, and heterogeneous costumings of our returned parties. We have ample work in repairing these and restoring the disturbed order of our domestic life. The men feel the effects of their journey, but are very content in their comfortable quarters. A pack of cards, grog at dinner, and the promise of a three days' holiday, have made the decks happy with idleness and laughter."

I give the general results of the party; referring to the Appendix for the detailed account of Messrs. McGary and Bonsall.

They left the brig, as may be remembered, on the 20th of September, and they reached Cape Russell on the 25th. Near this spot I had, in my former journey of reconnoissance, established a cairn; and here, as by previously-concerted arrangement, they left their first cache of pemmican, together with some bread and alcohol for fuel.

On the 28th, after crossing a large bay, they met a low cape about thirty miles to the northeast of the first depôt. Here they made a second cache of a hundred and ten pounds of beef and pemmican, and about thirty of a mixture of pemmican and Indian meal, with a bag of bread.

The day being too foggy for sextant observations for position, or even for a reliable view of the landmarks, they built a substantial cairn, and buried the provision at a distance of ten paces from its centre, bearing by compass, E. by N. ½ N. The point on which this cache stood I subsequently named after Mr. Bonsall, one of the indefatigable leaders of the party.

I will give the geographical outline of the track of this party in a subsequent part of this narrative, when I have spoken of the after-travel and surveys which confirmed and defined it. But I should do injustice both to their exertions and to the results of them, were I to omit mention of the difficulties which they encountered.

On the twenty-fifth day of their outward journey they met a great glacier, which I shall describe hereafter. It checked their course along the Greenland coast abruptly; but they still endeavored to make their way outside its edge to seaward, with the commendable object of seeking a more northern point for the provision depôt. This journey was along the base of an icy wall, which constantly threw off its discharging bergs, breaking up the ice for miles around, and compelling the party to ferry themselves and their sledge over the cracks by rafts of ice.

One of these incidents I give nearly in the language of Mr. Bonsall.

They had camped, on the night of 5th October, under the lee of some large icebergs, and within hearing of the grand artillery of the glacier. The floe on which their tent was pitched was of recent and transparent ice; and the party, too tired to seek a safer asylum, had turned in to rest; when, with a crack like the snap of a gigantic whip, the ice opened directly beneath them. This was, as nearly as they could estimate the time, at about one o'clock in the morning. The darkness was intense; and the cold, about 10° below zero, was increased by a wind which blew from the northeast over the glacier. They gathered together their tent and sleeping furs, and lashed them, according to the best of their ability, upon the sledge.

CAMP UNDER GLACIER—OCTOBER FIFTH.

Repeated intonations warned them that the ice was breaking up; a swell, evidently produced by the avalanches from the glacier, caused the platform on which they stood to rock to and fro.

Mr. McGary derived a hope from the stable character of the bergs near them: they were evidently not adrift. He determined to select a flat piece of ice, place the sledge upon it, and, by the aid of tent-poles and cooking-utensils, paddle to the old and firm fields which clung to the bases of the bergs. The party waited in anxious expectation until the returning day-light permitted this attempt; and, after a most adventurous passage, succeeded in reaching the desired position.

My main object in sending them out was the deposit of provisions, and I had not deemed it advisable to complicate their duties by any organization for a survey. They reached their highest latitude on the 6th of October; and this, as determined by dead reckoning, was in latitude 79°50′, and longitude 76°20′. From this point they sighted and took sextant bearings of land to the north,* having a trend or inclination west by north and east by south, at an estimated distance of thirty miles. They were at this time entangled in the icebergs; and it was from the lofty summit of one of these, in the midst of a scene of surpassing desolation, that they made their observations.

They began the third or final cache, which was the main object of the journey, on the 10th of October; placing it on a low island at the base of the large

---

* I may mention that the results of their observations were not used in the construction of our charts, except their interesting sextant bearings. These were both numerous and valuable, but not sustained at the time by satisfactory astronomical observations for position.

glacier which checked their further march along the coast.

Before adopting this site, they had perseveringly skirted the base of the glacier, in a fruitless effort to cross it to the north. In spite of distressing cold, and the nearly constant winds from the ice-clothed shore, they carried out all my instructions for securing this important depôt. The stores were carefully buried in a natural excavation among the cliffs; and heavy rocks, brought with great labor, were piled above them. Smaller stones were placed over these, and incorporated into one solid mass by a mixture of sand and water. The power of the bear in breaking up a provision cache is extraordinary; but the Esquimaux to the south had assured me that frozen sand and water, which would wear away the animal's claws, were more effective against him than the largest rocks. Still, knowing how much trouble the officers of Commodore Austin's Expedition experienced from the destruction of their caches, I had ordered the party to resort to a combination of these expedients.[33]

They buried here six hundred and seventy pounds of pemmican, forty of Borden's meat biscuit, and some articles of general diet; making a total of about eight hundred pounds. They indicated the site by a large cairn, bearing E. ½ S. from the cache, and at the distance of thirty paces. The landmarks of the cairn itself were sufficiently evident, but were afterwards fixed by bearings, for additional certainty.

The island which was so judiciously selected as the seat of this cache was named after my faithful friend and excellent second officer, Mr. James McGary, of New London.

MCGARY'S CACHE.

CHAPTER XIII.

WALRUS-HOLES—ADVANCE OF DARKNESS—DARKNESS—THE COLD
—"THE ICE-BLINK"—FOX-CHASE—ESQUIMAUX HUTS—OCCULTA-
TION OF SATURN—PORTRAIT OF OLD GRIM.

"OCTOBER 28, Friday.—The moon has reached her greatest northern declination of about 25° 35'. She is a glorious object: sweeping around the heavens, at the lowest part of her curve, she is still 14° above the horizon. For eight days she has been making her circuit with nearly unvarying brightness. It is one of those sparkling nights that bring back the memory of sleigh-bells and songs and glad communings of hearts in lands that are far away.

"Our fires and ventilation-fixtures are so arranged that we are able to keep a mean temperature below of 65°, and on deck, under our housing, above the freezing-point. This is admirable success; for the weather outside is at 25° below zero, and there is quite a little breeze blowing.

"The last remnant of walrus did not leave us until the second week of last month, when the temperature had sunk below zero. Till then they found open

Engraved at J. M. Butler's establishment 84 Chestnut St.

MIDNIGHT IN SEPTEMBER.

(From a sketch by Dr Kane.)

G. Ulman

water enough to sport and even sleep in, between
the fields of drift, as they opened with the tide; but
they had worked numerous breathing-holes besides, in
the solid ice nearer shore.*   Many of these were inside the capes of Rensselaer Harbor.   They had the
same circular, cleanly-finished margin as the seals',
but they were in much thicker ice, and the radiating

WALRUS SPORTING.

lines of fracture round them much more marked.
The animal evidently used his own buoyancy as a
means of starting the ice.

"Around these holes the ice was much discolored:

---

* The walrus often sleeps on the surface of the water while his
fellows are playing around him.   In this condition I frequently surprised the young ones, whose mothers were asleep by their side.

numbers of broken clam-shells were found near them, and, in one instance, some gravel, mingled with about half a peck of the coarse shingle of the beach. The use of the stones which the walrus swallows is still an interesting question. The ussuk or bearded seal has the same habit.

"November 7, Monday.—The darkness is coming on with insidious steadiness, and its advances can only be

WALRUS-HOLE.

perceived by comparing one day with its fellow of some time back. We still read the thermometer at noonday without a light, and the black masses of the hills are plain for about five hours with their glaring patches of snow; but all the rest is darkness. Lanterns are always on the spar-deck, and the lard-lamps never extinguished below. The stars of the sixth magnitude shine out at noonday.

"Except upon the island of Spitzbergen, which has

the advantages of an insular climate and tempered by ocean currents, no Christians have wintered in so high a latitude as this. They are Russian sailors who make the encounter there, men inured to hardships and cold. I cannot help thinking of the sad chronicles of the early

NOONDAY IN NOVEMBER.

Dutch, who perished year after year, without leaving a comrade to record their fate.

"Our darkness has ninety days to run before we shall get back again even to the contested twilight of to-day. Altogether, our winter will have been sunless for one hundred and forty days.

"It requires neither the 'Ice-foot' with its growing ramparts, nor the rapid encroachments of the night, nor the record of our thermometers, to portend for us a winter of unusual severity. The mean temperatures of October and September are lower than those of Parry for the same months at Melville Island. Thus far we have no indications of that deferred fall cold which marks the insular climate.

"November 9, Wednesday.—Wishing to get the altitude of the cliffs on the southwest cape of our bay before the darkness set in thoroughly, I started in time to reach them with my Newfoundlanders at noonday. Although it was but a short journey, the rough shore-ice and a slight wind rendered the cold severe. I had been housed for a week with my wretched rheumatism, and felt that daily exposure was necessary to enable me to bear up against the cold. The thermometer indicated twenty-three degrees below zero.

"Fireside astronomers can hardly realize the difficulties in the way of observations at such low temperatures. The mere burning of the hands is obviated by covering the metal with chamois-skin; but the breath, and even the warmth of the face and body, cloud the sextant-arc and glasses with a fine hoarfrost. Though I had much clear weather, we barely succeeded by magnifiers in reading the verniers. It is, moreover, an unusual feat to measure a base-line in the snow at fifty-five degrees below freezing.

"November 16, Wednesday.—The great difficulty is

to keep up a cheery tone among the men. Poor Hans has been sorely homesick. Three days ago he bundled up his clothes and took his rifle to bid us all good-bye. It turns out that besides his mother there is another one of the softer sex at Fiskernaes that the boy's heart is dreaming of. He looked as wretched as any lover of a milder clime. I hope I have treated his nostalgia successfully, by giving him first a dose of salts, and, secondly, promotion. He has now all the dignity of henchman. He harnesses my dogs, builds my traps, and walks with me on my ice-tramps; and, except hunting, is excused from all other duty. He is really attached to me, and as happy as a fat man ought to be.

"November 21, Monday.—We have schemes innumerable to cheat the monotonous solitude of our winter. We are getting up a fancy ball; and to-day the first number of our Arctic newspaper, 'The Ice-Blink,' came out, with the motto, 'IN TENEBRIS SERVARE FIDEM.' The articles are by authors of every nautical grade: some of the best from the forecastle. I transfer a few of them to my Appendix; but the following sketch is a fac-simile of the vignette of our little paper.

"November 22, Tuesday.—I offered a prize to-day of a Guernsey shirt to the man who held out longest in a 'fox-chase' round the decks. The rule of the sport was, that 'Fox' was to run a given circuit between galley and capstan, all hands following on his track; every four minutes a halt to be called to blow, and the fox making the longest run to take the prize; each of

"IN TENEBRIS SERVARE FIDEM."

the crew to run as fox in turn. William Godfrey sustained the chase for fourteen minutes, and *wore* off the shirt.

"November 27, Sunday.—I sent out a volunteer party some days ago with Mr. Bonsall, to see whether the Esquimaux have returned to the huts we saw empty at the cape. The thermometer was in the neighborhood of 40° below zero, and the day was too dark to read at noon. I was hardly surprised when they returned after camping one night upon the snow. Their sledge broke down, and they were obliged to leave tents and every thing else behind them. It must have been very cold, for a bottle of Monongahela whiskey of good stiff proof froze under Mr. Bonsall's head.

"Morton went out on Friday to reclaim the things they had left; and to-day at 1 P.M. he returned successful. He reached the wreck of the former party, making nine miles in three hours,—pushed on six miles farther on the Ice-foot,—then camped for the night; and, making a sturdy march the next day without luggage, reached the huts, and got back to his camp to sleep. This journey of his was, we then thought, really an achievement,—sixty-two miles in three marches, with a mean temperature of 40° below zero, and a noonday so dark that you could hardly see a hummock of ice fifty paces ahead.

"Under more favoring circumstances, Bonsall, Morton, and myself made eighty-four miles in three consecutive marches. I go for the system of forced marches on journeys that are not over a hundred and fifty miles. A practised walker unencumbered by weight does twenty miles a day nearly as easily as ten: it is the uncomfortable sleeping that wears a party out.

"Morton found no natives; but he saw enough to satisfy me that the huts could not have been deserted long before we came to this region. The foxes had been at work upon the animal remains that we found there, and the appearances which we noted of recent habitation had in a great degree disappeared. Where these Esquimaux have travelled to is matter for conjecture. The dilapidated character of the huts we have seen farther to the north seems to imply that they cannot have gone in that direction. They have more probably migrated southward, and, as the spring opens, may return, with the walrus and seal, to their former haunts. We shall see them, I think, before we leave our icy moorings.

"December 12, Monday.—A grand incident in our great monotony of life! We had an occultation of Saturn at 2 A.M., and got a most satisfactory observation. The emersion was obtained with greater accuracy than would have been expected from the excessive atmospheric undulation of these low temperatures. My little Fraunhöfer sustained its reputation well. We can now fix our position without a cavil.

"December 15, Thursday.—We have lost the last vestige of our mid-day twilight. We cannot see print, and hardly paper: the fingers cannot be counted a foot from the eyes. Noonday and midnight are alike, and, except a vague glimmer on the sky that seems to define the hill outlines to the south, we have nothing to tell us that this Arctic world of ours has a sun. In one week more we shall reach the midnight of the year.

"December 22, Thursday.—There is an excitement in our little community that dispenses with reflections upon the solstitial night. 'Old Grim' is missing, and has been for more than a day. Since the lamented demise of Cerberus, my leading Newfoundlander, he has been patriarch of our scanty kennel.

"Old Grim was 'a character' such as peradventure may at some time be found among beings of a higher order and under a more temperate sky. A profound hypocrite and time-server, he so wriggled his adulatory tail as to secure every one's good graces and nobody's respect. All the spare morsels, the cast-off delicacies of the mess, passed through the winnowing jaws of 'Old Grim,'—an illustration not so much of his eclecticism as his universality of taste. He was never known to refuse any thing offered or approachable, and never known to be satisfied, however prolonged and abundant the bounty or the spoil.

"Grim was an ancient dog: his teeth indicated many winters, and his limbs, once splendid tractors for the sledge, were now covered with warts and ringbones. Somehow or other, when the dogs were harnessing for a journey, 'Old Grim' was sure not to be found; and upon one occasion, when he was detected hiding away in a cast-off barrel, he incontinently became lame. Strange to say, he has been lame ever since except when the team is away without him.

"Cold disagrees with Grim; but by a system of patient watchings at the door of our deck-house, accompanied by a discriminating use of his tail, he became at last the one privileged intruder. My seal-skin coat has been his favorite bed for weeks together. Whatever love for an individual Grim expressed by his tail, he could never be induced to follow him on the ice after the cold darkness of the winter set in; yet the dear good old sinner would wriggle after you to the very threshold of the gangway, and bid you good-bye with a deprecatory wag of the tail which disarmed resentment.

"His appearance was quite characteristic:—his muzzle roofed like the old-fashioned gable of a Dutch garret-window; his forehead indicating the most meagre capacity of brains that could consist with his sanity as a dog; his eyes small; his mouth curtained by long black dewlaps; and his hide a mangy russet studded with chestnut-burrs: if he has gone indeed, we 'ne'er shall look upon his like again.' So much for old Grim!

"When yesterday's party started to take soundings, I thought the exercise would benefit Grim, whose time-serving sojourn on our warm deck had begun to render him over-corpulent. A rope was fastened round him; for at such critical periods he was obstinate and even ferocious; and, thus fastened to the sledge, he commenced his reluctant journey. Reaching a stopping-place after a while, he jerked upon his line, parted it a foot or two from its knot, and, dragging the remnant behind him, started off through the darkness in the direction of our brig. He has not been seen since.

"Parties are out with lanterns seeking him; for it is feared that his long cord may have caught upon some of the rude pinnacles of ice which stud our floe, and thus made him a helpless prisoner. The thermometer is at 44°.6 below zero, and old Grim's teeth could not gnaw away the cord.

"December 23, Friday.—Our anxieties for old Grim might have interfered with almost any thing else; but they could not arrest our celebration of yesterday. Dr. Hayes made us a well-studied oration, and Morton a

capital punch; add to these a dinner of marled beef,—
we have two pieces left, for the sun's return and the
Fourth of July,—and a bumper of champagne all
round; and the elements of our frolic are all registered.

"We tracked old Grim to-day through the snow to
within six hundred yards of the brig, and thence to
that mass of snow-packed sterility which we call the
shore. His not rejoining the ship is a mystery quite
in keeping with his character."

PORTRAIT OF OLD GRIM

CHAPTER XIV.

MY journal for the first two months of 1854 is so devoid of interest, that I spare the reader the task of following me through it. In the darkness and consequent inaction, it was almost in vain that we sought to create topics of thought, and by a forced excitement to ward off the encroachments of disease. Our observatory and the dogs gave us our only regular occupations.

On the 9th of January we had again an occultation of Saturn. The emersion occurred during a short interval of clear sky, and our observation of it was quite satisfactory; the limit of the moon's disc and that of the planet being well defined : the mist prevented our seeing the immersion. We had a recurrence of the same phenomenon on the 5th of February, and an occultation of Mars on the 14th; both of them observed under favorable circumstances, the latter especially.

152

Our magnetic observations went on; but the cold made it almost impossible to adhere to them with regularity. Our observatory was, in fact, an ice-house of the coldest imaginable description. The absence of snow prevented our backing the walls with that important non-conductor. Fires, buffalo-robes, and an arras of investing sail-cloth, were unavailing to bring

THE OBSERVATORY.

up the mean temperature to the freezing-point at the level of the magnetometer;* and it was quite common

---

* We had a good unifilar, that had been loaned to us by Professor Bache, of the Coast Survey, and a dip instrument, a Barrow's circle, obtained from the Smithsonian Institution, through the kindness of Col. Sabine. I owe much to Mr. Sontag, Dr. Hayes, and Mr. Bonsall, who bore the brunt of the term-day observations; it was only toward the close of the season that I was enabled to take my share

to find the platform on which the observer stood full fifty degrees lower, (—20°.) Our astronomical observations were less protracted, but the apartment in which they were made was of the same temperature with the outer air. The cold was, of course, intense; and some of our instruments, the dip-circle particularly, became difficult to manage in consequence of the unequal contraction of the brass and steel.

On the 17th of January, our thermometers stood at forty-nine degrees below zero; and on the 20th, the range of those at the observatory was at —64° to —67°. The temperature on the floes was always somewhat higher than at the island; the difference being due, as I suppose, to the heat conducted from the sea-water, which was at a temperature of +29°; the suspended instruments being affected by radiation.

On the 5th of February, our thermometers began to show unexampled temperature. They ranged from 60° to 75° below zero, and one very reliable instrument stood upon the taffrail of our brig at —65°. The reduced mean of our best spirit-standards gave —67°, or 99° below the freezing-point of water.

At these temperatures chloric ether became solid, and carefully-prepared chloroform exhibited a granu-

---

of them. In addition to these, we had weekly determinations of variation of declination, extending through the twenty-four hours, besides observations of intensity, deflection, inclination, and total force, with careful notations of temperature.

lar pellicle on its surface. Spirit of naphtha froze at —54°, and oil of sassafras at —49°. The oil of wintergreen was in a flocculent state at —56°, and solid at —63° and —65°.*[34]

The exhalations from the surface of the body invested the exposed or partially-clad parts with a wreath of vapor. The air had a perceptible pungency upon inspiration, but I could not perceive the painful sensation which has been spoken of by some Siberian travellers. When breathed for any length of time, it imparted a sensation of dryness to the air-passages. I noticed that, as it were involuntarily, we all breathed guardedly, with compressed lips.

The first traces of returning light were observed at noon on the 21st of January, when the southern horizon had for a short time a distinct orange tint. Though the sun had perhaps given us a band of illumination before, it was not distinguishable from the cold light of the planets. We had been nearing the sunshine for thirty-two days, and had just reached that degree of mitigated darkness which made the extreme midnight of Sir Edward Parry in latitude 74° 47'. Even as late as the 31st, two very sensitive daguerreotype plates, treated with iodine and bromine, failed to indicate any solar influence when exposed to the southern horizon at noon; the camera being used in-doors, to escape the effects of cold.

---

* I repeated my observations on the effects of these low temperatures with great care. A further account of them will be seen in the Appendix.

The influence of this long, intense darkness was most depressing. Even our dogs, although the greater part of them were natives of the Arctic circle, were unable to withstand it. Most of them died from an anomalous form of disease, to which, I am satisfied, the absence of light contributed as much as the extreme cold. I give a little extract from my journal of January 20th.

"This morning at five o'clock—for I am so afflicted with the insomnium of this eternal night, that I rise at any time between midnight and noon—I went upon deck. It was absolutely dark; the cold not permitting a swinging lamp. There was not a glimmer came to me through the ice-crusted window-panes of the cabin. While I was feeling my way, half puzzled as to the best method of steering clear of whatever might be before me, two of my Newfoundland dogs put their cold noses against my hand, and instantly commenced the most exuberant antics of satisfaction. It then occurred to me how very dreary and forlorn must these poor animals be, at atmospheres of $+10°$ in-doors and $—50°$ without,—living in darkness, howling at an accidental light, as if it reminded them of the moon,— and with nothing, either of instinct or sensation, to tell them of the passing hours, or to explain the long-lost daylight. They shall see the lanterns more frequently."

I may recur to the influence which our long winter night exerted on the health of these much-valued animals. The subject has some interesting bearings; but

I content myself for the present with transcribing another passage from my journal of a few days later.

"January 25, Wednesday.—The mouse-colored dogs, the leaders of my Newfoundland team, have for the past fortnight been nursed like babies. No one can

THE DECKS BY LAMPLIGHT.

tell how anxiously I watch them. They are kept below, tended, fed, cleansed, caressed, and *doctored*, to the infinite discomfort of all hands. To-day I give up the last hope of saving them. Their disease is as clearly mental as in the case of any human being. The more material functions of the poor brutes go on without interruption: they eat voraciously, retain their

strength, and sleep well. But all the indications beyond this go to prove that the original epilepsy, which
was the first manifestation of brain disease among
them, has been followed by a true lunacy. They
bark frenziedly at nothing, and walk in straight and
curved lines with anxious and unwearying perseverance.

"They fawn on you, but without seeming to appreciate the notice you give them in return; pushing
their heads against your person, or oscillating with a
strange pantomime of fear. Their most intelligent
actions seem automatic: sometimes they claw you, as
if trying to burrow into your seal-skins; sometimes
they remain for hours in moody silence, and then start
off howling as if pursued, and run up and down for
hours.

"So it was with poor Flora, our 'wise dog.' She
was seized with the endemic spasms, and, after a few
wild violent paroxysms, lapsed into a lethargic condition, eating voraciously, but gaining no strength.
This passing off, the same crazy wildness took possession of her, and she died of brain disease (*arachnoidal
effusion*) in about six weeks. Generally, they perish
with symptoms resembling locked-jaw in less than
thirty-six hours after the first attack."

On the 22d, I took my first walk on the great floe,
which had been for so long a time a crude, black labyrinth. I give the appearance of things in the words
of my journal.

"The floe has changed wonderfully. I remember it

sixty-four days ago, when our twilight was as it now is, a partially snow-patched plain, chequered with ridges of sharp hummocks, or a series of long icy levels, over which I coursed with my Newfoundlanders. All this has gone. A lead-colored expanse stretches its 'rounding gray' in every direction, and the old angular hummocks are so softened down as to blend in rolling dunes with the distant obscurity. The snow upon the levels shows the same remarkable evaporation. It is now in crisp layers, hardly six inches thick, quite undisturbed by drift. I could hardly recognise any of the old localities.

"We can trace the outline of the shore again, and even some of the long horizontal bands of its stratification. The cliffs of Sylvia Mountain, which open toward the east, are, if any thing, more covered with snow than the ridges fronting west across the bay.

"But the feature which had changed most was the ice-belt. When I saw it last, it was an investing zone of ice, coping the margin of the floe. The constant accumulation by overflow of tides and freezing has turned this into a bristling wall, twenty feet high, (20 ft. 8 in.) No language can depict the chaos at its base. It has been rising and falling throughout the long winter, with a tidal wave of thirteen perpendicular feet. The fragments have been tossed into every possible confusion, rearing up in fantastic equilibrium, surging in long inclined planes, dipping into dark valleys, and piling in contorted hills, often high above the ice-foot.

"The frozen rubbish has raised the floe itself, for a width of fifty yards, into a broken level of crags. To pass over this to our rocky island, with its storehouse, is a work of ingenious pilotage and clambering, only practicable at favoring periods of the tide, and often

THE ICE-FOOT.

impossible for many days together. Fortunately for our observatory, a long table of heavy ice has been so nicely poised on the crest of the ice-foot, that it swings like a seesaw with the changing water-level, and has formed a moving beach to the island, on which the floes could not pile themselves. Shoreward between Medary and the 'terrace,' the shoal-water has reared

up the ice-fields, so as to make them almost as impassable as the floes; and between Fern Rock and the
gravestone, where I used to pass with my sledges,
there is built a sort of garden-wall of crystal, fully
twenty feet high. It needs no iron spikes or broken
bottles to defend its crest from trespassers.

THE BELT-ICES.

"Mr. Sontag amuses me quite as much as he does
himself with his daily efforts to scale it."

My next extract is of a few days later.

"February 1, Wednesday.—The ice-foot is the most
wonderful and unique characteristic of our high
northern position. The spring-tides have acted on it

very powerfully, and the coming day enables us now to observe their stupendous effects. This ice-belt, as I have sometimes called it, is now twenty-four feet in solid thickness by sixty-five in mean width: the second or appended ice is thirty-eight feet wide; and the third thirty-four feet. All three are ridges of immense ice-tables, serried like the granite blocks of a rampart, and investing the rocks with a triple circumvallation. We know them as the belt-ices.

"The separation of the true ice-foot from our floe was at first a simple interval, which by the recession and advance of the tides gave a movement of about six feet to our brig. Now, however, the compressed ice grinds closely against the ice-foot, rising into inclined planes, and freezing so as actually to push our floe farther and farther from the shore. The brig has already moved twenty-eight feet, without the slightest perceptible change in the cradle which imbeds her."

I close my notice of these dreary months with a single extract more. It is of the date of February the 21st.

"We have had the sun, for some days, silvering the ice between the headlands of the bay; and to day, toward noon, I started out to be the first of my party to welcome him back. It was the longest walk and toughest climb that I have had since our imprisonment; and scurvy and general debility have made me 'short o' wind.' But I managed to attain my object. I saw him once more; and upon a projecting crag nestled in the sunshine. It was like bathing in perfumed water."

The month of March brought back to us the perpetual day. The sunshine had reached our deck on the last day of February: we needed it to cheer us. We were not as pale as my experience in Lancaster Sound had foretold; but the scurvy-spots that mottled our faces gave sore proof of the trials we had undergone. It was plain that we were all of us unfit for arduous travel on foot at the intense temperatures of the nominal spring; and the return of the sun, by increasing the evaporation from the floes, threatened us with a recurrence of still severer weather.

But I felt that our work was unfinished. The great object of the expedition challenged us to a more northward exploration. My dogs, that I had counted on so largely, the nine splendid Newfoundlanders and thirty-five Esquimaux of six months before, had perished; there were only six survivors of the whole pack, and one of these was unfit for draught. Still, they formed my principal reliance, and I busied myself from the very beginning of the month in training them to run together. The carpenter was set to work upon a small sledge, on an improved model, and adapted to the reduced force of our team; and, as we had exhausted our stock of small cord to lash its parts together, Mr. Brooks rigged up a miniature rope-walk, and was preparing a new supply from part of the material of our deep-sea lines. The operations of shipboard, however, went on regularly; Hans and occasionally Petersen going out on the hunt, though rarely returning successful.

Meanwhile we talked encouragingly of spring hopes
and summer prospects, and managed sometimes to force
an occasion for mirth out of the very discomforts of our
unyielding winter life.

This may explain the tone of my diary.

RETURNING DAY.

CHAPTER XV.

"MARCH 7, Tuesday.—I have said very little in this business journal about our daily Arctic life. I have had no time to draw pictures.

"But we have some trials which might make up a day's adventures. Our Arctic observatory is cold beyond any of its class, Kesan, Pulkowa, Toronto, or even its shifting predecessors, Bossetop and Melville Island. Imagine it a term-day, a magnetic term-day.

"The observer, if he were only at home, would be the 'observed of all observers.' He is clad in a pair of seal-skin pants, a dog-skin cap, a reindeer jumper, and walrus boots. He sits upon a box that once held a transit instrument. A stove, glowing with at least a bucketful of anthracite, represents pictorially a heating apparatus, and reduces the thermometer as near as may be to ten degrees below zero. One hand holds a chronometer, and is left bare to warm it: the other luxuriates in a fox-skin mitten. The right hand and the left take it 'watch and watch about.' As one burns with cold, the chronometer shifts to the other, and the mitten takes its place.

THE MAGNETIC OBSERVATORY.

"Perched on a pedestal of frozen gravel is a magnetometer; stretching out from it, a telescope: and, bending down to this, an abject human eye. Every six minutes, said eye takes cognizance of a finely-divided arc, and notes the result in a cold memorandum-book. This process continues for twenty-four hours, two sets of eyes taking it by turns; and, when twenty-four hours are over, term-day is over too.

"We have such frolics every week. I have just been relieved from one, and after a few hours am to be called out of bed in the night to watch and dot again. I have been engaged in this way when the thermometer gave 20° above zero at the instrument, 20° below at two feet above the floor, and 43° below at the floor itself: on my person, facing the little lobster-red fury of a stove, 94° above; on my person, away from the stove, 10° below zero. 'A grateful country' will of course appreciate the value of these labors, and, as it cons over hereafter the four hundred and eighty results which go to make up our record for each week, will never think of asking '*Cui bono* all this?'

"But this is no adventure. The adventure is the travel to and fro. We have night now only half the time; and half the time can go and come with eyes to help us. It was not so a little while since.

"Taking an ice-pole in one hand, and a dark-lantern in the other, you steer through the blackness for a lump of greater blackness, the Fern Rock knob. Stumbling over some fifty yards, you come to a wall: your black knob has disappeared, and nothing but gray indefinable ice is before you. Turn to the right; plant your pole against that inclined plane of slippery smoothness, and jump to the hummock opposite: it is the same hummock you skinned your shins upon the last night you were here. Now wind along, half serpentine, half zigzag, and you cannot mistake that

twenty-feet wall just beyond, creaking and groaning
and even nodding its crest with a grave cold welcome: it is the 'seam of the second ice.' Tumble
over it at the first gap, and you are upon the first
ice: tumble over that, and you are at the ice-foot;
and there is nothing else now between you and the
rocks, and nothing after them between you and the
observatory.

"But be a little careful as you come near this ice-foot.
It is munching all the time at the first ice, and you
have to pick your way over the masticated fragments.
Don't trust yourself to the half-balanced, half-fixed,
half-floating ice-lumps, unless you relish a bath like
Marshal Suwarrow's,—it might be more pleasant if
you were sure of getting out,—but feel your way
gingerly, with your pole held crosswise, not disdaining
lowly attitudes,—hands and knees, or even full length.
That long wedge-like hole just before you, sending
up its puffs of steam into the cold air, is the 'seam
of the ice-foot:' you have only to jump it and you
are on the smooth level ice-foot itself. Scramble up
the rocks now, get on your wooden shoes, and go to
work observing an oscillating needle for some hours
to come.

"Astronomy, as it draws close under the pole-star,
cannot lavish all its powers of observation on things
above. It was the mistake of Mr. Sontag some months
ago; when he wandered about for an hour on his way
to the observatory, and was afraid after finding it to
try and wander back. I myself had a slide down an

inclined plane, whose well-graded talus gave me ample time to contemplate the contingencies at its base;—a chasm peradventure, for my ice-pole was travelling ahead of me and stopped short with a clang; or it might be a pointed hummock—there used to be one just below; or by good luck it was only a water-pool, in which my lantern made the glitter. I exulted to find myself in a cushion of snow.

"March 9, Thursday.—How do we spend the day when it is not term-day, or rather the twenty-four hours? for it is either all day here, or all night, or a twilight mixture of both. How do we spend the twenty-four hours?

"At six in the morning, McGary is called, with all hands who have *slept in*. The decks are cleaned, the ice-hole opened, the refreshing beef-nets examined, the ice-tables measured, and things aboard put to rights. At half-past seven, all hands rise, wash on deck, open the doors for ventilation, and come below for breakfast. We are short of fuel, and therefore cook in the cabin. Our breakfast, for all fare alike, is hard tack, pork, stewed apples frozen like molasses-candy, tea and coffee, with a delicate portion of raw potato. After breakfast, the smokers take their pipe till nine: then all hands turn to, idlers to idle and workers to work; Ohlsen to his bench, Brooks to his 'preparations' in canvas. McGary to play tailor, Whipple to make shoes, Bonsall to tinker, Baker to skin birds,—and the rest to the 'Office!' Take a look into the Arctic Bureau! One table one salt-pork lamp with rusty chlorinated flame,

three stools, and as many waxen-faced men with their
legs drawn up under them, the deck at zero being too
cold for the feet. Each has his department: Kane is
writing, sketching, and projecting maps; Hayes copying
logs and meteorologicals; Sontag reducing his work at
Fern Rock. A fourth, as one of the working members

VISITING THE OBSERVATORY.

of the hive, has long been defunct: you will find him
in bed, or studying 'Littell's Living Age.' At twelve,
a business round of inspection, and orders enough to
fill up the day with work. Next, the drill of the Esquimaux dogs,—my own peculiar recreation,—a dog-
trot, specially refreshing to legs that creak with every
kick, and rheumatic shoulders that chronicle every

descent of the whip.   And so we get on to dinner-time; the occasion of another gathering, which misses the tea and coffee of breakfast, but rejoices in pickled cabbage and dried peaches instead.

"At dinner as at breakfast the raw potato comes in, our hygienic luxury.   Like doctor-stuff generally, it is not as appetizing as desirable.   Grating it down nicely, leaving out the ugly red spots liberally, and adding the utmost oil as a lubricant, it is as much as I can do to persuade the mess to shut their eyes and bolt it, like Mrs. Squeers's molasses and brimstone at Dotheboys Hall.   Two absolutely refuse to taste it.   I tell them of the Silesians using its leaves as spinach, of the whalers in the South Seas getting drunk on the molasses which had preserved the large potatoes of the Azores,—I point to this gum, so fungoid and angry the day before yesterday, and so flat and amiable to-day,— all by a potato poultice: my eloquence is wasted: they persevere in rejecting the admirable compound.

"Sleep, exercise, amusement, and work at will, carry on the day till our six o'clock supper, a meal something like breakfast and something like dinner, only a little more scant: and the officers come in with the reports of the day.   Doctor Hayes shows me the log, I sign it; Sontag the weather, I sign the weather; Mr. Bonsall the tides and thermometers.   Thereupon comes in mine ancient, Brooks; and I enter in his journal No. 3 all the work done under his charge, and discuss his labors for the morrow.

"McGary comes next, with the cleaning-up arrangement, inside, outside, and on decks; and Mr. Wilson follows with ice-measurements. And last of all comes my own record of the day gone by; every line, as I look back upon its pages, giving evidence of a weakened body and harassed mind.

WINTER LIFE ON BOARD SHIP.

"We have cards sometimes, and chess sometimes,— and a few magazines, Mr. Littell's thoughtful present, to cheer away the evening.

"March 11, Saturday.—All this seems tolerable for commonplace routine; but there is a lack of comfort

which it does not tell of. Our fuel is limited to three
bucketfuls of coal a day, and our mean temperature
outside is 40° below zero; 46° below as I write. London Brown Stout, and somebody's Old Brown Sherry,
freeze in the cabin lockers; and the carlines overhead
are hung with tubs of chopped ice, to make water for
our daily drink. Our lamps cannot be persuaded to
burn salt lard; our oil is exhausted; and we work by
muddy tapers of cork and cotton floated in saucers.
We have not a pound of fresh meat, and only a barrel
of potatoes left.

"Not a man now, except Pierre and Morton, is ex-
empt from scurvy; and, as I look around upon the pale
faces and haggard looks of my comrades, I feel that we
are fighting the battle of life at disadvantage, and that
an Arctic night and an Arctic day age a man more
rapidly and harshly than a year anywhere else in all
this weary world.

"March 13, Monday.—Since January, we have been
working at the sledges and other preparations for travel.
The death of my dogs, the rugged obstacles of the ice,
and the intense cold have obliged me to reorganize our
whole equipment. We have had to discard all our
India-rubber fancy-work: canvas shoe-making, fur-sock-
ing, sewing, carpentering, are all going on; and the
cabin, our only fire-warmed apartment, is the work-
shop, kitchen, parlor, and hall. Pemmican cases are
thawing on the lockers; buffalo robes are drying
around the stove; camp equipments occupy the cor-
ners; and our wo-begone French cook, with an in-

finitude of useless saucepans, insists on monopolizing the stove.

"March 15, Wednesday.—The mean temperature of the last five days has been,

March 10.. . —46°.03
11.. —45°.60
12.. —46°.64
13.. —46°.56
14.. —46°.65

giving an average of —46° 30′, with a variation between the extremes of less than three-quarters of a degree.

"These records are remarkable. The coldest month of the Polar year has heretofore been February; but we are evidently about to experience for March a mean temperature not only the lowest of our own series, but lower than that of any other recorded observations.

"This anomalous temperature seems to disprove the idea of a diminished cold as we approach the Pole. It will extend the isotherm of the solstitial month higher than ever before projected.

"The mean temperature of Parry for March (in lat. 74° 30′) was —29°; our own will be at least 41° below zero.

"At such temperatures, the ice or snow covering offers a great resistance to the sledge-runners. I have noticed this in training my dogs. The dry snow in its finely-divided state resembles sand, and the runners

creak as they pass over it. Baron Wrangell notes the
same fact in Siberia at —40°.

"The difficulties of draught, however, must not interfere with my parties. I am only waiting until the sun,
now 13° high at noon, brings back a little warmth to
the men in sleeping. The mean difference between
bright clear sunshine and shade is now 5°. But on
the 10th, at noon, the shade gave —42° 2', and the
sun —28°; a difference of more than fourteen degrees.
This must make an impression before long.

"March 17, Friday.—It is nine o'clock, P. M., and the
thermometer outside at —46°. I am anxious to have
this depôt party off; but I must wait until there is a
promise of milder weather. It must come soon. The
sun is almost at the equator. On deck, I can see to
the northward all the bright glare of sunset, streaming
out in long bands of orange through the vapors of the
ice-foot, and the frost-smoke exhaling in wreaths like
those from the house-chimneys a man sees in the
valleys as he comes down a mountain-side."

I must reserve for my official report the detailed
story of this ice-foot and its changes.

The name is adopted on board ship from the Danish
"Eis-fod," to designate a zone of ice which extends
along the shore from the untried north beyond us
almost to the Arctic circle. To the south it breaks
up during the summer months, and disappears as high
as Upernavik or even Cape Alexander; but in this
our high northern winter harbor, it is a perennial
growth, clinging to the bold faces of the cliffs, follow-

ing the sweeps of the bays and the indentations of rivers.

This broad platform, although changing with the seasons, never disappears. It served as our highway

MARY LEIPER RIVER—THE ICE-BELT.

of travel, a secure and level sledge-road, perched high above the grinding ice of the sea, and adapting itself to the tortuosities of the land. As such I shall call it the "ice-belt."

I was familiar with the Arctic shore-ices of the Asiatic and American explorers, and had personally studied the same formations in Wellington Channel, where, previously to the present voyage, they might have been supposed to reach their greatest development. But this wonderful structure has here assumed a form which none of its lesser growths to the south had exhibited. As a physical feature, it may be regarded as hardly second, either in importance or prominence, to the glacier; and as an agent of geological change, it is in the highest degree interesting and instructive.

Although subject to occasional disruption, and to loss of volume from evaporation and thaws, it measures the severity of the year by its rates of increase. Rising with the first freezings of the late summer, it crusts the sea-line with curious fretwork and arabesques: a little later, and it receives the rude shock of the drifts, and the collision of falling rocks from the cliffs which margin it: before the early winter has darkened, it is a wall, resisting the grinding floes; and it goes on gathering increase and strength from the successive freezing of the tides, until the melted snows and water-torrents of summer for a time check its progress. During our first winter at Rensselaer Harbor, the ice-belt grew to three times the size which it had upon our arrival; and, by the middle of March, the islands and adjacent shores were hemmed in by an investing plane of nearly thirty feet high (27 feet) and one hundred and twenty wide.

The ice-foot at this season was not, however, an unbroken level. It had, like the floes, its barricades, serried and irregular; which it was a work of great labor

and some difficulty to traverse. Our stores were in consequence nearly inaccessible; and, as the ice-foot still
continued to extend itself, piling ice-table upon ice-table,
it threatened to encroach upon our anchorage and peril
the safety of the vessel. The ridges were already

ICE-BELT OF EARLY WINTER.

within twenty feet of her, and her stern was sensibly
lifted up by their pressure. We had, indeed, been puzzled for six weeks before, by remarking that the floe
we were imbedded in was gradually receding from the
shore; and had recalled the observation of the Danes
of Upernavik, that their nets were sometimes forced
away strangely from the land. The explanation is,

perhaps, to be found in the alternate action of the tides and frost; but it would be out of place to enter upon the discussion here.

"March 18, Saturday.—To day our spring-tides gave to the massive ice which sustains our little vessel a rise and fall of seventeen feet. The crunching and grinding, the dashing of the water, the gurgling of the eddies, and the toppling over of the nicely-poised ice-tables, were unlike the more brisk dynamics of hum-

ICE-BELT AND FLOE.

mock action, but conveyed a more striking expression of power and dimension.

"The thermometer at four o'clock in the morning was minus 49°; too cold still, I fear, for our sledgemen to set out. But we packed the sledge and strapped on the boat, and determined to see how she would drag. Eight men attached themselves to the lines, but were scarcely able to move her. This may be due in part to an increase of friction produced by the excessive cold, according to the experience of the Siberian travellers; but I have no doubt it is principally caused by the very thin runners of our Esquimaux sledge cutting through the snow-crust.

"The excessive refraction this evening, which entirely lifted up the northern coast as well as the icebergs, seems to give the promise of milder weather. In the hope that it may be so, I have fixed on to-morrow for the departure of the sledge, after very reluctantly dispensing with more than two hundred pounds of her cargo, besides the boat. The party think they can get along with it now.

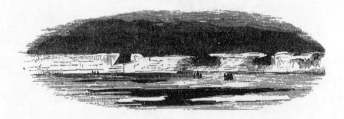

EXCESSIVE REFRACTION OF BERGS.

"March 20, Monday.—I saw the depôt party off yesterday. They gave the usual three cheers, with three for myself. I gave them the whole of my brother's great wedding-cake and my last two bottles of Port, and they pulled the sledge they were harnessed to famously. But I was not satisfied. I could see it was hard work; and, besides, they were without the boat, or enough extra pemmican to make their deposit of importance. I followed them, therefore, and found that they encamped at 8 P.M. only five miles from the brig.

J. Hamilton.

Engraved at J.M.Butlers establishment 84 Chestnut St.

A.W. Graham.

THE PACK OFF SYLVIA HEADLAND.

(From a sketch by Dr. Kane.)

"When I overtook them, I said nothing to discourage them, and gave no new orders for the morning; but after laughing at good Ohlsen's rueful face, and listening to all Petersen's assurances that the cold and nothing but the cold retarded his Greenland sledge, and that no sledge of any other construction could have been moved at all through minus 40° snow, I quietly bade them good-night, leaving all hands under their buffaloes.

"Once returned to the brig, all my tired remainder-men were summoned: a large sled with broad runners, which I had built somewhat after the neat Admiralty model sent me by Sir Francis Beaufort, was taken down, scraped, polished, lashed, and fitted with track-ropes and *rue-raddies;* the lines arranged to draw as near as possible in a line with the centre of gravity. We made an entire cover of canvas, with snugly-adjusted fastenings; and by one in the morning we had our discarded excess of pemmican and the boat once more in stowage.

"Off we went for the camp of the sleepers. It was very cold, but a thoroughly Arctic night; the snow just tinged with the crimson stratus above the sun, which, equinoctial as it was, glared beneath the northern horizon like a smelting-furnace. We found the tent of the party by the bearings of the stranded bergs. Quietly and stealthily we hauled away their Esquimaux sledge, and placed her cargo upon 'the Faith.' Five men were then rue-raddied to the track-lines; and with the whispered word, 'Now, boys, when

Mr. Brooks gives his third snore, off with you!' off they went, and 'the Faith' after them, as free and nimble as a volunteer. The trial was a triumph. We awakened the sleepers with three cheers; and, giving them a second good-bye, returned to the brig, carrying the dishonored vehicle along with us. And now, bating mishaps past anticipation, I shall have a depôt for my long trip.

"The party were seen by McGary from aloft, at noon to-day, moving easily, and about twelve miles from the brig. The temperature too is rising, or rather unmistakably about to rise. Our lowest was —43°, but our highest reached —22°; this extreme range, with the excessive refraction and a gentle misty air from about the S.E., makes me hope that we are going to have a warm spell. The party is well off. Now for my own to follow them!"

CHAPTER XVI.

"MARCH 21, Tuesday.—All hands at work house-cleaning. Thermometer —48°. Visited the fox-traps with Hans in the afternoon, and found one poor animal frozen dead. He was coiled up, with his nose buried in his bushy tail, like a fancy foot-muff or the *prie-dieu* of a royal sinner. A hard thing about his fate was that he had succeeded in effecting his escape from the trap; but, while working his way underneath, had been frozen fast to a smooth stone by the moisture of his own breath. He was not probably aware of it before the moment when he sought to avail himself of his hard-gained liberty. These saddening thoughts did not impair my appetite at supper, where the little creature looked handsomer than ever.

"March 22, Wednesday.—We took down the forward bulkhead to-day, and moved the men aft, to save fuel. All hands are still at work clearing up the

183

decks, the scrapers sounding overhead, and the hickory brooms crackling against the frozen woodwork. Afternoon comes, and McGary brings from the traps two foxes, a blue and a white. Afternoon passes, and we skin them. Evening passes, and we eat them. Never were foxes more welcome visitors, or treated more like domestic animals.

" March 23, Thursday.—The accumulated ice upon our housing shows what the condensed and frozen moisture of the winter has been. The average thickness of this curious deposit is five inches, very hard and well crystallized. Six cart-loads have been already chopped out, and about four more remain.

" It is very far from a hardship to sleep under such an ice-roof as this. In a climate where the intense cold approximates all ice to granite, its thick air-tight coating contributes to our warmth, gives a beautiful and cheerful lustre to our walls, and condenses any vapors which our cooks allow to escape the funnels. I only remove it now because I fear the effects of damp in the season of sunshine.

" March 27, Monday.—We have been for some days in all the flurry of preparation for our exploration trip: buffalo-hides, leather, and tailoring-utensils everywhere. Every particle of fur comes in play for mits and muffs and wrappers. Poor Flora is turned into a pair of socks, and looks almost as pretty as when she was heading the team.

" The wind to-day made it intensely cold. In riding but four miles to inspect a fox-trap, the movement froze my cheeks twice. We avoid masks with great care, reserving them for the severer weather: the jaw when protected recovers very soon the sensibility which exposure has subdued.

"Our party is now out in its ninth day. It has had some trying weather:

On the 19th	—42°.3
20th	—35°.4
21st	—19°.37
22d	— 7°.47
23d	— 9°.07
24th	—18°.32
25th	—34°.80
26th	—42°.8
27th	—34°.38

of mean daily temperature; making an average of 27°.13 below zero.

"March 29, Wednesday.—I have been out with my dog-sledge, inspecting the ice to-day from the north-western headland. There seems a marked difference between this sound and other estuaries, in the number of ice-bergs. Unlike Prince Regent's, or Wellington, or Lancaster Sounds, the shores here are lined with glaciers, and the water is everywhere choked and harassed by their discharges. This was never so apparent to me as this afternoon. The low sun lit up line after line of lofty bergs, and the excessive refraction elevated them so much, that I thought I could see a chain of continuous ice running on toward the north until it was lost in illimitable distance.

"March 31, Friday.—I was within an ace to-day of losing my dogs, every one of them. When I reached the ice-foot, they balked:—who would not?—the tide was low, the ice rampant, and a jump of four feet necessary to reach the crest. The howling of the wind and the whirl of the snow-drift confused the

NORTHWESTERN HEADLAND.

poor creatures; but it was valuable training for them, and I strove to force them over. Of course I was on foot, and they had a light load behind them. 'Now, Stumpy! Now, Whitey!' 'Good dogs!' 'Tu-lee-ēē-ēē! Tuh!' They went at it like good stanch brutes, and the next minute the whole team was rolling in a lump, some sixteen feet below me, in the chasm of the ice-foot. The drift was such that at first I could not see

them. The roaring of the tide and the subdued wail
of the dogs made me fear for the worst. I had to walk
through the broken ice, which rose in toppling spires
over my head, for nearly fifty yards, before I found an
opening to the ice-face, by which I was able to climb
down to them. A few cuts of a sheath-knife released
them, although the caresses of the dear brutes had like
to have been fatal to me, for I had to straddle with
one foot on the fast ice and the other on loose piled
rubbish. But I got a line attached to the cross-pieces
of the sledge-runners, flung it up on the ice-foot, and
then piloted my dogs out of their slough. In about
ten minutes, we were sweating along at eight miles an
hour."

Every thing looked promising, and we were only
waiting for intelligence that our advance party had deposited its provisions in safety to begin our transit of
the bay. Except a few sledge-lashings and some trifling
accoutrements to finish, all was ready.

We were at work cheerfully, sewing away at the
skins of some moccasins by the blaze of our lamps,
when, toward midnight, we heard the noise of steps
above, and the next minute Sontag, Ohlsen, and Petersen came down into the cabin. Their manner startled
me even more than their unexpected appearance on
board. They were swollen and haggard, and hardly
able to speak.

Their story was a fearful one. They had left their
companions in the ice, risking their own lives to bring

us the news: Brooks, Baker, Wilson, and Pierre were all lying frozen and disabled. Where? They could not tell: somewhere in among the hummocks to the north and east; it was drifting heavily round them when they parted. Irish Tom had stayed by to feed and care for the others; but the chances were sorely against them. It was in vain to question them further. They had evidently travelled a great distance, for they were sinking with fatigue and hunger, and could hardly be rallied enough to tell us the direction in which they had come.

THE RESCUE PARTY.

My first impulse was to move on the instant with an unencumbered party: a rescue, to be effective or even hopeful, could not be too prompt. What pressed on my mind most was, where the sufferers were to be looked for among the drifts. Ohlsen seemed to have his faculties rather more at command than his associates, and I thought that he might assist us as a guide; but he was sinking with exhaustion, and if he went with us we must carry him.

There was not a moment to be lost. While some were still busy with the new-comers and getting ready a hasty meal, others were rigging out the "Little Willie" with a buffalo-cover, a small tent, and a package of pemmican; and, as soon as we could hurry through our arrangements, Ohlsen was strapped on in a fur bag, his legs wrapped in dog-skins and eider-down, and we were off upon the ice. Our party consisted of nine men and myself. We carried only the clothes on our backs. The thermometer stood at —46°, seventy-eight degrees below the freezing-point.

A well-known peculiar tower of ice, called by the men the "Pinnacly Berg," served as our first landmark: other icebergs of colossal size, which stretched in long beaded lines across the bay, helped to guide us afterward; and it was not until we had travelled for sixteen hours that we began to lose our way.

We knew that our lost companions must be somewhere in the area before us, within a radius of forty miles. Mr. Ohlsen, who had been for fifty hours without rest, fell asleep as soon as we began to move, and awoke now with unequivocal signs of mental disturbance. It became evident that he had lost the bearing of the icebergs, which in form and color endlessly repeated themselves; and the uniformity of the vast field of snow utterly forbade the hope of local landmarks.

Pushing ahead of the party, and clambering over some rugged ice-piles, I came to a long level floe, which I thought might probably have attracted the eyes of weary men in circumstances like our own. It was a light conjecture; but it was enough to turn the scale, for there was no other to balance it. I gave orders to abandon the sledge, and disperse in search of foot-marks. We raised our tent, placed our pemmican in *cache*, except a small allowance for each man to carry

PINNACLY BERG.

on his person; and poor Ohlsen, now just able to keep his legs, was liberated from his bag. The thermometer had fallen by this time to —49°.3, and the wind was setting in sharply from the northwest. It was out of the question to halt: it required brisk exercise to keep us from freezing. I could not even melt ice for water; and, at these temperatures, any resort to snow for the purpose of allaying thirst was followed by bloody lips and tongue: it burnt like caustic.

It was indispensable then that we should move on, looking out for traces as we went. Yet when the men were ordered to spread themselves, so as to multiply the chances, though they all obeyed heartily, some painful impress of solitary danger, or perhaps it may have been the varying configuration of the ice-field, kept them closing up continually into a single group. The strange manner in which some of us were affected I now attribute as much to shattered nerves as to the direct influence of the cold. Men like McGary and Bonsall, who had stood out our severest marches, were seized with trembling-fits and short breath; and, in spite of all my efforts to keep up an example of sound bearing, I fainted twice on the snow.

We had been nearly eighteen hours out without water or food, when a new hope cheered us. I think it was Hans, our Esquimaux hunter, who thought he saw a broad sledge-track. The drift had nearly effaced it, and we were some of us doubtful at first whether it was not one of those accidental rifts which the gales make in the surface-snow. But, as we traced it on to the deep snow among the hummocks, we were led to footsteps; and, following these with religious care, we at last came in sight of a small American flag fluttering from a hummock, and lower down a little Masonic banner hanging from a tent-pole hardly above the drift. It was the camp of our disabled comrades: we reached it after an unbroken march of twenty-one hours.

The little tent was nearly covered. I was not among the first to come up; but, when I reached the tent-curtain, the men were standing in silent file on each side of it. With more kindness and delicacy of feeling than is often supposed to belong to sailors, but which is almost characteristic, they intimated their wish that I should go in alone. As I crawled in, and, coming upon the darkness, heard before me the burst of welcome gladness that came from the four poor fellows stretched on their backs, and then for the first time the cheer outside, my weakness and my gratitude together almost overcame me. "They had expected me: they were sure I would come!"

We were now fifteen souls; the thermometer seventy-five degrees below the freezing-point; and our sole accommodation a tent barely able to contain eight persons: more than half our party were obliged to keep from freezing by walking outside while the others slept. We could not halt long. Each of us took a turn of two hours' sleep; and we prepared for our homeward march.

We took with us nothing but the tent, furs to protect the rescued party, and food for a journey of fifty hours. Every thing else was abandoned. Two large buffalo-bags, each made of four skins, were doubled up, so as to form a sort of sack, lined on each side by fur, closed at the bottom but opened at the top. This was laid on the sledge; the tent, smoothly folded, serving as a floor. The sick, with their limbs sewed up carefully in reindeer-skins, were placed upon the bed of buffalo-robes, in a half-reclining posture; other skins and blanket-bags were thrown above them; and the whole litter was lashed together so as to allow but a single opening opposite the mouth for breathing.

This necessary work cost us a great deal of time and effort; but it was essential to the lives of the sufferers. It took us no less than four hours to strip and refresh them, and then to embale them in the manner I have described. Few of us escaped without frost-bitten fingers: the thermometer was at 55°.6 below zero, and a slight wind added to the severity of the cold.

It was completed at last, however; all hands stood round; and, after repeating a short prayer, we set out on our retreat. It was fortunate indeed that we were not inexperienced in sledging over the ice. A great part of our track lay among a succession of hummocks; some of them extending in long lines, fifteen and twenty feet high, and so uniformly steep that we had to turn them by a considerable deviation from our direct course; others that we forced our way through, far above our heads in height, lying in parallel ridges, with the space between too narrow for the sledge to be lowered into it safely, and yet not wide enough for the runners to cross without the aid of ropes to stay them. These spaces too were generally choked with light snow, hiding the openings between the ice-fragments. They were fearful traps to disengage a limb from, for every man knew that a fracture or a sprain even would cost him his life. Besides all this, the sledge was top-heavy with its load: the maimed men could not bear to be lashed down tight enough to secure them against falling off. Notwithstanding our caution in rejecting every superfluous burden, the weight, including bags and tent, was eleven hundred pounds.

And yet our march for the first six hours was very cheering. We made by vigorous pulls and lifts nearly a mile an hour, and reached the new floes before we were absolutely weary. Our sledge sustained the trial admirably. Ohlsen, restored by hope, walked steadily at the leading belt of the sledge-lines; and I began to feel certain of reaching our halfway station of the day before, where we had left our tent. But we were still nine miles from it, when, almost without premonition, we all became aware of an alarming failure of our energies.

I was of course familiar with the benumbed and almost lethargic sensation of extreme cold; and once, when exposed for some hours in the midwinter of Baffin's Bay, I had experienced symptoms which I compared to the diffused paralysis of the electro-galvanic shock. But I had treated the *sleepy comfort* of freezing as something like the embellishment of romance. I had evidence now to the contrary.

Bonsall and Morton, two of our stoutest men, came to me, begging permission to sleep: "they were not cold: the wind did not enter them now: a little sleep was all they wanted." Presently Hans was found nearly stiff under a drift; and Thomas, bolt upright, had his eyes closed, and could hardly articulate. At last, John Blake threw himself on the snow, and refused to rise. They did not complain of feeling cold; but it was in vain that I wrestled, boxed, ran, argued, jeered, or reprimanded: an immediate halt could not be avoided.

We pitched our tent with much difficulty. Our hands were too powerless to strike a fire: we were obliged to do without water or food. Even the spirits (whisky) had frozen at the men's feet, under all the coverings. We put Bonsall, Ohlsen, Thomas, and Hans, with the other sick men, well inside the tent, and crowded in as many others as we could. Then, leaving the party in charge of Mr. McGary, with orders to come on after four hours' rest, I pushed ahead with William Godfrey, who volunteered to be my companion. My aim was to reach the halfway tent, and thaw some ice and pemmican before the others arrived.

The floe was of level ice, and the walking excellent. I cannot tell how long it took us to make the nine miles; for we were in a strange sort of stupor, and had little apprehension of time. It was probably about four hours. We kept ourselves awake by imposing on each other a continued articulation of words; they must have been incoherent enough. I recall these hours as among the most wretched I have ever gone through: we were neither of us in our right senses, and retained a very confused recollection of what preceded our arrival at the tent. We both of us, however, remember a bear, who walked leisurely before us and tore up as he went a jumper that Mr. McGary had improvidently thrown off the day before. He tore it

into shreds and rolled it into a ball, but never offered
to interfere with our progress. I remember this, and
with it a confused sentiment that our tent and buffalo-
robes might probably share the same fate. Godfrey,
with whom the memory of this day's work may atone
for many faults of a later time, had a better eye than
myself; and, looking some miles ahead, he could see
that our tent was undergoing the same unceremonious
treatment. I thought I saw it too, but we were so
drunken with cold that we strode on steadily, and, for
aught I know, without quickening our pace.

Probably our approach saved the contents of the
tent; for when we reached it the tent was uninjured,
though the bear had overturned it, tossing the buffalo-
robes and pemmican into the snow; we missed only a
couple of blanket-bags. What we recollect, however,
and perhaps all we recollect, is, that we had great difficulty in raising it. We crawled into our reindeer
sleeping-bags, without speaking, and for the next three
hours slept on in a dreamy but intense slumber.
When I awoke, my long beard was a mass of ice,
frozen fast to the buffalo-skin: Godfrey had to cut me
out with his jack-knife. Four days after our escape, I
found my woollen comfortable with a goodly share of
my beard still adhering to it.

We were able to melt water and get some soup
cooked before the rest of our party arrived: it took
them but five hours to walk the nine miles. They
were doing well, and, considering the circumstances, in
wonderful spirits. The day was most providentially

windless, with a clear sun. All enjoyed the refreshment we had got ready: the crippled were repacked in their robes; and we sped briskly toward the hummock-ridges which lay between us and the Pinnacly Berg.

The hummocks we had now to meet came properly under the designation of squeezed ice. A great chain of bergs stretching from northwest to southeast, moving with the tides, had compressed the surface-floes; and, rearing them up on their edges, produced an area more like the volcanic pedragal of the basin of Mexico than any thing else I can compare it to.

It required desperate efforts to work our way over it,—literally desperate, for our strength failed us anew, and we began to lose our self-control. We could not abstain any longer from eating snow: our mouths swelled, and some of us became speechless. Happily the day was warmed by a clear sunshine, and the thermometer rose to —4° in the shade: otherwise we must have frozen.

Our halts multiplied, and we fell half-sleeping on the snow. I could not prevent it. Strange to say, it refreshed us. I ventured upon the experiment myself, making Riley wake me at the end of three minutes; and I felt so much benefited by it that I timed the men in the same way. They sat on the runners of the sledge, fell asleep instantly, and were forced to wakefulness when their three minutes were out.

By eight in the evening we emerged from the floes. The sight of the Pinnacly Berg revived us. Brandy, an invaluable resource in emergency, had already been served out in tablespoonful doses. We now took a longer rest, and a last but stouter dram, and reached the brig at 1 P.M., we believe without a halt.

I say *we believe;* and here perhaps is the most decided proof of our sufferings: we were quite delirious, and had ceased to entertain a sane apprehension of the circumstances about us. We moved on like men in a dream. Our footmarks seen afterward showed that we had steered a bee-line for the brig. It must have been by a sort of instinct, for it left no impress on the memory. Bonsall was sent staggering ahead, and reached the brig, God knows how, for he had fallen repeatedly at the track-lines; but he delivered with punctilious accuracy the messages I had sent by him to Dr. Hayes. I thought myself the soundest of all, for I went through all the formula of sanity, and can recall the muttering delirium of my comrades when we got back into the cabin of our brig. Yet I have been told since of some speeches and some orders too of mine, which I should have remembered for their absurdity if my mind had retained its balance.

Petersen and Whipple came out to meet us about two miles from the brig. They brought my dog-team, with the restoratives I had sent for by Bonsall. I do not remember their coming. Dr. Hayes entered with judicious energy upon the treatment our condition called for, administering morphine freely, after the usual frictions. He reported none of our brain-symptoms as serious, referring them properly to the class of those indications of exhausted power which yield to generous diet and rest. Mr. Ohlsen suffered some time from strabismus and blindness: two others underwent amputation of parts of the foot, without unpleasant consequences; and two died in spite of all our efforts. This rescue party had been out for seventy-two hours. We had halted in all eight hours, half of our number sleeping at a time. We travelled between eighty and ninety miles, most of the way dragging a heavy sledge. The mean temperature of the whole time, including the warmest hours of three days, was at minus 41°.2. We had no water except at our two halts, and were at no time able to intermit vigorous exercise without freezing.

"April 4, Tuesday.—Four days have passed, and I am again at my record of failures, sound but aching still in every joint. The rescued men are not out of danger, but their gratitude is very touching. Pray God that they may live!"

INSIDE OF TENT.

CHAPTER XVII.

THE week that followed has left me nothing to remember but anxieties and sorrow. Nearly all our
party, as well the rescuers as the rescued, were tossing
in their sick-bunks, some frozen, others undergoing
amputations, several with dreadful premonitions of
tetanus. I was myself among the first to be about:
the necessities of the others claimed it of me.

Early in the morning of the 7th I was awakened by
a sound from Baker's throat, one of those the most
frightful and ominous that ever startle a physician's
ear. The lock-jaw had seized him,—that dark visitant
whose foreshadowings were on so many of us. His
symptoms marched rapidly to their result: he died on
the 8th of April. We placed him the next day in his
coffin, and, forming a rude but heartfull procession,
bore him over the broken ice and up the steep side of
the ice-foot to Butler Island; then, passing along the

snow-level to Fern Rock, and, climbing the slope of the
Observatory, we deposited his corpse upon the pedestals
which had served to support our transit-instrument
and theodolite.   We read the service for the burial of
the dead, sprinkling over him snow for dust, and repeated the Lord's Prayer; and then, icing up again
the opening in the walls we had made to admit the
coffin, left him in his narrow house.

Jefferson Baker was a man of kind heart and true
principles.   I knew him when we were both younger.
I passed two happy seasons at a little cottage adjoining
his father's farm.   He thought it a privilege to join
this expedition, as in those green summer days when
I had allowed him to take a gun with me on some
shooting-party.   He relied on me with the affectionate
confidence of boyhood, and I never gave him a harsh
word or a hard thought.

We were watching in the morning at Baker's death-
bed, when one of our deck-watch, who had been cutting
ice for the melter, came hurrying down into the cabin
with the report, "People hollaing ashore!"   I went up,
followed by as many as could mount the gangway;
and there they were, on all sides of our rocky harbor,
dotting the snow-shores and emerging from the blackness of the cliffs,—wild and uncouth, but evidently
human beings.

As we gathered on the deck, they rose upon the
more elevated fragments of the land-ice, standing singly
and conspicuously like the figures in a tableau of the
opera, and distributing themselves around almost in a

half-circle. They were vociferating as if to attract our
attention, or perhaps only to give vent to their surprise; but I could make nothing out of their cries,
except "Hoah, ha, ha!" and "Ka, kăāh! ka, kăāh!"
repeated over and over again.

MEETING THE ESQUIMAUX.

There was light enough for me to see that they
brandished no weapons, and were only tossing their
heads and arms about in violent gesticulations. A
more unexcited inspection showed us, too, that their
numbers were not as great nor their size as Pata-

gonian as some of us had been disposed to fancy at
first. In a word, I was satisfied that they were natives
of the country; and, calling Petersen from his bunk to
be my interpreter, I proceeded, unarmed and waving
my open hands, toward a stout figure who made himself conspicuous and seemed to have a greater number
near him than the rest. He evidently understood the
movement, for he at once, like a brave fellow, leaped
down upon the floe and advanced to meet me fully
half-way.

He was nearly a head taller than myself, extremely
powerful and well-built, with swarthy complexion and
piercing black eyes. His dress was a hooded *capôte*
or jumper of mixed white and blue fox-pelts, arranged
with something of fancy, and booted trousers of white
bear-skin, which at the end of the foot were made to
terminate with the claws of the animal.

I soon came to an understanding with this gallant
diplomatist. Almost as soon as we commenced our
parley, his companions, probably receiving signals
from him, flocked in and surrounded us; but we had
no difficulty in making them know positively that they
must remain where they were, while Metek went with
me on board the ship. This gave me the advantage
of negotiating, with an important hostage.

Although this was the first time he had ever seen
a white man, he went with me fearlessly; his companions staying behind on the ice. Hickey took them
out what he esteemed our greatest delicacies,—slices
of good wheat bread, and corned pork, with exorbitant

lumps of white sugar; but they refused to touch them
They had evidently no apprehension of open violence
from us. I found afterward that several among them
were singly a match for the white bear and the walrus,
and that they thought us a very pale-faced crew.

METEK.

Being satisfied with my interview in the cabin, I
sent out word that the rest might be admitted to the
ship; and, although they, of course, could not know
how their chief had been dealt with, some nine or ten
of them followed with boisterous readiness upon the
bidding. Others in the mean time, as if disposed to

give us their company for the full time of a visit, brought up from behind the land-ice as many as fifty-six fine dogs, with their sledges, and secured them within two hundred feet of the brig, driving their lances into the ice, and picketing the dogs to them by the seal-skin traces. The animals understood the operation perfectly, and lay down as soon as it commenced. The sledges were made up of small frag-

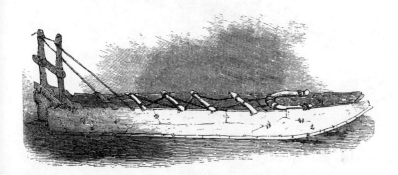

NATIVE SLEDGE, (KOOMETIK,)—CELLULAR BONE OF WHALE.

ments of porous bone, admirably knit together by thongs of hide; the runners, which glistened like burnished steel, were of highly-polished ivory, obtained from the tusks of the walrus.

The only arms they carried were knives, concealed in their boots; but their lances, which were lashed to the sledges, were quite a formidable weapon. The staff was of the horn of the narwhal, or else of the thigh-bones of the bear, two lashed together, or sometimes the mirabilis of the walrus, three or four of them

united.   This last was a favorite material also for the
cross-bars of their sledges.   They had no wood.   A
single rusty hoop from a current-drifted cask might
have furnished all the knives of the party; but the

HOOP-IRON KNIFE, (SEVIK)

fleam-shaped tips of their lances were of unmistakable
steel, and were riveted to the tapering bony point
with no mean skill.   I learned afterward that the
metal was obtained in traffic from the more southern
tribes.

WALRUS LANCE.

I give drawings of the lance-head, and of the knives
which the party carried.   They were clad much as I
have described Metek, in jumpers, boots, and white
bear-skin breeches, with their feet decorated like his.

en griffe. A strip of knotted leather worn round the neck, very greasy and dirty-looking, which no one could be persuaded to part with for an instant, was mistaken at first for an ornament by the crew: it was not until mutual hardships had made us better acquainted that we learned its mysterious uses.

NESSAK, (JUMPER-HOOD,) IN HIS TRAVELLING DRESS.

When they were first allowed to come on board, they were very rude and difficult to manage. They spoke three or four at a time, to each other and to us, laughing heartily at our ignorance in not understanding them, and then talking away as before. They were incessantly in motion, going everywhere, trying doors, and squeezing themselves through dark passages,

round casks and boxes, and out into the light again,
anxious to touch and handle every thing they saw,
and asking for, or else endeavoring to steal, every thing
they touched. It was the more difficult to restrain
them, as I did not wish them to suppose that we were
at all intimidated. But there were some signs of our
disabled condition which it was important they should
not see: it was especially necessary to keep them out
of the forecastle, where the dead body of poor Baker
was lying: and, as it was in vain to reason or persuade, we had at last to employ the "gentle laying-on
of hands," which, I believe, the laws of all countries
tolerate, to keep them in order.

Our whole force was mustered and kept constantly
on the alert; but, though there may have been something of discourtesy in the occasional shoulderings and
hustlings that enforced the police of the ship, things
went on good-humouredly. Our guests continued
running in and out and about the vessel, bringing in
provisions, and carrying them out again to their dogs
on the ice, in fact, stealing all the time, until the
afternoon; when, like tired children, they threw themselves down to sleep. I ordered them to be made
comfortable in the hold; and Morton spread a large
buffalo-robe for them, not far from a coal-fire in the
galley-stove.

They were lost in barbarous amaze at the new fuel,
—too hard for blubber, too soft for firestone;—but they
were content to believe it might cook as well as seals'-
fat. They borrowed from us an iron pot and some

melted water, and parboiled a couple of pieces of walrus-meat; but the real *pièce de resistance*, some five pounds a head, they preferred to eat raw. Yet there was something of the *gourmet* in their mode of assorting their mouthfuls of beef and blubber. Slices of each, or rather strips, passed between the lips, either together or in strict alternation, and with a regularity of sequence that kept the molars well to their work.

They did not eat all at once, but each man when and as often as the impulse prompted. Each slept after eating, his raw chunk lying beside him on the buffalo-skin; and, as he woke, the first act was to eat, and the next to sleep again. They did not lie down, but slumbered away in a sitting posture, with the head declined upon the breast, some of them snoring famously.

In the morning they were anxious to go; but I had given orders to detain them for a parting interview with myself. It resulted in a treaty, brief in its terms, that it might be certainly remembered, and mutually beneficial, that it might possibly be kept. I tried to make them understand what a powerful Prospero they had had for a host, and how beneficent he would prove himself so long as they did his bidding. And, as an earnest of my favor, I bought all the walrus-meat they had to spare, and four of their dogs, enriching them in return with needles and beads and a treasure of old cask-staves.

In the fulness of their gratitude, they pledged themselves emphatically to return in a few days with more meat, and to allow me to use their dogs and sledges for

my excursions to the north. I then gave them leave
to go. They yoked in their dogs in less than two
minutes, got on their sledges, cracked their two-fathom-
and-a-half-long seal-skin whips, and were off down the
ce to the southwest at a rate of seven knots an hour.

WILD DOG TEAM.

They did not return: I had read enough of treaty-
makings not to expect them too confidently. But the
next day came a party of five, on foot; two old men,
one of middle age, and a couple of gawky boys. We
had missed a number of articles soon after the first
party left us, an axe, a saw, and some knives. We
found afterward that our storehouse at Butler Island
had been entered: we were too short-handed to guard

it by a special watch. Besides all this, reconnoitring stealthily beyond Sylvia Head, we discovered a train of sledges drawn up behind the hummocks.

There was cause for apprehension in all this; but I felt that I could not afford to break with the rogues. They had it in their power to molest us seriously in our sledge-travel; they could make our hunts around the harbor dangerous; and my best chance of obtaining an abundant supply of fresh meat, our great desideratum, was by their agency. I treated the new party with marked kindness, and gave them many presents; but took care to make them aware that, until all the missing articles were restored, no member of the tribe would be admitted again as a guest on board the brig. They went off with many pantomimic protestations of innocence; but McGary, nevertheless, caught the incorrigible scamps stealing a coal-barrel as they passed Butler Island, and expedited their journey homeward by firing among them a charge of small shot.

Still, one peculiar worthy—we thought it must have been the venerable of the party, whom I knew afterward as a stanch friend, old Shang-huh—managed to work round in a westerly direction, and to cut to pieces my India-rubber boat, which had been left on the floe since Mr. Brooks's disaster, and to carry off every particle of the wood.

A few days after this, an agile, elfin youth drove up to our floe in open day. He was sprightly and good-looking, and had quite a neat turn-out of sledge and

dogs. He told his name with frankness, "*Myouk*,
I am,"—and where he lived. We asked him about
the boat; but he denied all knowledge of it, and refused either to confess or repent. He was surprised
when I ordered him to be confined to the hold. At
first he refused to eat, and sat down in the deepest

MYOUK.

grief; but after a while he began to sing, and then to
talk and cry, and then to sing again; and so he kept
on rehearsing his limited *solfeggio*,—

and crying and talking by turns, till a late hour of the

night. When I turned in, he was still noisily disconsolate.

There was a simplicity and *bonhommie* about this boy that interested me much; and I confess that when I made my appearance next morning—I could hardly conceal it from the gentleman on duty, whom I affected to censure—I was glad my bird had flown. Some time during the morning-watch, he had succeeded in throwing off the hatch and escaping. We suspected that he had confederates ashore, for his dogs had escaped with as much address as himself. I was convinced, however, that I had the truth from him, where he lived and how many lived with him; my cross-examination on these points having been very complete and satisfactory.

It was a sad business for some time after these Esquimaux left us, to go on making and registering our observations at Fern Rock. Baker's corpse still lay in the vestibule, and it was not long before another was placed by the side of it. We had to pass the bodies as often as we went in or out; but the men, grown feeble and nervous, disliked going near them in the night-time. When the summer thaw came and we could gather stones enough, we built up a grave on a depression of the rocks, and raised a substantial cairn above it.

"April 19, Wednesday.—I have been out on the floe again, breaking in my dogs. My reinforcement from the Esquimaux makes a noble team for me. For the last five days I have been striving with them, just as often and as long as my strength allowed me; and to-day I have my victory. The Society for Preventing Cruelty to Animals would have put me in custody, if they had been near enough; but, thanks to a merciless whip freely administered, I have been dashing along twelve miles in the last hour, and am back again; harness, sledge, and bones all unbroken. I am ready for another journey.

"April 22, Saturday.—Schubert has increasing symptoms of erysipelas around his amputated stump; and every one on board is depressed and silent except himself. He is singing in his bunk, as joyously as ever, 'Aux gens atrabilaires,' &c. Poor fellow! I am alarmed about him: it is a hard duty which compels me to take the field while my presence might cheer his last moments."

THE KAPETAH, OR JUMPER.

CHAPTER XVIII.

THE month of April was about to close, and the short season available for Arctic search was upon us. The condition of things on board the brig was not such as I could have wished for; but there was nothing to exact my presence, and it seemed to me clear that the time had come for pressing on the work of the expedition. The arrangements for our renewed exploration had not been intermitted, and were soon complete. I leave to my journal its own story.

"April 25, Tuesday.—A journey on the carpet; and the crew busy with the little details of their outfit: the officers the same.

"I have made a log-line for sledge-travel, with a contrivance for fastening it to the ice and liberating it at pleasure. It will give me my dead reckoning quite as well as on the water. I have a team now of seven dogs, four that I bought of the Esquimaux, and three

215

of my old stock.   They go together quite respectably.
Godfrey and myself will go with them on foot, following the first sledge on Thursday.

"April 26, Wednesday.—McGary went yesterday
with the leading sledge; and, as Brooks is still on his
back in consequence of the amputation, I leave Ohlsen
in charge of the brig.   He has my instructions in full:
among them I have dwelt largely upon the treatment
of the natives.

"These Esquimaux must be watched carefully, at
the same time that they are to be dealt with kindly,
though with a strict enforcement of our police-regula-
tions and some caution as to the freedom with which
they may come on board.   No punishments must be
permitted, either of them or in their presence, and no
resort to fire-arms unless to repel a serious attack.   I
have given orders, however, that if the contingency
does occur there shall be no firing over head.   The
prestige of the gun with a savage is in his notion of
its infallibility.   You may spare bloodshed by killing
a dog or even wounding him; but in no event should
you throw away your ball.   It is neither politic nor
humane.

"Our stowage-precautions are all arranged, to meet
the chance of the ice breaking up while I am away;
and a boat is placed ashore with stores, as the brig
may be forced from her moorings.

"The worst thought I have now in setting out is,
that of the entire crew I can leave but two behind in
able condition, and the doctor and Bonsall are the only

two officers who can help Ohlsen. This is our force, four able-bodied and six disabled to keep the brig: the commander and seven men, scarcely better upon the average, out upon the ice. Eighteen souls, thank God! certainly not eighteen bodies!——

"I am going this time to follow the ice-belt (Eis-fod) to the Great Glacier of Humboldt, and there load up with pemmican from our cache of last October. From this point I expect to stretch along the face of the glacier inclining to the west of north, and make an attempt to cross the ice to the American side. Once on smooth ice, near this shore, I may pass to the west, and enter the large indentation whose existence I can infer with nearly positive certainty. In this I may find an outlet, and determine the state of things beyond the ice-clogged area of this bay.

"I take with me pemmican and bread and tea, a canvas tent, five feet by six, and two sleeping-bags of reindeer-skin. The sledge has been built on board by Mr. Ohlsen. It is very light, of hickory, and but nine feet long. Our kitchen is a soup-kettle for melting snow and making tea, arranged so as to boil with either lard or spirits."

The pattern of the tent was suggested by our experience during the fall journeys. The greatest discomfort of the Arctic traveller when camping out is from the congealed moisture of the breath forming long feathers of frost against the low shelving roof of the tent within a few inches of his face. The remedy which I adopted was to run the tent-poles through grummet-holes in the canvas about eighteen inches above the floor, and allow the lower part of the sides to hang down vertically like a valance, before forming the floor-cloth. This arrangement gave ample room for breathing; it prevented the ice forming above the

THE TENT.

sleeper's head, and the melted rime from trickling down upon it.

"For instruments I have a fine Gambey sextant, in addition to my ordinary pocket-instrument, an artificial horizon, and a Barrow's dip-circle. These occupy little room upon the sledge. My telescope and chronometer I carry on my person.

"McGary has taken the 'Faith.' He carries few

stores, intending to replenish at the cache of Bonsall
Point, and to lay in pemmican at McGary Island.
Most of his cargo consists of bread, which we find it
hard to dispense with in eating cooked food. It has a
good effect in absorbing the fat of the pemmican, which
is apt to disagree with the stomach."

THE FAITH.

Godfrey and myself followed on the 27th, as I had
intended. The journey was an arduous one to be undertaken, even under the most favoring circumstances
and by unbroken men. It was to be the crowning
expedition of the campaign, to attain the Ultima
Thule of the Greenland shore, measure the waste that
lay between it and the unknown West, and seek round

the farthest circle of the ice for an outlet to the mysterious channels beyond. The scheme could not be carried out in its details. Yet it was prosecuted far enough to indicate what must be our future fields of labour, and to determine many points of geographical interest. Our observations were in general confirmatory of those which had been made by Mr. Bonsall; and they accorded so well with our subsequent surveys as to trace for us the outline of the coast with great certainty.

If the reader has had the patience to follow the pathway of our little brig, he has perceived that at Refuge Harbor, our first asylum, a marked change takes place in the line of direction of the coast. From Cape Alexander, which may be regarded as the westernmost cape of Greenland, the shore runs nearly north and south, like the broad channel of which it is the boundary; but on reaching Refuge Inlet it bends nearly at a right angle, and follows on from west to east till it has passed the 65th degree of longitude. Between Cape Alexander and the inlet it is broken by two indentations, the first of them near the Etah settlement, which was visited in 1855 by the Rescue Expedition under Lieutenant Hartstene, and which bears on my charts the name of that noble-spirited commander; the other remembered by us as Lifeboat Cove. In both of these the glaciers descend to the water-line, from an interior of lofty rock-clad hills.[35] My sketches give but a rude idea of their picturesque sublimity.

The coast-line is diversified, however, by numerous water-worn headlands,[36] which on reaching Cape Hatherton decline into rolling hills,[37] their margins studded with islands, which are the favorite breeding-places of the eider, the glaucous gull, and the tern.

ETAH, AND MY BROTHER JOHN'S GLACIER.

Cape Hatherton rises boldly above these, a mass of porphyritic rock.[38]

After leaving Refuge Harbor, the features of the coast undergo a change. There are no deep bays or discharging glaciers; and it is only as we approach Rensselaer Harbor, where the shore-line begins to incline once more to the north, that the deep recesses and ice-lined fiords make their appearance again.

The geological structure changes also,[39] and the

cliffs begin to assume a series of varied and picturesque outlines along the coast, that scarcely require the aid of imagination to trace in them the ruins of architectural structure. They come down boldly to the shore-line, their summits rising sometimes more than a thousand feet above the eye, and the long cones of rubbish at their base mingling themselves with the ice-foot.[40]

The coast retains the same character as far as the Great Glacier. It is indented by four great bays, all of them communicating with deep gorges, which are watered by streams from the interior ice-fields; yet none of them exhibit glaciers of any magnitude at the water-line. Dallas Bay shows a similar formation, and the archipelago beyond Cape Hunter retains it almost without change.[41]

The mean height of the table-land till it reaches the bed of the Great Glacier may be stated in round numbers at nine hundred feet, its tallest summit near the water at thirteen hundred, and the rise of the background above the general level at six hundred more.[42] The face of this stupendous ice-mass, as it defined the coast, was everywhere an abrupt and threatening precipice, only broken by clefts and deep ravines, giving breadth and interest to its wild expression.

The most picturesque portion of the North Greenland coast is to be found after leaving Cape George Russell and approaching Dallas Bay. The red sandstones contrast most favorably with the blank whiteness, associating the cold tints of the dreary Arctic landscape

with the warm coloring of more southern lands. The
seasons have acted on the different layers of the cliff
so as to give them the appearance of jointed masonry,
and the narrow line of greenstone at the top caps
them with well-simulated battlements.

THREE BROTHER TURRETS.

One of these interesting freaks of nature became
known to us as the "Three Brother Turrets."

The sloping rubbish at the foot of the coast-wall led
up, like an artificial causeway, to a gorge that was
streaming at noonday with the southern sun; while
everywhere else the rock stood out in the blackest
shadow. Just at the edge of this bright opening rose

the dreamy semblance of a castle, flanked with triple
towers, completely isolated and defined. These were
the "Three Brother Turrets."

I was still more struck with another of the same
sort, in the immediate neighborhood of my halting-
ground beyond Sunny Gorge, to the north of latitude
79°. A single cliff of greenstone, marked by the slaty
limestone that once encased it, rears itself from a
crumbled base of sandstones, like the boldly-chiselled
rampart of an ancient city. At its northern extremity,
on the brink of a deep ravine which has worn its way
among the ruins, there stands a solitary column or
minaret-tower, as sharply finished as if it had been
cast for the Place Vendôme. Yet the length of the
shaft alone is four hundred and eighty feet; and it
rises on a plinth or pedestal itself two hundred and
eighty feet high.

I remember well the emotions of my party as it
first broke upon our view. Cold and sick as I was, I
brought back a sketch of it, which may have interest
for the reader, though it scarcely suggests the imposing
dignity of this magnificent landmark. Those who are
happily familiar with the writings of Tennyson, and
have communed with his spirit in the solitudes of a
wilderness, will apprehend the impulse that inscribed
the scene with his name.

Still beyond this, comes the archipelago which bears
the name of our brig, studded with the names of those
on board of her who adhered to all the fortunes of the
expedition; and at its eastern cape spreads out the

J Hamilton.   Engraved at J M Butler's establishment 84 Chestnut St.   J McGoffin.

TENNYSONS MONUMENT.

(From a sketch by Dr. Kane.)

Great Glacier of Humboldt. My recollections of this glacier are very distinct. The day was beautifully clear on which I first saw it; and I have a number of sketches made as we drove along in view of its magnificent face. They disappoint me, giving too much white surface and badly-fading distances, the grandeur of the few bold and simple lines of nature being almost entirely lost.

I will not attempt to do better by florid description. Men only rhapsodize about Niagara and the ocean. My notes speak simply of the "long ever-shining line of cliff diminished to a well-pointed wedge in the perspective;" and again, of "the face of glistening ice, sweeping in a long curve from the low interior, the facets in front intensely illuminated by the sun." But this line of cliff rose in solid glassy wall three hundred feet above the water-level, with an unknown unfathomable depth below it; and its curved face, sixty miles in length from Cape Agassiz to Cape Forbes, vanished into unknown space at not more than a single day's railroad-travel from the Pole. The interior with which it communicated, and from which it issued, was an unsurveyed *mer de glace*, an ice-ocean, to the eye of boundless dimensions.[43]

It was in full sight—the mighty crystal bridge which connects the two continents of America and Greenland. I say continents; for Greenland, however insulated it may ultimately prove to be, is in mass strictly continental. Its least possible axis, measured from Cape Farewell to the line of this glacier, in the neighborhood of the 80th parallel, gives a length of more than twelve hundred miles, not materially less than that of Australia from its northern to its southern cape.[44]

GREAT GLACIER.

Imagine, now, the centre of such a continent, occupied through nearly its whole extent by a deep unbroken sea of ice, that gathers perennial increase from the water-shed of vast snow-covered mountains and all the precipitations of the atmosphere upon its own surface. Imagine this, moving onward like a great glacial river, seeking outlets at every fiord and valley, rolling

icy cataracts into the Atlantic and Greenland seas;
and, having at last reached the northern limit of the
land that has borne it up, pouring out a mighty frozen
torrent into unknown Arctic space.[45]

It is thus, and only thus, that we must form a just
conception of a phenomenon like this Great Glacier.
I had looked in my own mind for such an appearance,

GLACIER PROTRUDING AT CACHE ISLAND.

should I ever be fortunate enough to reach the northern coast of Greenland. But now that it was before
me, I could hardly realize it. I had recognised, in my
quiet library at home, the beautiful analogies which
Forbes and Studer have developed between the glacier
and the river. But I could not comprehend at first
this complete substitution of ice for water.

It was slowly that the conviction dawned on me,

that I was looking upon the counterpart of the great river-system of Arctic Asia and America. Yet here were no water-feeders from the south. Every particle of moisture had its origin within the Polar circle, and had been converted into ice. There were no vast alluvions, no forest or animal traces borne down by liquid torrents. Here was a plastic, moving, semi-solid mass, obliterating life, swallowing rocks and islands, and ploughing its way with irresistible march through the crust of an investing sea.

CHAPTER XIX.

"It is now the 20th of May, and for the first time I am able, propped up by pillows and surrounded by sick messmates, to note the fact that we have failed again to force the passage to the north.

"Godfrey and myself overtook the advance party under McGary two days after leaving the brig. Our dogs were in fair travelling condition, and, except snow-blindness, there seemed to be no drawback to our efficiency. In crossing Marshall Bay, we found the snow so accumulated in drifts, that, with all our efforts to pick out a track, we became involved: we could not force our sledges through. We were forced to unload and carry forward the cargo on our backs, beating a path for the dogs to follow in. In this way we plodded on to the opposite headland, Cape William Wood, where the waters of Mary Minturn River, which had delayed the freezing of the ice, gave us a long reach of level travel. We then made a better rate; and our days' marches were such as to carry us by the 4th of May nearly to the glacier.

"This progress, however, was dearly earned. As early as the 3d of May, the winter's scurvy reappeared painfully among our party. As we struggled through the snow along the Greenland coast we sank up to our middle, and the dogs, floundering about, were so buried as to preclude any attempts at hauling. This excessive snow-deposit seemed to be due to the precipitation of cold condensing wind suddenly wafted from the neighboring glacier; for at Rensselaer Harbor we had only four inches of general snow depth. It obliged us to unload our sledges again, and carry their cargo, a labor which resulted in dropsical swellings with painful prostration. Here three of the party were taken with snow-blindness, and George Stephenson had to be condemned as unfit for travel altogether, on account of chest-symptoms accompanying his scorbutic troubles. On the 4th, Thomas Hickey also gave in, although not quite disabled for labor at the tracklines.

"Perhaps we would still have got on; but, to crown all, we found that the bears had effected an entrance into our pemmican-casks, and destroyed our chances of reinforcing our provisions at the several caches. This great calamity was certainly inevitable; for it is simple justice to the officers under whose charge the provision-depôts were constructed, to say that no means in their power could have prevented the result. The pemmican was covered with blocks of stone which it had required the labor of three men to adjust; but the extraordinary strength of the bear had enabled him to force aside the heaviest rocks, and his pawing had broken the iron casks which held our pemmican literally into chips. Our alcohol-cask, which it had cost me a separate and special journey in the late fall to deposit, was so completely destroyed that we could not find a stave of it.

APPROACHING DALLAS BAY.

"Off Cape James Kent, about eight miles from 'Sunny Gorge,' while taking an observation for latitude, I was myself seized with a sudden pain and fainted. My limbs became rigid, and certain obscure tetanoid symptoms of our late winter's enemy disclosed themselves. In this condition I was unable to make more than nine miles a day. I was strapped upon the sledge, and the march continued as usual; but my powers diminished so rapidly that I could not resist even the otherwise comfortable temperature of 5° below zero. My left foot becoming frozen up to the metatarsal joint, caused a

vexatious delay; and the same night it became evident
that the immovability of my limbs was due to dropsical effusion.

"On the 5th, becoming delirious, and fainting every
time that I was taken from the tent to the sledge, I
succumbed entirely. I append the report of our surgeon
made upon my return. This will best exhibit the
diseased condition of myself and party, and explain, in
stronger terms than I can allow myself to use, the
extent of my efforts to contend against it.[46]

"My comrades would kindly persuade me that, even
had I continued sound, we could not have proceeded
on our journey. The snows were very heavy, and
increasing as we went; some of the drifts perfectly
impassable, and the level floes often four feet deep in
yielding snow. The scurvy had already broken out
among the men, with symptoms like my own; and
Morton, our strongest man, was beginning to give way.
It is the reverse of comfort to me that they shared my
weakness. All that I should remember with pleasu-
rable feeling is, that to five brave men, Morton, Riley,
Hickey, Stephenson, and Hans, themselves scarcely
able to travel, I owe my preservation. They carried
me back by forced marches, after cacheing our stores
and India-rubber boat near Dallas Bay, in lat. 79°.5,
lon. 66°.

"I was taken into the brig on the 14th. Since then,
fluctuating between life and death, I have by the blessing of God reached the present date, and see feebly
in prospect my recovery. Dr. Hayes regards my attack

as one of scurvy, complicated by typhoid fever. George Stephenson is similarly affected. Our worst symptoms are dropsical effusion and night-sweats.

"May 22, Monday.—Let me, if I can, make up my record for the time I have been away or on my back.

"Poor Schubert is gone. Our gallant merry-hearted companion left us some ten days ago, for, I trust, a more genial world. It is sad, in this dreary little homestead of ours, to miss his contented face and the joyous troll of his ballads.

"The health of the rest has, if any thing, improved. Their complexions show the influence of sunlight, and I think several have a firmer and more elastic step. Stephenson and Thomas are the only two beside myself who are likely to suffer permanently from the effects of our break-down. Bad scurvy both: symptoms still serious.

"Before setting out a month ago, on a journey that should have extended into the middle of June, I had broken up the establishment of Butler Island, and placed all the stores around the brig upon the heavy ice. My object in this was a double one. First, to remove from the Esquimaux the temptation and ability to pilfer. Second, to deposit our cargo where it could be re-stowed by very few men, if any unforeseen change in the ice made it necessary. Mr. Ohlsen, to whose charge the brig was committed, had orders to stow the hold slowly, remove the forward housing, and fit up the forecastle for the men to inhabit it again.

"All of these he carried out with judgment and

energy. I find upon my return the brig so stowed and refitted that four days would prepare us for sea. The quarter-deck alone is now boarded in; and here all the officers and sick are sojourning. The wind makes this wooden shanty a somewhat airy retreat; but, for the

THE BRIG IN MAY.

health of our maimed scorbutic men, it is infinitely preferable to the less-ventilated quarters below. Some of the crew, with one stove, are still in the forecastle; but the old cabin is deserted.

"I left Hans as hunter. I gave him a regular exemption from all other labor, and a promised present to his lady-love on reaching Fiskernaes. He signalized his

promotion by shooting two deer, *Tukkuk*, the first yet
shot.   We have now on hand one hundred and forty-
five pounds of fine venison, a very gift of grace to our
diseased crew.   But, indeed, we are not likely to want
for wholesome food, now that the night is gone, which
made our need of it so pressing.   On the first of May,
those charming little migrants the snow-birds, *ultima
cœlicolum*, which only left us on the 4th of November,
returned to our ice-crusted rocks, whence they seem to
'fill the sea and air with their sweet jargoning.'   Seal
literally abound too.   I have learned to prefer this flesh
to the reindeer's, at least that of the female seal, which
has not the fetor of her mate's.

"By the 12th, the sides of the Advance were free
from snow, and her rigging clean and dry.   The floe is
rapidly undergoing its wonderful processes of decay;
and the level ice measures but six feet in thickness.
To-day they report a burgomaster gull seen: one of the
earliest but surest indications of returning open water.
It is not strange, ice-leaguered exiles as we are, that
we observe and exult in these things.   They are the
pledges of renewed life, the olive-branch of this dreary
waste: we feel the spring in all our pulses.

"The first thing I did after my return was to send
McGary to Life-boat Cove, to see that our boat and its
buried provisions were secure.   He made the journey
by dog-sledge in four days, and has returned reporting
that all is safe: an important help for us, should
this heavy ice of our more northern prison refuse to
release us.

"But the pleasantest feature of his journey was the disclosure of open water, extending up in a sort of tongue, with a trend of north by east to within two miles of Refuge Harbor, and there widening as it expanded to the south and west.

"Indeed, some circumstances which he reports seem to point to the existence of a north water all the year round; and the frequent water-skies, fogs, &c., that we have seen to the southwest during the winter, go to confirm the fact. The breaking up of the Smith Strait's ice commences much earlier than this; but as yet it has not extended farther than Littleton Island, where I should have wintered if my fall journey had not pointed to the policy of remaining here. The open water undoubtedly has been the cause of the retreat of the Esquimaux. Their sledge-tracks have been seen all along the land-foot; but, except a snow house at Esquimaux Point, we have met nothing which to the uninitiated traveller would indicate that they had rested upon this desert coast.

"As soon as I had recovered enough to be aware of my failure, I began to devise means for remedying it. But I found the resources of the party shattered. Pierre had died but a week before, and his death exerted an unfavorable influence. There were only three men able to do duty. Of the officers, Wilson, Brooks, Sontag, and Petersen were knocked up. There was no one except Sontag, Hayes, or myself, who was qualified to conduct a survey; and, of us three, Dr. Hayes was the only one on his feet.

"The quarter to which our remaining observations were to be directed lay to the north and east of the Cape Sabine of Captain Inglefield. The interruption our progress along the coast of Greenland had met from the Great Glacier, and the destruction of our provision-caches by the bears, left a blank for us of the entire northern coast-line. It was necessary to ascertain whether the farthermost expansion of Smith's Strait did not find an outlet in still more remote channels; and this became our duty the more plainly, since our theodolite had shown us that the northern coast trended off to the eastward, and not toward the west, as our predecessor had supposed. The angular difference of sixty degrees between its bearings on his charts and our own left me completely in the dark as to what might be the condition of this unknown area.

"I determined to trust almost entirely to the dogs for our travel in the future, and to send our parties of exploration, one after the other, as rapidly as the strength and refreshing of our team would permit.

"Dr. Hayes was selected for that purpose; and I satisfied myself that, with a little assistance from my comrades, I could be carried round to the cots of the sick, and so avail myself of his services in the field.

"He was a perfectly fresh man, not having yet undertaken a journey. I gave him a team and my best driver, William Godfrey. He is to cross Smith's Straits above the inlet, and make as near as may be a straight course for Cape Sabine. My opinion is that by keeping well south he will find the ice less clogged and

easier sledging. Our experience proves, I think, that
the transit of this broken area must be most impeded
as we approach the glacier. The immense discharge
of icebergs cannot fail to break it up seriously for
travel.

"I gave him the small sledge which was built by Mr.
Ohlsen. The snow was sufficiently thawed to make it
almost unnecessary to use fire as a means of obtaining
water: they could therefore dispense with tallow or

THE TEAM.

alcohol, and were able to carry pemmican in larger
quantities. Their sleeping-bags were a very neat article of a light reindeer-skin. The dogs were in excellent condition too, no longer foot-sore, but well rested
and completely broken, including the four from the
Esquimaux, animals of great power and size. Two
of these, the stylish leaders of the team, a span of
thoroughly wolfish iron-grays, have the most powerful
and wild-beast-like bound that I have seen in animals
of their kind.

"I made up the orders of the party on the 19th, the first day that I was able to mature a plan; and with commendable zeal they left the brig on the 20th.

"May 23, Tuesday.—They have had superb weather, thank heaven!—a profusion of the most genial sunshine, bringing out the seals in crowds to bask around their breathing-holes. A ptarmigan was killed to-day, a male, with but two brown feathers on the back of his little neck to indicate the return of his summer-plumage.

"The winter is gone! The Andromeda has been found on shore under the snow, with tops vegetating and green! I have a shoot of it in my hand.

"May 25, Thursday.—Bands of soft mist hide the tops of the hills: the unbroken transparency of last month's atmosphere has disappeared, and the sky has all the ashen or pearly obscurity of the Arctic summer.

"May 26, Friday.—I get little done; but I have too much to attend to in my weak state to journalize. Thermometer above freezing-point, without the sun to-day.

"May 27, Saturday.—Every thing showing that the summer changes have commenced. The ice is rapidly losing its integrity, and a melting snow has fallen for the last two days,—one of those comforting home-snows that we have not seen for so long.

"May 28, Sunday.—Our day of rest and devotion. It was a fortnight ago last Friday since our poor friend Pierre died. For nearly two months he had been struggling against the enemy with a resolute will and mirthful spirit, that seemed sure of victory. But he sunk in spite of them.

"The last offices were rendered to him with the same careful ceremonial that we observed at Baker's funeral. There were fewer to walk in the procession; but the body was encased in a decent pine coffin and carried to Observatory Island, where it was placed side-by-side with that of his messmate. Neither could yet be buried; but it is hardly necessary to say that the frost has embalmed their remains. Dr. Hayes read the chapter from Job which has consigned so many to their last resting-place, and a little snow was sprinkled upon the face of the coffin. Pierre was a volunteer not only of our general expedition, but of the party with which he met his death-blow. He was a gallant man, a universal favorite on board, always singing some Béranger ballad or other, and so elastic in his merriment that even in his last sickness he cheered all that were about him."

CHAPTER XX.

"MAY 30, Tuesday.—We are gleaning fresh water
from the rocks, and the icebergs begin to show commencing streamlets. The great floe is no longer a
Sahara, if still a desert. The floes are wet, and their
snows dissolve readily under the warmth of the foot,
and the old floe begins to shed fresh water into its
hollows. Puddles of salt water collect around the
ice-foot. It is now hardly recognizable,—rounded,
sunken, broken up with water-pools overflowing its
base. Its diminished crusts are so percolated by the
saline tides, that neither tables nor broken fragments
unite any longer by freezing. It is lessening so rapidly
that we do not fear it any longer as an enemy to

the brig. The berg indeed vanished long before the sun-thermometers indicated a noon-temperature above 32°.

"The changes of this ice at temperatures far below the freezing-point confirm the views I formed upon my last cruise as to the limited influence of direct thaw. I am convinced that the expansion of the ice after the contraction of low temperatures, and the infiltrative or endosmometric changes thus induced,—the differing temperatures of sea-water and ice, and their chemical relations,—the mechanical action of pressure, collapse, fracture, and disruption,—the effects of sun-heated snow-surfaces, falls of warm snow, currents, wind, drifts, and wave-action,—all these leave the great mass of the Polar ice-surfaces so broken, disintegrated, and reduced, when the extreme cold abates, and so changed in structure and molecular character, that the few weeks of summer thaw have but a subsidiary office to perform in completing their destruction.

SEAL SCREEN.

"Seal of the Hispid variety, the Netsik of the Esquimaux and Danes, grow still more numerous on the level floes, lying cautiously in the sun beside their *atluks*.[47] By means of the Esquimaux stratagem of a white screen pushed forward on a sledge until the concealed hunter comes within range, Hans has shot four of them. We have more fresh meat than we can eat.

For the past three weeks we have been living on ptarmigan, rabbits, two reindeer, and seal.

SHOOTING SEAL.

"They are fast curing our scurvy.   With all these
resources,—coming to our relief so suddenly too,—how
can my thoughts turn despairingly to poor Franklin
and his crew?

" . . . . Can they have survived?   No man can
answer with certainty; but no man without presump-
tion can answer in the negative.

"If, four months ago,—surrounded by darkness and
bowed down by disease,—I had been asked the question, I would have turned toward the black hills and
the frozen sea, and responded in sympathy with them,
'No.'   But with the return of light a savage people
come down upon us, destitute of any but the rudest

appliances of the chase, who were fattening on the most wholesome diet of the region, only forty miles from our anchorage, while I was denouncing its scarcity.

"For Franklin, every thing depends upon locality : but, from what I can see of Arctic exploration thus far, it would be hard to find a circle of fifty miles' diameter entirely destitute of animal resources. The most solid winter-ice is open here and there in pools and patches worn by currents and tides. Such were the open spaces that Parry found in Wellington Channel; such are the stream-holes (stromhols) of the Greenland coast, the polynia of the Russians; and such we have ourselves found in the most rigorous cold of all.

"To these spots, the seal, walrus, and the early birds crowd in numbers. One which kept open, as we find from the Esquimaux, at Littleton Island, only forty miles from us, sustained three families last winter until the opening of the north water. Now, if we have been entirely supported for the past three weeks by the hunting of a single man,—seal-meat alone being plentiful enough to subsist us till we turn homeward,—certainly a party of tolerably skilful hunters might lay up an abundant stock for the winter. As it is, we are making caches of meat under the snow, to prevent its spoiling on our hands, in the very spot which a few days ago I described as a Sahara. And, indeed, it was so for nine whole months, when this flood of animal life burst upon us like fountains of water and pastures and date-trees in a southern desert.

"I have undergone one change in opinion. It is of the ability of Europeans or Americans to inure themselves to an ultra-Arctic climate. God forbid, indeed, that civilized man should be exposed for successive years to this blighting darkness! But around the Arctic circle, even as high as 72°, where cold and cold only is to be encountered, men may be acclimatized, for there is light enough for out-door labor.

"Of the one hundred and thirty-six picked men of Sir John Franklin in 1846, Northern Orkney men, Greenland whalers, so many young and hardy constitutions, with so much intelligent experience to guide them, I cannot realize that some may not yet be alive; that some small squad or squads, aided or not aided by the Esquimaux of the expedition, may not have found a hunting-ground, and laid up from summer to summer enough of fuel and food and seal-skins to brave three or even four more winters in succession.

"I speak of the miracle of this bountiful fair season. I could hardly have been much more surprised if these black rocks, instead of sending out upon our solitude the late inroad of yelling Esquimaux, had sent us naturalized Saxons. Two of our party at first fancied they were such.

"The mysterious compensations by which we adapt ourselves to climate are more striking here than in the tropics. In the Polar zone the assault is immediate and sudden, and, unlike the insidious fatality of hot countries, produces its results rapidly. It requires hardly a single winter to tell who are to be the heat-making and acclimatized men. Petersen, for instance, who has resided for two years at Upernavik, seldom enters a room with a fire. Another of our party, George Riley, with a vigorous constitution, established habits of free exposure, and active cheerful temperament, has so inured himself to the cold, that he sleeps on our sledge-journeys without a blanket or any other covering than his walking-suit, while the outside temperature is 30° below zero. The half-breeds of the coast rival the Esquimaux in their powers of endurance.

"There must be many such men with Franklin. The North British sailors of the Greenland seal and whale fisheries I look upon as inferior to none in capacity to resist the Arctic climates.

"My mind never realizes the complete catastrophe, the destruction of all Franklin's crews. I picture them to myself broken into detachments, and my mind fixes itself on one little group of some thirty, who have found the open spot of some tidal eddy, and under the teachings of an Esquimaux or perhaps one of their own Greenland whalers, have set bravely to work, and trapped the fox, speared the bear, and killed the seal and walrus and whale. I think of them ever with hope. I sicken not to be able to reach them.

"It is a year ago to-day since we left New York. I am not as sanguine as I was then: time and experience have chastened me. There is every thing about me to check enthusiasm and moderate hope. I am here in forced inaction, a broken-down man, oppressed by cares, with many dangers before me, and still under the shadow of a hard wearing winter, which has crushed two of my best associates. Here on the spot, after two unavailing expeditions of search, I hold my opinions unchanged; and I record them as a matter of duty upon a manuscript which may speak the truth when I can do so no longer.

"June 1, Thursday.—At ten o'clock this morning the wail of the dogs outside announced the return of Dr. Hayes and William Godfrey. Both of them were completely snow-blind, and the doctor had to be led to my bedside to make his report. In fact, so exhausted was he, that in spite of my anxiety I forbore to question him until he had rested. I venture to say, that both he and his companion well remember their astonishing performance over stewed apples and seal-meat.

"The dogs were not so foot-sore as might have been expected; but two of them, including poor little 'Jenny,' were completely knocked up. All attention was bestowed upon these indispensable essentials of Arctic search, and soon they were more happy than their masters."

Dr. Hayes's Journey.

Dr. Hayes made a due north line on leaving the brig; but, encountering the "squeezed ices" of my own party in March, he wisely worked to the eastward. I had advised him to descend to Smith's Sound, under a conviction that the icebergs there would be less numerous, and that the diminished distance from land to land would make his transit more easy. But he managed to effect the object by a less circuitous route than I had anticipated; for, although he made but fifteen miles on the 20th, he emerged the next day from the heavy ice, and made at least fifty. On this day his meridian observation gave the latitude of 79° 8′ 6″, and from a large berg he sighted many points of the coast.

On the 22d, he encountere a wall of hummocks, exceeding twenty feet in height, and extending in a long line to the northeast.

After vain attempts to force them, becoming embarrassed in fragmentary ice, worn, to use his own words, into "deep pits and valleys," he was obliged to camp, surrounded by masses of the wildest character, some of them thirty feet in height.

The next three days were spent in struggles through this broken plain; fogs sometimes embarrassed them, but at intervals land could be seen to the northwest. On the 27th, they reached the north side of the bay, passing over but few miles of new and unbroken floe.

The excessively broken and rugged character of this ice they had encountered must be due to the discharges from the Great Glacier of Humboldt, which arrest the floes and make them liable to excessive disruption under the influence of winds and currents.

Dr. Hayes told me, that in many places they could not have advanced a step but for the dogs. Deep cavities filled with snow intervened between lines of ice-barricades, making their travel as slow and tedious as the same obstructions had done to the party of poor Brooks before their eventful rescue last March.

Their course was now extremely tortuous; for, although from the headlands of Rensselaer Harbor to the point which they first reached on the northern coast

DOGS AMONG BERGS.

was not more than ninety miles as the crow flies, yet by the dead reckoning of the party they must have had an actual travel of two hundred and seventy.

For the details of this passage I refer the reader to the appended report of Dr. Hayes. His gravest and most insurmountable difficulty was snow-blindness, which so affected him that for some time he was not able to use the sextant. His journal-entry referring to the 23d, while tangled in the ice, says, "I was so snow-blind that I could not see; and as riding, owing to the jaded condition of the dogs, was seldom possible, we were obliged to lay to."

It was not until the 25th that their eyesight was sufficiently restored to enable them to push on. In these devious and untrodden ice-fields, even the instinct of the dogs would have been of little avail to direct their course. It was well for the party that during this compulsory halt the temperatures were mild and endurable. From their station of the 25th, they obtained reliable sights of the coast, trending to the northward and eastward, and a reliable determination of latitude, in 79° 24' 4". A fine headland, bearing nearly due northwest, I named Cape Hayes, in commemoration of the gentleman who discovered it.

Instead, however, of making for the land, which could not have aided their survey, they followed the outer ice, at the same time edging in toward a lofty bluff whose position they had determined by intersection. They hoped here to effect a landing, but encountered a fresh zone of broken ice in the attempt. The hummocks could not be turned. The sledge had to be lifted over them by main strength, and it required the most painful efforts of the whole party to liberate it from the snow between them.

On the 26th, disasters accumulated. William Godfrey, one of the sturdiest travellers, broke down; and the dogs, the indispensable reliance of the party, were in bad working trim. The rude harness, always apt to become tangled and broken, had been mended so often and with such imperfect means as to be scarcely serviceable.

CAPE HAYES.

This evil would seem the annoyance of an hour to the travellers in a stage-coach, but to a sledge-party on the ice-waste it is the gravest that can be conceived. The Esquimaux dog, as I before mentioned, is driven by a single trace, a long thin thong of seal or walrus-hide, which passes from his chest over his haunches to the sledge. The team is always driven abreast, and the traces are of course tangling and twisting themselves up incessantly, as the half-wild or terrified brutes bound right or left from their prescribed positions. The consequence is, that the seven or nine or fourteen lines have a marvellous aptitude at knotting themselves up beyond the reach of skill and patience. If the weather is warm enough to thaw the snow, they become utterly soft and flaccid, and the naked hand, if applied ingeniously, may dispense with a resort to the Gordian process. But in the severe cold, such as I experienced in my winter journeys of 1854, the knife is often the only appliance; an unsafe one if invoked too often, for every new attachment shortens your harness, and you may end by drawing your dogs so close that they cannot pull. I have been obliged to halt and camp on the open floe, till I could renew enough of warmth and energy and patience to disentangle the knots of my harness. Oh, how charitably have I remembered Doctor Slop!

It was only after appropriating an undue share of his seal-skin breeches that the leader of the party succeeded in patching up his mutilated dog-lines. He was rewarded, however, for he shortly after found an old floe, over which his sledge passed happily to the north coast. It was the first time that any of our parties had succeeded in penetrating the area to the north. The ice had baffled three organized foot-parties. It could certainly never have been traversed without the aid of dogs; but it is equally certain that the effort must again have failed, even with their aid, but for the energy and determination of Dr. Hayes, and the endurance of his partner, William Godfrey. The latitude by observation was 79° 45′ N., the longitude 69° 12′ W. The coast here trended more to the westward than it had done. It was sighted for thirty miles to the northward and eastward. This was the culminating point of his survey, beyond which his observations did not extend. Two large headlands, Capes Joseph Leidy and John Frazer, indicate it.

The cliffs were of mingled limestone and sandstone, corresponding to those on the southern side of Peabody Bay. To the north they exceeded two thousand feet in height, while to the southward they diminished to twelve hundred. The ice-foot varied from fifty to one hundred and fifty feet in width, and stood out against the dark debris thrown down by the cliffs in a clean naked shelf of dazzling white.

The party spent the 28th in mending the sledge, which was completely broken, and feeding up their dogs for a renewal of the journey. But, their provisions being limited, Dr. Hayes did not deem himself justified in continuing to the north. He determined to follow and survey the coast toward Cape Sabine.

His pemmican was reduced to eighteen pounds; there was apparently no hope of deriving resources from the hunt; and the coasts were even more covered with snow than those he had left on the southern side. His return was a thing of necessity.

The course of the party to the westward along the land-ice was interrupted by a large indentation, which

they had seen and charted while approaching the
coast. It is the same which I surveyed in April,
1855, and which now bears the name of the Secretary
of the Navy, Mr. Dobbin.   A sketch which I made of
it gives an idea of the appearance of the bay and

DOBBIN BAY.

of two islands which Dr. Hayes discovered near its
entrance. He saw also on its southwestern side a
lofty pyramid, truncated at its summit, which corre-
sponded both in its bearings and position with the
survey of my April journey. I append a sketch of
this interesting landmark.

The latter portion of Dr. Hayes's journey was full

of incident. The land-ice was travelled for a while at the rate of five or six miles an hour; but, after crossing Dobbin Bay, the snows were an unexpected impediment, and the ice-foot was so clogged that they made but fifteen miles from camp to camp on the floes. After

FLETCHER WEBSTER HEADLAND.

fixing the position of Cape Sabine, and connecting it with the newly-discovered coast-line to the north and east, he prepared to cross the bay farther to the south.

Most providentially they found this passage free from bergs; but their provisions were nearly gone, and their dogs were exhausted. They threw away their sleeping-bags, which were of reindeer-skin and weighed about twelve pounds each, and abandoned besides clothing enough to make up a reduction in weight of nearly fifty pounds. With their load so lightened, they were enabled to make good the crossing of the bay. They landed at Peter Force Bay, and reached the brig on the 1st of June.

This journey connected the northern coast with the survey of my predecessor; but it disclosed no channel or any form of exit from this bay.

It convinced me, however, that such a channel must exist; for this great curve could be no cul-de-sac. Even were my observations since my first fall journey of September, 1853, not decisive on this head, the general movement of the icebergs, the character of the tides, and the equally sure analogies of physical geography, would point unmistakably to such a conclusion.

To verify it, I at once commenced the organization of a double party. This, which is called in my Report the Northeast Party, was to be assisted by dogs, but was to be subsisted as far as the Great Glacier by provisions carried by a foot-party in advance.

For the continuation of my plans I again refer to my journal.

"June 2, Friday.—There is still this hundred miles wanting to the northwest to complete our entire circuit of this frozen water. This is to be the field for our next party. I am at some loss how to organize it; for myself, I am down with scurvy. Dr. Hayes is just from the field, worn out and snow-blind. His health-roll makes a sorry parade. It runs thus:—

Officers.

MR. BROOKS............................Unhealed stump.
MR. WILSON ....   do.
MR. SONTAG............................Down with scurvy
MR. BONSALL..........................Scurvy knee, but mending.
MR. PETERSEN.................. ....General scurvy.
MR. GOODFELLOW......................Scurvy.
MR. OHLSEN...........................Well.
MR. McGARY...........................Well.

Crew.

WILLIAM MORTON.....................Nearly recovered.
THOMAS HICKEY.......................Well.
GEORGE WHIPPLE.....................Scurvy.
JOHN BLAKE..........................Scurvy.
HANS CRISTIAN.......................Well.
GEORGE RILEY ....Sound.
GEORGE STEPHENSON.................Scurvy from last journey.
WILLIAM GODFREY...................Snow-blind.

"June 3, Saturday.—McGary, Bonsall, Hickey, and Riley were detailed for the first section of the new parties: they will be accompanied by Morton, who has orders to keep himself as fresh as possible, so as to enter on his own line of search to the greatest possible advantage. I keep Hans a while to recruit the dogs, and do the hunting and locomotion generally for the rest of us; but I shall soon let him follow, unless things grow so much worse on board as to make it impossible.

"They start light, with a large thirteen-feet sledge, arranged with broad runners on account of the snow, and are to pursue my own last track, feeding at the caches which I deposited, and aiming directly for the glacier-barrier on the Greenland side. Here, sustained as I hope by the remnants of the great cache of last fall, they will survey and attempt to scale the ice, to look into the interior of the great *mer de glace*.

"My notion is, that the drift to the southward both of berg and floe, not being reinforced from the glacier, may leave an interval of smooth frozen ice; but, if this route should fail, there ought still to be a chance by sheering to the southward and westward and looking out for openings among the hummocks.

"I am intensely anxious that this party should succeed: it is my last throw. They have all my views, and I believe they will carry them out unless overruled by a higher Power.

"Their orders are, to carry the sledge forward as far as the base of the Great Glacier, and fill up their provisions from the cache of my own party of last May. Hans will then join them with the dogs; and, while McGary and three men attempt to scale and survey the glacier, Morton and Hans will push to the north across the bay with the dog-sledge, and advance along the more distant coast. Both divisions are provided with clampers, to steady them and their sledges on the irregular ice-surfaces; but I am not without apprehensions that, with all their efforts, the glacier cannot be surmounted.

"In this event, the main reliance must be on Mr. Morton: he takes with him a sextant, artificial horizon, and pocket chronometer, and has intelligence, courage, and the spirit of endurance, in full measure. He is withal a long-tried and trustworthy follower.

"June 5, Monday.—The last party are off: they left yesterday at 2 P. M. I can do nothing more but await the ice-changes that are to determine for us our liberation or continued imprisonment.

"The sun is shining bravely, and the temperature feels like a home summer.

"A *Sanderling*, the second migratory land-bird we have seen, came to our brig to-day,—and is now a specimen.

"June 6, Tuesday.—We are a parcel of sick men, affecting to keep ship till our comrades get back. Except Mr. Ohlsen and George Whipple, there is not a sound man among us. Thus wearily in our Castle of Indolence, for 'labor dire it was, and weary woe,' we have been watching the changing days, and noting bird and insect and vegetable, as it tells us of the coming summer. One fly buzzed around William Godfrey's head to-day,—he could not tell what the species was; and Mr. Petersen brought in a cocoon from which the grub had eaten its way to liberty. Hans gives us a seal almost daily, and for a passing luxury we have ptarmigan and hare. The little snow-birds have crowded to Butler Island, and their songs penetrate the cracks of our rude housing. Another snipe too was mercilessly shot the very day of his arrival.

"The andromeda shows green under its rusty winter-dried stems; the willows are sappy and puffing, their catskins of last year dropping off. Draba, lichens, and stellaria, can be detected by an eye accustomed to this dormant vegetation, and the stonecrops are really green and juicy in their centres: all this under the snow. So we have assurance that summer is coming; though our tide-hole freezes every night alongside, and the ice-floe seems to be as fast as ever.

"June 8, Thursday.—Hans brings us in to-day a couple of seal: all of them as yet are of the Rough or Hispid species. The flesh of this seal is eaten universally by the Danes of Greenland, and is almost the staple diet of the Esquimaux. When raw, it has a flabby look, more like coagulated blood than muscular fibre: cooking gives it a dark soot-color. It is close-grained, but soft and tender, with a flavor of lamp-oil—a mere *soupçon*, however, for the blubber, when fresh, is at this season sweet and delicious.

" The seal are shot lying by their *atluk* or breathing-holes. As the season draws near midsummer, they are more approachable; their eyes being so congested by the glare of the sun that they are sometimes nearly blind. Strange to say, a few hours' exposure of a recently-killed animal to the sun blisters and destroys the hide; or, as the sealers say, cooks it. We have lost several skins in this way. Each seal yields a liberal supply of oil, the average thus far being five gallons each."

Besides the Hispid seal, the only species which visited Rensselaer Harbor was the *Phoca barbata*, the large bearded seal, or *usuk* of the Esquimaux. I have measured these ten feet in length and eight in circumference, of such unwieldy bulk as not unfrequently to be mistaken for the walrus.

The Netsik will not perforate ice of more than one season's growth, and are looked for, therefore, where there was open water the previous year. But the bearded seals have no *atluk*. They depend for respiration upon the accidental chasms in the ice, and are found wherever the bergs or floes have been in motion. They are thus more diffused in their range than their sun-basking little brethren, who crowd together in communities, and in some places absolutely throng the level ices.

The *Usuk* appears a little later than the *Netsik*, and his coming is looked for anxiously by the Esquimaux. The lines, *atlunak*, which are made from his skin, are the lightest and strongest and most durable of any in use. They are prized by the hunters in their contests with the walrus.

To obtain the atlunak in full perfection, the animal is skinned in a spiral, so as to give a continuous coil from head to tail. This is carefully chewed by the teeth of the matrons, and, after being well greased with the burnt oil of their lamps, is hung up in their huts to season. At the time referred to in my journal, Anoatok was completely festooned with them.

On one occasion, while working my way toward the Esquimaux huts, I saw a large *Usuk* basking asleep upon the ice. Taking off my shoes, I commenced a somewhat refrigerating process of stalking, lying upon my belly, and crawling along step by step behind the little knobs of floe. At last, when I was within long rifle-shot, the animal gave a sluggish roll to one side, and suddenly lifted his head. The movement was evidently independent of me, for he strained his neck in nearly the opposite direction. Then, for the first time, I found that I had a rival seal-hunter in a large bear, who was, on his belly like myself, waiting with

THE ATLUK, OR SEAL-HOLE.

commendable patience and cold feet for a chance of nearer approach.

What should I do?—the bear was doubtless worth more to me than the seal: but the seal was now within shot, and the bear "a bird in the bush." Besides, my bullet once invested in the seal would leave me defenceless. I might be giving a dinner to the bear and saving myself for his dessert. These meditations were soon brought to a close; for a second movement of the seal so aroused my hunter's instincts that I pulled the trigger. My cap alone exploded. Instantly, with a floundering splash, the seal descended into the deep, and the bear, with three or four rapid leaps, stood disconsolately by the place of his descent. For a single moment we stared each other in the face, and then, with that discretion which is the better part of valor, the bear ran off in one direction, and I followed his example in the other.

The generally-received idea of the Polar bear battling with the walrus meets little favor among the Esquimaux of Smith's Straits. My own experience is directly adverse to the truth of the story. The walrus is never out of reach of water, and, in his peculiar element, is without a rival. I have seen the bear follow the ussuk by diving; but the tough hide and great power of the walrus forbid such an attack.

"June 9, Friday.—To-day I was able to walk out upon the floe for the first time. My steps were turned to the observatory, where, close beside the coffins of Baker and Schubert, Sontag was at work with the unifilar, correcting the winter disturbances. Our local deviation seems to have corrected itself: the iron in our comfortless little cell seems to have been so distributed that our results were not affected by it.

"I was very much struck by the condition of the

floe-ice. Hitherto I have been dependent upon the accounts of my messmates, and believed that the work of thaw was going on with extreme rapidity. They are mistaken: we have a late season. The ice-foot has not materially changed either in breadth or level, and its base has been hardly affected at all, except by the overflow of the tides. The floe, though undergoing the ordinary molecular changes which accompany elevation of temperature, shows less surface-change than the Lancaster Sound ices in early May. All this, but especially the condition of the ice-foot, warns me to prepare for the contingency of not escaping. It is a momentous warning. We have no coal for a second winter here; our stock of fresh provisions is utterly exhausted; and our sick need change, as essential to their recovery.

"The willows are tolerably forward on Butler Island. Poor, stunted crawlers, they show their expanded leaflets against the gray rocks. Among these was the Bear berry, (*S. uva ursi:*) knowing its reputation with the Esquimaux to the south as a remedy for scurvy, I gleaned leaves enough for a few scanty mouthfuls. The lichens are very conspicuous; but the mosses and grasses and heaths have not yet made their appearance in the little valley between the rocks."

DRAGGING SEAL

CHAPTER XXI.

PROGRESS OF SEASON—PLANTS IN WINTER—BIRDS RETURNING—
COCHLEARIA—THE PLANTS.

"JUNE 10, Saturday.—Hans was ordered yesterday
to hunt in the direction of the Esquimaux huts, in the
hope of determining the position of the open water.
He did not return last night; but Dr. Hayes and Mr.
Ohlsen, who were sent after him this morning with
the dog-sledge, found the hardy savage fast asleep not

five miles from the brig. Alongside of him was a large usuk or bearded seal, (*P. barbata,*) shot, as usual, in the head. He had dragged it for seven hours over the ice-foot. The dogs having now recruited, he started light to join Morton at the glacier.

"June 11, Sunday.—Another walk on shore showed me the andromeda in flower, and the saxifrages and carices green under the dried tufts of last year. This rapidly-maturing vegetation is of curious interest. The andromeda tetragona had advanced rapidly toward fructification without a corresponding development of either stalk or leaflet. In fact, all the heaths—and there were three species around our harbor—had a thoroughly moorland and stunted aspect. Instead of the graceful growth which should characterize them, they showed only a low scrubby sod or turf, yet studded with flowers. The spots from which I gathered them were well infiltrated with melted snows, and the rocks enclosed them so as to aid the solar heat by reverberation. Here, too, silene and cerathium, as well as the characteristic flower-growths of the later summer, the poppy, and sorrel, and saxifrages, were already recognisable.

"Few of us at home can realize the protecting value of this warm coverlet of snow. No eider-down in the cradle of an infant is tucked in more kindly than the sleeping-dress of winter about this feeble flower-life. The first warm snows of August and September falling on a thickly-pleached carpet of grasses, heaths, and willows, enshrine the flowery growths which nestle round them in a non-conducting air-chamber; and, as each successive snow increases the thickness of the cover, we have, before the intense cold of winter sets in, a light cellular bed covered by drift, six, eight, or ten feet deep, in which the plant retains its vitality. The frozen subsoil does not encroach upon this narrow zone of vegetation. I have found in midwinter, in this high latitude of 78° 50′, the surface so nearly moist as to be friable to the touch; and upon the ice-floes, commencing with a surface-temperature of —30°, I found at two feet deep a temperature of —8°, at four feet +2°, and at eight feet +26°. This was on the largest of a range of east and west hummock-drifts in the open way off Cape Stafford. The glacier which we became so familiar with afterward at Etah yields an uninterrupted stream throughout the year.

"My experiments prove that the conducting power of the snow is proportioned to its compression by winds, rains, drifts, and congelation. The early spring and late fall and summer snows are more cellular and less condensed than the nearly impalpable powder of winter. The drifts, therefore, that accumulate during nine months of the year, are dispersed in well-defined layers of differing density. We have first the warm cellular snows of fall which surround the plant, next the fine impacted snow-dust of winter, and above these the later humid deposits of the spring.

"It is interesting to observe the effects of this disposition of layers upon the safety of the vegetable growths below them. These, at least in the earlier summer, occupy the inclined slopes that face the sun, and the several strata of snow take of course the same inclination. The consequence is that as the upper snow is dissipated by the early thawings, and sinks upon the more compact layer below, it is to a great extent arrested, and runs off like rain from a slope of clay. The plant reposes thus in its cellular bed, guarded from the rush of waters, and protected too from the nightly frosts by the icy roof above it.

"June 16, Friday.—Two long-tailed ducks (*Harelda glacialis*) visited us, evidently seeking their breeding-grounds. They are beautiful birds, either at rest or on the wing. We now have the snow-birds, the snipe, the burgomaster gull, and the long-tailed duck, enlivening our solitude; but the snow-birds are the only ones in numbers, crowding our rocky islands, and making our sunny night-time musical with home-remembered songs. Of each of the others we have but a solitary pair, who seem to have left their fellows for this far northern mating-ground in order to live unmolested. I long for specimens; but they shall not be fired at.

The ptarmigan show a singular backwardness in assuming the summer feathering. The male is still entirely white; except, in some specimens, a few brown feathers on the crown of the head. The female has made more progress, and is now well coated with her new plumage, the coverts and quill-feathers still remaining white. At Upernavik, in lat. 73°, they are already in full summer costume.

"June 18, Sunday.—Another pair of long-tailed

ducks passed over our bay, bound for farther breeding-grounds; we saw also an ivory-gull and two great northern divers, (*Colymbus glacialis,*) the most imposing birds of their tribe. These last flew very high, emitting at regular intervals their reed-like 'kawk.'

"Mr. Ohlsen and Dr. Hayes are off on an overland tramp. I sent them to inspect the open water to the southward. The immovable state of the ice-foot gives me anxiety: last year, a large bay above us was closed all summer; and the land-ice, as we find it here, is as perennial as the glacier.

"June 20, Tuesday.—This morning, to my great surprise, Petersen brought me quite a handful of scurvy-grass, (*C. fenestrata.*) In my fall list of the stinted flora here, it had quite escaped my notice. I felt grateful to him for his kindness, and, without the affectation of offering it to any one else, ate it at once. Each plant stood about one inch high, the miniature leaves expanding throughout a little radius of hardly one inch more. Yet, dwarfed as it was, the fructifying process was nearly perfected; the buds already expanding and nearly ready to burst. We found cochlearia afterward at Littleton Island, but never in any quantity north of Cape Alexander. Although the melted snows distil freely over the darker rocks, (porphyries and green-stones,) it is a rare exception to note any vegetable discoloration of the surface beneath. There are few signs of those confervaceous growths which are universal as high as Upernavik. The nature of this narrative does not permit me to indulge in matters unconnected with my story: I cite these in passing as among the indications of our high northern latitude.

"June 21, Wednesday.—A snow, moist and flaky, melting upon our decks, and cleaning up the dingy surface of the great ice-plain with a new garment. We are at the summer solstice, the day of greatest solar light! Would that the traditionally-verified but meteorologically-disproved equinoctial storm could break upon us, to destroy the tenacious floes!

"June 22, Thursday.—The ice changes slowly, but the progress of vegetation is excessively rapid. The growth on the rocky group near our brig is surprising.

"June 23, Friday.—The eiders have come back: a pair were seen in the morning, soon followed by four ducks and drakes. The poor things seemed to be seeking breeding-grounds, but the ice must have scared them. They were flying southward.

"June 25, Sunday.—Walked on shore and watched the changes: andromeda in flower, poppy and ranunculus the same: saw two snipe and some tern.

"Mr. Ohlsen returned from a walk with Mr. Petersen. They saw reindeer, and brought back a noble specimen of the king duck. It was a solitary male, resplendent with the orange, black, and green of his head and neck.

"Stephenson is better; and I think that a marked improvement, although a slow one, shows itself in all of us. I work the men lightly, and allow plenty of basking in the sun. In the afternoon we walk on shore, to eat such succulent plants as we can find amid

the snow. The pyrola I have not found, nor the cochlearia, save in one spot, and then dwarfed. But we
have the lychnis, the young sorrel, the andromeda, the
draba, and the willow-bark; this last an excellent
tonic, and, in common with all the Arctic vegetable
astringents, I think, powerfully antiscorbutic."

CHAPTER XXII.

MR. BONSALL'S RETURN — HIS STORY — THE BEAR IN CAMP — HIS
FATE — BEARS AT SPORT — THE THAWS.

"June 27, Tuesday.—McGary and Bonsall are back
with Hickey and Riley. They arrived last evening:
all well, except that the snow has affected their eyesight badly, owing to the scorbutic condition of their
systems. Mr. McGary is entirely blind, and I fear will
be found slow to cure. They have done admirably.
They bring back a continued series of observations,
perfectly well kept up, for the further authentication
of our survey. They had a good chronometer, artificial horizon, and sextant, and their results correspond
entirely with those of Mr. Sontag and myself. They
are connected too with the station at Chimney Rock,
Cape Thackeray, which we have established by theodolite. I may be satisfied now with our projection of
the Greenland coast. The different localities to the
south have been referred to the position of our winter

272

harbor, and this has been definitely fixed by the labors of Mr. Sontag, our astronomer. We have therefore not only a reliable base, but a set of primary triangulations which, though limited, may support the minor field-work of our sextants.

Journey of Messrs. McGary and Bonsall.

"They left the brig on the 3d, and reached the Great Glacier on the 15th, after only twelve days of travel. They showed great judgment in passing the bays; and, although impeded by the heavy snows, would have been able to remain much longer in the field, but for the destruction of our provision-depôts by the bears.

"I am convinced, however, that no efforts of theirs could have scaled the Great Glacier; so that the loss of our provisions, though certainly a very serious mishap, cannot be said to have caused their failure. They were well provided with pointed staves, foot-clampers, and other apparatus for climbing ice; but, from all they tell me, any attempt to scale this stupendous glacial mass would have been madness, and I am truly glad that they desisted from it before fatal accident befell them.

"Mr. Bonsall is making out his report of the daily operations of this party. It seems that the same heavy snow which had so much interfered with my travel in April and May still proved their greatest drawback. It was accumulated particularly between the headlands of the bays; and, as it was already affected by the warm sun, it called for great care in crossing it. They encountered drifts which were altogether impenetrable, and in such cases could only advance by long circuits, after reconnoitring from the top of icebergs.

"I have tried in vain to find out some good general rule, when traversing the ice near the coast, to avoid the accumulation of snows and hummock-ridges. It appears that the direct line between headland and headland or cape and cape is nearly always obstructed by broken ice; while in the deep recesses the grounded ice is even worse. I prefer a track across the middle of the bay, outside of the grounded ices and inside of the hummock-ridges; unless, as sometimes happens, the late fall-ice is to be found extending in level flats outside.

"This is evidently the season when the bears are in most abundance. Their tracks were everywhere, both on shore and upon the floes. One of them had the audacity to attempt intruding itself upon the party during one of their halts upon the ice; and Bonsall tells a good story of the manner in which they received and returned his salutations. It was about half an hour after midnight, and they were all sleeping away a long day's fatigue, when McGary either heard or felt, he could hardly tell which, something that was scratching at the snow immediately by his head. It waked him just enough to allow him to recognise a huge animal actively engaged in reconnoitring the circuit of the tent. His startled outcry aroused his companion-

inmates, but without in any degree disturbing the unwelcome visitor; specially unwelcome at that time and
place, for all the guns had been left on the sledge, a
little distance off, and there was not so much as a
walking-pole inside. There was of course something

THE BEAR IN CAMP

of natural confusion in the little council of war. The
first impulse was to make a rush for the arms; but
this was soon decided to be very doubtfully practicable,
if at all, for the bear, having satisfied himself with his
observations of the exterior, now presented himself at
the tent-opening. Sundry volleys of lucifer matches
and some impromptu torches of newspaper were fired

without alarming him, and, after a little while, he planted himself at the doorway and began making his supper upon the carcass of a seal which had been shot the day before.

"Tom Hickey was the first to bethink him of the military device of a sortie from the postern, and, cutting a hole with his knife, crawled out at the rear of the tent. Here he extricated a boat-hook, that formed one of the supporters of the ridge-pole, and made it the instrument of a right valorous attack. A blow well administered on the nose caused the animal to retreat for the moment a few paces beyond the sledge, and Tom, calculating his distance nicely, sprang forward, seized a rifle, and fell back in safety upon his comrades. In a few seconds more, Mr. Bonsall had sent a ball through and through the body of his enemy. I was assured that after this adventure the party adhered to the custom I had enjoined, of keeping at all times a watch and fire-arms inside the camping-tent.

"The final cache, which I relied so much upon, was entirely destroyed. It had been built with extreme care, of rocks which had been assembled by very heavy labor, and adjusted with much aid often from capstan-bars as levers. The entire construction was, so far as our means permitted, most effective and resisting. Yet these tigers of the ice seemed to have scarcely encountered an obstacle. Not a morsel of pemmican remained except in the iron cases, which, being round with conical ends, defied both claws and teeth. They had rolled and pawed them in every direction, tossing

them about like footballs, although over eighty pounds
in weight. An alcohol-case, strongly iron-bound, was
dashed into small fragments, and a tin can of liquor
mashed and twisted almost into a ball. The claws of

THE CACHE DESTROYED.

the beast had perforated the metal, and torn it up as
with a cold chisel.

"They were too dainty for salt meats: ground coffee
they had an evident relish for: old canvas was a favorite for some reason or other; even our flag, which had
been reared 'to take possession' of the waste, was
gnawed down to the very staff. They had made a
regular frolic of it; rolling our bread-barrels over the

ice-foot and into the broken outside ice; and, unable to masticate our heavy India-rubber cloth, they had tied it up in unimaginable hard knots.

"McGary describes the whole area around the cache as marked by the well-worn paths of these animals; and an adjacent slope of ice-covered rock, with an angle of 45°, was so worn and covered with their hair, as to suggest the idea that they had been amusing themselves by sliding down it on their haunches. A performance, by-the-way, in which I afterward caught them myself.

"June 28, Wednesday.—Hans came up with the party on the 17th. Morton and he are still out. They took a day's rest; and then, 'following the old tracks,' as McGary reports, 'till they were clear of the cracks near the islands, pushed northward at double-quick time. When last seen, they were both of them walking, for the snow was too soft and deep for them to ride with their heavy load.' Fine weather, but the ice yields reluctantly."

While thus watching the indications of advancing summer, my mind turned anxiously to the continued absence of Morton and Hans. We were already beyond the season when travel upon the ice was considered practicable by our English predecessors in Wellington Channel, and, in spite of the continued solidity around us, it was unsafe to presume too much upon our high northern position.

The ice, although seemingly as unbroken as ever, was no longer fit for dog-travel; the floes were covered

with water-pools, many of which could not be forded
by our team; and, as these multiplied with the rapidly-
advancing thaws, they united one with another,
chequering the level waste with an interminable repe-
tition of confluent lakes. These were both embarrassing
and dangerous. Our little brig was already so thawed
out where her sides came in contact with her icy cradle
as to make it dangerous to descend without a gangway,
and our hunting parties came back wet to the skin.

It was, therefore, with no slight joy that on the
evening of the 10th, while walking with Mr. Bonsall,
a distant sound of dogs caught my ear. These faithful
servants generally bayed their full-mouthed welcome
from afar off, but they always dashed in with a wild
speed which made their outcry a direct precursor of
their arrival. Not so these well-worn travellers. Hans
and Morton staggered beside the limping dogs, and
poor Jenny was riding as a passenger upon the sledge.
It was many hours before they shared the rest and comfort of our ship.

CHAPTER XXIII.

MR. MORTON left the brig with the relief party of
McGary on the 4th of June. He took his place at the
track-lines like the others; but he was ordered to avoid
all extra labor, so as to husband his strength for the
final passage of the ice.

On the 15th he reached the base of the Great Glacier, and on the 16th was joined by Hans with the
dogs. A single day was given to feed and refresh the
animals, and on the 18th the two companies parted.
Morton's account I have not felt myself at liberty to

alter. I give it as nearly as possible in his own words, without affecting any modification of his style.

Morton's Journey.

The party left Cache Island at 12.35 A. M., crossing the land-ices by portage, and going south for about a mile to avoid a couple of bad seams caused by the breakage of the glacier. Here Morton and Hans separated from the land-party, and went northward, keeping parallel with the glacier, and from five to seven miles distant. The ice was free from hummocks, but heavily covered with snow, through which they walked knee deep. They camped about eight miles from the glacier, at 7.45, travelling that night about twenty-eight miles. Here a crack allowed them to measure the thickness of the ice: it was seven feet five inches. The thermometer at 6 A. M. gave +28° for the temperature of the air; 29.2 for the water.

They started again at half-past nine. The ice, at first, was very heavy, and they were frequently over their knees in the dry snow; but, after crossing certain drifts, it became hard enough to bear the sledge, and the dogs made four miles an hour until twenty minutes past four, when they reached the middle of Peabody Bay. They then found themselves among the bergs which on former occasions had prevented other parties from getting through. These were generally very high, evidently newly separated from the glacier. Their surfaces were fresh and glassy, and not like those generally met with in Baffin's Bay,—less worn, and bluer, and looking in all respects like the face of the Grand Glacier. Many were rectangular, some of them regular squares, a quarter of a mile each way; others, more than a mile long.

They could not see more than a ship's-length ahead, the icebergs were so unusually close together. Old icebergs bulge and tongue out below, and are thus prevented from uniting; but these showed that they were lately launched, for they approached each other so nearly that the party were sometimes forced to squeeze through places less than four feet wide, through which the dogs could just draw the sledge. Sometimes they could find no passage between two bergs, the ice being so crunched up between them that they could not force their way. Under these circumstances, they would either haul the sledge over the low tongues of the berg, or retrace their steps, searching through the drift for a practicable road.

This they were not always fortunate in finding, and it was at best a tedious and in some cases a dangerous alternative, for oftentimes they could not cross them; and, when they tried to double, the compass, their only guide, confused them by its variation.

It took them a long while to get through into smoother ice. A tolerably wide passage would appear between two bergs, which they would gladly follow; then a narrower one; then no opening in front, but one to the side. Following that a little distance, a blank ice-cliff would close the way altogether, and they were forced to retrace their steps and begin again. Constantly baffled, but, like true fellows, determined to "go ahead," they at last found a lane some six miles to the west, which led upon their right course. But they were from eight o'clock at night till two or three of the next morning, puzzling their way out of the maze, like a blind man in the streets of a strange city.

June 19, Monday.—At 8.45 A. M. they encamped. Morton then climbed a berg, in order to select their best road. Beyond some bergs he caught glimpses of a great white plain, which proved to be the glacier seen far into the interior; for, on getting up another berg farther on, he saw its face as it fronted on the bay. This was near its northern end. It looked full of stones and earth, while large rocks projected out from it and rose above it here and there.

They rested till half-past ten, having walked all the time to spare the dogs. After starting, they went on for ten miles, but were then arrested by wide seams in the ice, bergs, and much broken ice. So they turned about, and reached their last camp by twelve, midnight. They then went westward, and, after several trials, made a way, the dogs running well. It took them but two hours to reach the better ice, for the bergs were in a narrow belt.

The chasms between them were sometimes four feet wide, with water at the bottom. These they bridged in our usual manner; that is to say, they attacked the nearest large hummocks with their axes, and, chopping them down, rolled the heaviest pieces they could move into the fissure, so that they wedged each other in. They then filled up the spaces between the blocks with smaller lumps of ice as well as they could, and so contrived a rough sort of bridge to coax the dogs over. Such a seam would take about an hour and a half to fill up well and cross.

On quitting the berg-field, they saw two dovekies in a crack, and shot one. The other flew to the northeast. Here they sighted the northern shore, ("West Land,") mountainous, rolling, but very distant, perhaps fifty or sixty miles off. They drove on over the best ice they had met due north. After passing about twelve miles of glacier, and seeing thirty of opposite shore, they camped at 7.20 A. M.

They were now nearly abreast of the termination of the Great Glacier. It was mixed with earth and rocks. The snow sloped from the land to the ice, and the two seemed to be mingled together for eight or ten miles to the north, when the land became solid, and the glacier was lost. The height of this land seemed about four hundred feet, and the glacier lower.

June 21, Wednesday.—They stood to the north at 11.30 P. M., and made for what Morton thought a cape, seeing a vacancy between it and the West Land. The ice was good, even, and free from bergs, only two or three being in sight. The atmosphere became thick and misty, and the west shore, which they saw faintly on Tuesday, was not visible. They could only see the cape for which they steered. The cold was sensibly felt, a very cutting wind blowing N.E. by N. They reached the opening seen to the westward of the cape by Thursday, 7 A.M. It proved to be a channel; for, as they moved on in the misty weather, a sudden lifting of the fog showed them the cape and the western shore.

ENTERING THE CHANNEL—CAPES ANDREW JACKSON AND JOHN BARROW.

The ice was weak and rotten, and the dogs began to tremble. Proceeding at a brisk rate, they had got upon unsafe ice before they were aware of it. Their course was at the time nearly up the middle of the channel; but, as soon as possible, they turned, and, by a backward circuit, reached the shore. The dogs, as their fashion is, at first lay down and refused to

proceed, trembling violently. The only way to in
duce the terrified, obstinate brutes to get on was for
Hans to go to a white-looking spot where the ice was
thicker, the soft stuff looking dark; then, calling the
dogs coaxingly by name, they would crawl to him on
their bellies. So they retreated from place to place,
until they reached the firm ice they had quitted. A
half-mile brought them to comparatively safe ice, a
mile more to good ice again.

In the midst of this danger they had during the lift-
ings of the fog sighted open water, and they now saw
it plainly. There was no wind stirring, and its face
was perfectly smooth. It was two miles farther up the
channel than the firm ice to which they had retreated.
Hans could hardly believe it. But for the birds that
were seen in great numbers, Morton says he would not
have believed it himself.

The ice covered the mouth of the channel like a
horseshoe. One end lapped into the west side a considerable distance up the channel, the other covered
the cape for about a mile and a half, so that they
could not land opposite their camp, which was about a
mile and a half from the cape.

That night they succeeded in climbing on to the
level by the floe-pieces, and walked around the turn of
the cape for some distance, leaving their dogs behind.
They found a good ice-foot, very wide, which extended
as far as the cape. They saw a good many birds on
the water, both eider-ducks and dovekies, and the rocks
on shore were full of sea-swallows. There was no ice.

A fog coming on, they turned back to where the dogs
had been left.

They started again at 11.30 A.M. of the 21st.   On
reaching the land-ice they unloaded, and threw each
package of provision from the floe up to the ice-foot,

MAKING THE LAND-ICE, (CLIMBING.)

which was eight or nine feet above them.   Morton
then climbed up with the aid of the sledge, which they
converted into a ladder for the occasion.   He then
pulled the dogs up by the lines fastened round their
bodies, Hans lending a helping hand and then climbing up himself.   They then drew up the sledge.   The
water was very deep, a stone the size of Morton's head

taking twenty-eight seconds to reach the bottom, which was seen very clearly.

As they had noticed the night before, the ice-foot lost its good character on reaching the cape, becoming a mere narrow ledge hugging the cliffs, and looking as if it might crumble off altogether into the water at any moment. Morton was greatly afraid there would be no land-ice there at all when they came back. Hans and he thought they might pass on by climbing along the face of the crag; in fact they tried a path about fifty feet high, but it grew so narrow that they saw they could not get the dogs past with their sledge-load of provisions. He therefore thought it safest to leave some food, that they might not starve on the return in case the ice-foot should disappear. He accordingly cached enough provision to last them back, with four days' dog-meat.

At the pitch of the cape the ice-ledge was hardly three feet wide; and they were obliged to unloose the dogs and drive them forward alone. Hans and he then tilted the sledge up, and succeeded in carrying it past the narrowest place. The ice-foot was firm under their tread, though it crumbled on the verge.

The tide was running very fast. The pieces of heaviest draught floated by nearly as fast as the ordinary walk of a man, and the surface-pieces passed them much faster, at least four knots. On their examination the night before, the tide was from the north, running southward, carrying very little ice. The ice which was now moving so fast to northward seemed to be the broken land-ice around the cape, and the loose edge of the south ice. The thermometer in the water gave +36°, seven degrees above the freezing-point of sea-water at Rensselaer Harbor.

They now yoked in the dogs, and set forward over the worst sort of mashed ice for three-quarters of a mile. After passing the cape, they looked ahead, and saw nothing but open water. The land to the west-ward seemed to overlap the land on which they stood, a long distance ahead: all the space between was open water. After turning the cape,—that which is marked on the chart as Cape Andrew Jackson,—they found a good smooth ice-foot in the entering curve of a bay, since named after the great financier of the American Revolution, Robert Morris. It was glassy ice, and the dogs ran on it full speed. Here the sledge made at least six miles an hour. It was the best day's travel they made on the journey.

After passing four bluffs at the bottom and sides of the bay, the land grew lower; and presently a long low country opened on the land-ice, a wide plain between large headlands, with rolling hills through it. A flock of Brent geese were coming down the valley of this low land, and ducks were seen in crowds upon the open water. When they saw the geese first, they were apparently coming from the eastward; they made a curve out to seaward, and then, turning, flew far ahead over the plain, until they were lost to view, showing that their destination was inland. The general line of flight of the flock was to the northeast. Eiders and dovekies were also seen; and tern were very numerous, hundreds of them squealing and screeching in flocks. They were so tame that they came within a few yards of the party. Flying high overhead, their notes echoing from the rocks, were large white birds, which they took for burgomasters. Ivory gulls and mollemokes were seen farther on. They did not lose sight of the birds after this, as far as they went. The ivory gulls flew very high, but the mollemokes alit, and fed on the water, flying over it well out to sea, as we had seen them do in Baffin's Bay. Separate from these flew a dingy bird unknown to Morton. Never had they seen the birds so numerous: the water was actually black with dovekies, and the rocks crowded.[48]

The part of the channel they were now coasting was narrower, but as they proceeded it seemed to widen again. There was some ice arrested by a bend of the channel on the eastern shore; and, on reaching a low gravel point, they saw that a projection of land shut them in just ahead to the north. Upon this ice numerous seal were basking, both the netsik and ussuk.

To the left of this, toward the West Land, the great channel (Kennedy Channel) of open water continued. There was broken ice floating in it, but with passages fifteen miles in width and perfectly clear. The end of the point—"Gravel Point," as Morton called it—was covered with hummocks and broken ice for about two miles from the water. This ice was worn and full of gravel. Six miles inland, the point was flanked by mountains.

A little higher up, they noticed that the pieces of ice in the middle of the channel were moving up, while the lumps near shore were floating down. The channel was completely broken up, and there would have been no difficulty in a frigate standing anywhere. The little

APPEARANCE OF CHANNEL.

brig, or "a fleet of her like," could have beat easily to the northward.

The wind blew strong from the north, and continued to do so for three days, sometimes blowing a gale, and very damp, the tops of the hills becoming fixed with dark foggy clouds. The damp falling mist prevented their seeing any distance. Yet they saw no ice borne down from the northward during all this time; and, what was more curious, they found, on their return south, that no ice had been sent down during the gale. On the contrary, they then found the channel perfectly clear from shore to shore.

June 22, Thursday.—They camped at 8.30 A. M., on a ledge of low rock, having made in the day's journey forty-eight miles in a straight line. Morton thought they were at least forty miles up the channel. The ice was here moving to the southward with the tide. The channel runs northwardly, and is about thirty-five miles wide. The opposite coast appears straight, but still sloping, its head being a little to the west of north. This shore is high, with lofty mountains of sugar-loaf shape at the tops, which, set together in ranges, looked like piles of stacked cannon-balls. It was too cloudy for observations when they camped, but they obtained several higher up. The eider were in such numbers here that Hans fired into the flocks, and killed two birds with one shot.

June 23, Friday.—In consequence of the gale of wind, they did not start till 12.30 midnight. They made about eight miles, and were arrested by the broken ice of the shore. Their utmost efforts could not pass the sledge over this; so they tied the dogs to it, and went ahead to see how things looked. They found the land-ice growing worse and worse, until at last it ceased, and the water broke directly against the steep cliffs.

They continued their course overland until they

came to the entrance of a bay, whence they could see
a cape and an island to the northward. They then
turned back, seeing numbers of birds on their way,
and, leaving the dogs to await their return, prepared
to proceed on foot.

This spot was the greenest that they had seen since
leaving the headlands of the channel. Snow patched the
valleys, and water was trickling from the rocks. Early-
as it was, Hans was able to recognise some of the flower-
life. He eat of the young shoots of the lychnis, and
brought home to me the dried pod (*siliqua*) of a hesperis, which had survived the wear and tear of winter.
Morton was struck with the abundance of little stonecrops, "about the size of a pea." I give in the appendix
his scanty list of recognised but not collected plants.

June 23, 24, Friday, Saturday.—At 3 A.M. they
started again, carrying eight pounds of pemmican and
two of bread, besides the artificial horizon, sextant, and
compass, a rifle, and the boat-hook. After two hours'
walking the travel improved, and, on nearing a plain
about nine miles from where they had left the sledge,
they were rejoiced to see a she-bear and her cub.
They had tied the dogs securely, as they thought; but
Toodla and four others had broken loose and followed
them, making their appearance within an hour. They
were thus able to attack the bear at once.

Hans, who to the simplicity of an Esquimaux united
the shrewd observation of a hunter, describes the con-
test which followed so graphically that I try to engraft
some of the quaintness of his description upon Mr.

Morton's report. The bear fled; but the little one being unable either to keep ahead of the dogs or to keep pace with her, she turned back, and, putting her head under its haunches, threw it some distance ahead. The cub safe for the moment, she would wheel round and face the dogs, so as to give it a chance to run away; but it always stopped just as it alighted, till she came up and threw it ahead again: it seemed to expect her aid, and would not go on without it. Sometimes the mother would run a few yards ahead, as if to coax the young one up to her, and when the dogs came up she would turn on them and drive them back; then, as they dodged her blows, she would rejoin the cub and push it on, sometimes putting her head under it, sometimes catching it in her mouth by the nape of the neck.

For a time she managed her retreat with great celerity, leaving the two men far in the rear. They had engaged her on the land-ice; but she led the dogs in-shore, up a small stony valley which opened into the interior. But, after she had gone a mile and a half, her pace slackened, and, the little one being jaded, she soon came to a halt.

The men were then only half a mile behind; and, running at full speed, they soon came up to where the dogs were holding her at bay. The fight was now a desperate one. The mother never went more than two yards ahead, constantly looking at the cub. When the dogs came near her, she would sit upon her haunches and take the little one between her hind legs, fighting the dogs with her paws, and roaring so that she could have been heard a mile off. "Never," said Morton, "was an animal more distressed." She would stretch her neck and snap at the nearest dog with her shining teeth, whirling her paws like the arms of a windmill. If she missed her aim, not daring to pursue one dog lest the others should harm the cub, she would give a great roar of baffled rage, and go on pawing, and snapping, and facing the ring, grinning at them with her mouth stretched wide.

When the men came up, the little one was perhaps rested, for it was able to turn round with her dam, no matter how quick she moved, so as to keep always in front of her belly. The five dogs were all the time frisking about her actively, tormenting her like so many gad-flies; indeed, they made it difficult to draw a bead on at her without killing them. But Hans, lying on his elbow, took a quiet aim and shot her through the head. She dropped and rolled over dead without moving a muscle.

The dogs sprang toward her at once; but the cub jumped upon her body and reared up, for the first time growling hoarsely. They seemed quite afraid of the little creature, she fought so actively and made so much noise; and, while tearing mouthfuls of hair from the dead mother, they would spring aside the minute the cub turned toward them. The men drove the dogs off for a time, but were obliged to shoot the cub at last, as she would not quit the body.

Hans fired into her head. It did not reach the

brain, though it knocked her down; but she was still able to climb on her mother's body and try to defend it still, "her mouth bleeding like a gutter-spout." They were obliged to despatch her with stones.

After skinning the old one they gashed its body, and the dogs fed upon it ravenously. The little one they cached for themselves on the return; and, with difficulty taking the dogs off, pushed on, crossing a small bay which extended from the level ground and had still some broken ice upon it. Hans was tired out, and was sent on shore to follow the curve of the bay, where the road was easier.

The ice over the shallow bay which Morton crossed was hummocked, with rents through it, making very hard travel. He walked on over this, and saw an opening not quite eight miles across, separating the two islands, which I have named after Sir John Franklin and his comrade Captain Crozier. He had seen them before from the entrance of the larger bay,—Lafayette Bay,—but had taken them for a single island, the channel between them not being then in sight. As he neared the northern land, at the east shore which led to the cape, (Cape Constitution,) which terminated his labors, he found only a very small ice-foot, under the lee of the headland and crushed up against the side of the rock. He went on; but the strip of land-ice broke more and more, until about a mile from the cape it terminated altogether, the waves breaking with a cross sea directly against the cape. The wind had moderated, but was still from the north, and the current ran up very fast, four or five knots perhaps.

The cliffs were here very high: at a short distance they seemed about two thousand feet; but the crags were so overhanging that Morton could not see the tops as

A SKETCH.

he drew closer. The echoes were confusing, and the clamor of half a dozen ivory gulls, who were frightened from their sheltered nooks, was multiplied a hundred-fold. The mollemokes were still numerous; but he now saw no ducks.

He tried to pass round the cape. It was in vain: there was no ice-foot; and, trying his best to ascend the cliffs, he could get up but a few hundred feet.　Here he fastened to his walking-pole the Grinnell flag of the *Antarctic*—a well-cherished little relic, which had now followed me on two Polar voyages.　This flag had been saved from the wreck of the United States sloop-of-war Peacock, when she stranded off the Columbia River; it had accompanied Commodore Wilkes in his far-southern discovery of an Antarctic continent.　It was now its strange destiny to float over the highest northern land, not only of America but of our globe.　Side by side with this were our Masonic emblems of the compass and the square.　He let them fly for an hour and a half from the black cliff over the dark rock-shadowed waters, which rolled up and broke in white caps at its base.

He was bitterly disappointed that he could not get round the cape, to see whether there was any land beyond; but it was impossible.　Rejoining Hans, they supped off their bread and pemmican, and, after a good nap, started on their return on Sunday, the 25th, at 1.30 P.M.　From Thursday night, the 22d, up to Sunday at noon, the wind had been blowing steadily from the north, and for thirty-six hours of the time it blew a gale.　But as he returned, he remarked that the more southern ice toward Kennedy Channel was less than it had been when he passed up.　At the mouth of the channel it was more broken than when he saw it before, but the passage above was clear.　About half-way between the farthest point which he reached and the channel, the few small lumps of ice which he ob-

served floating—they were not more than half a dozen
—were standing with the wind to the southward, while
the shore-current or tide was driving north.

His journal of Monday, 26th, says, " As far as I could
see, the open passages were fifteen miles or more wide,
with sometimes mashed ice separating them.   But it is
all small ice, and I think it either drives out to the
open space to the north, or rots and sinks,* as I could
see none ahead to the far north."[49]

The coast after passing the cape, he thought, must
trend to the eastward, as he could at no time when
below it see any land beyond.   But the west coast still
opened to the north: he traced it for about fifty miles.
The day was very clear, and he was able to follow the
range of mountains which crowns it much farther.
They were very high, rounded at their summits, not
peaked like those immediately abreast of him; though,
as he remarked, this apparent change of their character
might be referred to distance, for their undulations lost
themselves like a wedge in the northern horizon.

His highest station of outlook at the point where his
progress was arrested he supposed to be about three
hundred feet above the sea.   From this point, some six
degrees to the west of north, he remarked in the
farthest distance a peak truncated at its top like the
cliffs of Magdalena Bay.   It was bare at its summit,
but striated vertically with protruding ridges.   Our

---

* As I quote his own words, I do not think it advisable to comment
upon his view. Ice never sinks in a liquid of the same density as that
in which it formed.

united estimate assigned to it an elevation of from twenty-five hundred to three thousand feet. This peak, the most remote northern land known upon our globe, takes its name from the great pioneer of Arctic travel, Sir Edward Parry.

MOUNT PARRY AND VICTORIA RANGE, (ROUGH SKETCH BY MORTON.)

The range with which it was connected was much higher, Mr. Morton thought, than any we had seen on the southern or Greenland side of the bay. The summits were generally rounded, resembling, to use his own expression, a succession of sugar-loaves and stacked cannon-balls declining slowly in the perspective. I have named these mountains after the name of the lady sovereign under whose orders Sir John Franklin sailed, and the prince her consort. They are similar in their features to those of Spitzbergen; and, though I am aware how easy it is to be deceived in our judgment of distant heights, I am satisfied from the estimate of Mr. Morton, as well as from our measurements of the same range farther to the south, that they equal them in elevation, 2500 feet.

Two large indentations broke in upon the uniform margin of the coast. Everywhere else the spinal ridge seemed unbroken. Mr. Morton saw no ice.

It will be seen by the abstract of our " field-notes" in the Appendix, as well as by an analysis of the results which I have here rendered nearly in the very words of Mr. Morton, that, after travelling due north over a solid area choked with bergs and frozen fields, he was startled by the growing weakness of the ice: its surface became rotten, and the snow wet and pulpy. His dogs, seized with terror, refused to advance. Then for the first time the fact broke upon him, that a long dark band seen to the north beyond a protruding cape —Cape Andrew Jackson—was water. With danger and difficulty he retraced his steps, and, reaching sound ice, made good his landing on a new coast.

The journeys which I had made myself, and those of my different parties, had shown that an unbroken surface of ice covered the entire sea to the east, west, and south. From the southernmost ice, seen by Dr. Hayes only a few weeks before, to the region of this mysterious water, was, as the crow flies, one hundred and six miles. But for the unusual sight of birds and the unmistakable giving way of the ice beneath them, they would not have believed in the evidence of eyesight. Neither Hans nor Morton was prepared for it.

Landing on the cape, and continuing their exploration, new phenomena broke upon them. They were on the shores of a channel, so open that a frigate, or a fleet of frigates, might have sailed up it. The ice, already broken and decayed, formed a sort of horseshoe-shaped beach, against which the waves broke in surf. As they travelled north, this channel expanded into an iceless area; "for four or five small pieces"— lumps—were all that could be seen over the entire surface of its white-capped waters. Viewed from the cliffs, and taking thirty-six miles as the mean radius open to reliable survey, this sea had a justly-estimated extent of more than four thousand square miles.

Animal life, which had so long been a stranger to us to the south, now burst upon them. At Rensselaer Harbor, except the Netsik seal or a rarely-encountered Harelda, we had no life available for the hunt. But here the Brent goose, (*Anas bernicla*,) the eider, and the king duck, were so crowded together that our Esquimaux killed two at a shot with a single rifle-ball.

The Brent goose had not been seen before since entering Smith's Straits. It is well known to the Polar traveller as a migratory bird of the American continent. Like the others of the same family, it feeds upon vegetable matter, generally on marine plants with their adherent molluscous life. It is rarely or never seen in the interior, and from its habits may be regarded as singularly indicative of open water. The flocks of this bird, easily distinguished by their wedge-shaped line of flight, now crossed the water obliquely, and disappeared over the land to the north and east. I had shot these birds on the coast of Wellington Channel in latitude 74° 50′, nearly six degrees to the south : they were then flying in the same direction.

The rocks on shore were crowded with sea-swallows, (*Sterna Arctica,*) birds whose habits require open water, and they were already breeding.

It may interest others besides the naturalist to state, that all of these birds occupied the southern limits of the channel for the first few miles after reaching open water, but, as the party continued their progress to the north, they disappeared, and marine birds took their place. The gulls were now represented by no less than four species. The kittiwakes (*Larus tridactylis*)—reminding Morton of "old times in Baffin's Bay"—were again stealing fish from the water, probably the small whiting, (*Merlangus Polaris,*) and their grim cousins, the burgomasters, enjoying the dinner thus provided at so little cost to themselves. It was a picture of life all round.

Of the flora and its indications I can say but little ; still less can I feel justified in drawing from them any thermal inferences. The season was too early for a display of Arctic vegetation ; and, in the absence of specimens, I am unwilling to adopt the observations of Mr. Morton, who was no botanist. It seems clear, however, that many flowering plants, at least as developed as those of Rensselaer Harbor, had already made themselves recognisable; and, strange to say, the only specimen brought back was a crucifer, (*Hesperis pygmœa*—Durand,) the *siliquæ* of which, still containing seed, had thus survived the winter, to give evidence of its perfected growth. This plant I have traced to the Great Glacier, thus extending its range from the South Greenland zone. It has not, I believe, been described at Upernavik.[50]

It is another remarkable fact that, as they continued their journey, the land-ice and snow, which had served as a sort of pathway for their dogs, crumbled and melted, and at last ceased altogether; so that, during the final stages of their progress, the sledge was rendered useless, and Morton found himself at last toiling over rocks and along the beach of a sea, which, like the familiar waters of the south, dashed in waves at his feet.

Here for the first time he noticed the Arctic Petrel, (*Procellaria glacialis*,) a fact which shows the accuracy of his observation, though he was then unaware of its importance. This bird had not been met with since we left the North Water of the English whalers, more than two hundred miles south of the position on which he stood. Its food is essentially marine, the acalephæ, &c. &c.; and it is seldom seen in numbers, except in the highways of open water frequented by the whale and the larger representatives of ocean life. They were in numbers, flitting and hovering over the crests of the waves, like their relatives of kinder climates, the Cape of Good Hope Pigeons, Mother Carey's Chickens, and the petrels everywhere else.

As Morton, leaving Hans and his dogs, passed between Sir John Franklin Island and the narrow beach-line, the coast became more wall-like, and dark masses of porphyritic rock abutted into the sea. With growing difficulty, he managed to climb from rock to rock, in hopes of doubling the promontory and sighting the coasts beyond, but the water kept encroaching more and more on his track.

It must have been an imposing sight, as he stood at this termination of his journey, looking out upon the great waste of waters before him. Not a "speck of ice," to use his own words, could be seen. There, from a height of four hundred and eighty feet, which commanded a horizon of almost forty miles, his ears were gladdened with the novel music of dashing waves; and a surf, breaking in among the rocks at his feet, stayed his farther progress.

Beyond this cape all is surmise. The high ridges to the northwest dwindled off into low blue knobs, which blended finally with the air. Morton called the cape, which baffled his labors, after his commander; but I have given it the more enduring name of Cape Constitution.

The homeward journey, as it was devoted to the completion of his survey and developed no new facts,

I need not give.   But I am reluctant to close my notice
of this discovery of an open sea, without adding that
the details of Mr. Morton's narrative harmonized with
the observations of all our party.   I do not propose to
discuss here the causes or conditions of this phenomenon.   How far it may extend,—whether it exists
simply as a feature of the immediate region, or as part
of a great and unexplored area communicating with a
Polar basin,—and what may be the argument in favor
of one or the other hypothesis, or the explanation
which reconciles it with established laws,—may be
questions for men skilled in scientific deductions.   Mine
has been the more humble duty of recording what we
saw.   Coming as it did, a mysterious fluidity in the
midst of vast plains of solid ice, it was well calculated
to arouse emotions of the highest order; and I do not
believe there was a man among us who did not long for
the means of embarking upon its bright and lonely
waters.   But he who may be content to follow our
story for the next few months will feel, as we did,
that a controlling necessity made the desire a fruitless
one.

An open sea near the Pole, or even an open Polar
basin, has been a topic of theory for a long time, and
has been shadowed forth to some extent by actual or
supposed discoveries.   As far back as the days of
Barentz, in 1596, without referring to the earlier and
more uncertain chronicles, water was seen to the eastward of the northernmost cape of Novaia Zemlia; and,
until its limited extent was defined by direct observa-

J.Hamilton.

R.Hinshelwood.

Engraved at J.M.Butler's establishment 84 Chestnut St.

THE OPEN WATER FROM CAPE JEFFERSON.

(From description)

tion, it was assumed to be the sea itself. The Dutch fishermen above and around Spitzbergen pushed their adventurous cruises through the ice into open spaces varying in size and form with the season and the winds; and Dr. Scoresby, a venerated authority, alludes to such vacancies in the floe as pointing in argument to a freedom of movement from the north, inducing open water in the neighborhood of the Pole. Baron Wrangell, when forty miles from the coast of Arctic Asia, saw, as he thought, a "vast, illimitable ocean," forgetting for the moment how narrow are the limits of human vision on a sphere. So, still more recently, Captain Penny proclaimed a sea in Wellington Sound, on the very spot where Sir Edward Belcher has since left his frozen ships; and my predecessor Captain Inglefield, from the mast-head of his little vessel, announced an "open Polar basin," but fifteen miles off from the ice which arrested our progress the next year.

All these illusory discoveries were no doubt chronicled with perfect integrity; and it may seem to others, as since I have left the field it sometimes does to myself, that my own, though on a larger scale, may one day pass within the same category. Unlike the others, however, that which I have ventured to call an open sea has been travelled for many miles along its coast, and was viewed from an elevation of five hundred and eighty feet, still without a limit, moved by a heavy swell, free of ice, and dashing in surf against a rockbound shore.

It is impossible, in reviewing the facts which connect themselves with this discovery,—the melted snow upon the rocks, the crowds of marine birds, the limited but still advancing vegetable life, the rise of the thermometer in the water,—not to be struck with their bearing on the question of a milder climate near the Pole. To refer them all to the modification of temperature induced by the proximity of open water is only to change the form of the question; for it leaves the inquiry unsatisfied—What is the cause of the open water?

This, however, is not the place to enter upon such a discussion. There is no doubt on my mind, that at a time within historical and even recent limits, the climate of this region was milder than it is now. I might base this opinion on the fact, abundantly developed by our expedition, of a secular elevation of the coast-line. But, independently of the ancient beaches and terraces and other geological marks which show that the shore has risen, the stone huts of the natives are found scattered along the line of the bay in spots now so fenced in by ice as to preclude all possibility of the hunt, and of course of habitation by men who rely on it for subsistence.[51]

Tradition points to these as once favorite hunting-grounds near open water. At Rensselaer Harbor, called by the natives *Aunatok,* or the Thawing-Place, we met with huts in quite tolerable preservation, with the stone pedestals still standing which used to sustain the carcases of the captured seals and walrus. Sunny Gorge, and a large indentation in Dallas Bay which bears the Esquimaux name of the Inhabited Place, showed us the remains of a village, surrounded by the bones of seals, walrus, and whales—all now cased in ice. In impressive connection with the same facts, showing not only the former extension of the Esquimaux race to the higher north, but the climatic changes which may perhaps be still in progress there, is the sledge-runner which Mr. Morton saw on the shores of Morris Bay, in latitude 81°. It was made of the bone of a whale, and worked out with skilful labor.[52]

In this recapitulation of facts, I am not entering upon the question of a warmer climate impressed upon this region in virtue of a physical law which extends the isotherms toward the Pole. Still less am I disposed to express an opinion as to the influence which ocean-currents may exert on the temperature of these far-northern regions: there is at least one man, an officer in the same service with myself, and whose scientific investigations do it honor, with whom I am content to leave that discussion. But I would respectfully suggest to those whose opportunities facilitate the inquiry, whether it may not be that the Gulf Stream, traced already to the coast of Novaia Zemlia, is deflected by that peninsula into the space around the Pole. It would require a change in the mean summer temperature of only a few degrees to develop the periodical recurrence of open water. The conditions which define the line of perpetual snow and the limits of the glacier formation may have certainly a proximate application to the problem of such water-spaces near the Pole.[53]

CHAPTER XXIV.

Attempt to reach Beechy Island.

ALL the sledge-parties were now once more aboard
ship, and the season of Arctic travel had ended. For
more than two months we had been imprisoned in ice,
and throughout all that period, except during the enforced holiday of the midwinter darkness or while
repairing from actual disaster, had been constantly in
the field. The summer was wearing on, but still the
ice did not break up as it should. As far as we could
see, it remained inflexibly solid between us and the
North Water of Baffin's Bay. The questions and
speculations of those around me began to show that
they too had anxious thoughts for the coming year.
There was reason for all our apprehensions, as some
of my notes may show.

310

"July 8, Saturday.—Penny saw water to the south-ward in Barrow's Straits as early as June; and by the 1st of July the leads were within a mile of his harbor in Wellington Channel. Dr. Sutherland says he could have cut his way out by the 15th. Austin was not liberated till the 10th of August; but the water had worked up to within three miles and a half of him as early as the 1st, having advanced twenty miles in the preceding month. If, now, we might assume that the ice between us and the nearest water would give way as rapidly as it did in these two cases,—an assumption, by-the-way, which the difference of the localities is all against,—the mouth of our harbor should be reached in fifty days, or by the last day of August; and after that, several days or perhaps weeks must go by before the inside ice yields around our brig.

"I know by experience how soon the ice breaks up after it once begins to go, and I hardly think that it can continue advancing so slowly much longer. In-deed, I look for it to open, if it opens at all, about the beginning of September at farthest, somewhere near the date of Sir James Ross's liberation at Leopold. But then I have to remember that I am much farther to the north than my predecessors, and that by the 28th of last August I had already, after twenty days of unremitting labor, forced the brig nearly forty miles through the pack, and that the pack began to close on us only six days later, and that on the 7th of Septem-ber we were fairly frozen in. Yet last summer was a most favorable one for ice-melting. Putting all this together, it looks as if the winter must catch us before we can get halfway through the pack, even though we should begin warping to the south at the earliest moment that we can hope for water.

"It is not a pleasant conclusion of the argument; for there never was, and I trust never will be, a party worse armed for the encounter of a second Arctic winter. We have neither health, fuel, nor provisions. Dr. Hayes, and indeed all I have consulted about it indirectly, despond at the thought; and when I look round upon our diseased and disabled men, and think of the fearful work of the last long night, I am tempted to feel as they do.

"The alternative of abandoning the vessel at this early stage of our absence, even were it possible, would, I feel, be dishonoring; but, revolving the question as one of practicability alone, I would not undertake it. In the first place, how are we to get along with our sick and newly-amputated men? It is a dreary distance at the best to Upernavik or Beechy Island, our only seats of refuge, and a precarious traverse if we were all of us fit for moving; but we are hardly one-half in efficiency of what we count in number. Besides, how can I desert the brig while there is still a chance of saving her? There is no use of noting *pros* and *cons:* my mind is made up; I will not do it.

"But I must examine this ice-field for myself. I have been maturing through the last fortnight a scheme of relief, based upon a communication with the English squadron to the south, and to-morrow I set out to reconnoitre. Hans will go with me. We will fit out our poor travel-worn dogs with canvas shoes, and cross the floes to the true water-edge, or at least be satisfied that it is impossible. 'He sees best who uses his own eyes.' After that I have my course resolved on.

"July 11, Tuesday.—We got back last night: a sixty miles' journey,—comfortless enough, with only three hours' sleep on the ice. For thirty-five miles south the straits are absolutely tight. Off Refuge Inlet and Esquimaux Point we found driving leads; but between these points and the brig, not a crack. I pushed the dogs over the drift-ice, and, after a fair number of mischances, found the North Water. It was flowing and free; but since McGary saw it last May it has not advanced more than four miles. It would be absurd at this season of the year to attempt escaping in open boats with this ice between us and water. All that can be done is to reinforce our energies as we may, and look the worst in the face.

"In view of these contingencies, I have determined to attempt in person to communicate with Beechy Island, or at least make the effort. If I can reach Sir Edward Belcher's squadron, I am sure of all I want. I will take a light whaleboat, and pick my companions for a journey to the south and west. I may find perhaps the stores of the North Star at the Wolstenholme Islands, or by great good luck come

across some passing vessel of the squadron, and make
known our whereabouts and wants; or, failing these,
we will try and coast it along to Wellington Channel.

"A depôt of provisions and a seaworthy craft large
enough to carry us,—if I had these, every thing would
be right. Even Sir John Ross's launch, the Little
Mary, that he left at Union Bay, would serve our
purpose. If I had her, I could make a southern
passage after the fall tides. The great enemy of that
season is the young shore-ice, that would cut through
our frail boats like a saw. Or, if we can only renew
our stock of provisions for the winter, we may await
the chances of next year.

"I know it is a hazardous venture, but it is a necessary one, and under the circumstances an incumbent
duty. I should have been glad, for some reasons, if the
command of such an attempt could have been delegated
to a subordinate; but I feel that I have no right to
devolve this risk upon another, and I am, besides, the
only one possessed of the necessary local knowledge of
Lancaster Sound and its ice-movements.

"As a prelude to this solemn undertaking, I met my
officers in the evening, and showed them my ice-charts;
explaining, what I found needed little explanation, the
prospect immediately before us. I then discussed the
probable changes, and, giving them my personal opinion that the brig might after all be liberated at a late
date, I announced my project. I will not say how
gratified I was with the manner in which they received
it. It struck me that there was a sense of personal

relief experienced everywhere. I told them that I did
not choose to call a council or connect any of them
with the responsibilities of the measure, for it involved
only the personal safety of those who chose to share
the risk. Full instructions were then left for their
guidance during my absence.

"It was the pleasantest interview I ever had with
my associates. I believe every man on board would
have volunteered, but I confined myself to five active
men: James McGary, William Morton, George Riley,
Hans Christian, and Thomas Hickey, make up my
party."

Our equipment had been getting ready for some
time, though without its object being understood or
announced. The boat was our old "Forlorn Hope,"
mended up and revised for her new destinies. She was
twenty-three feet long, had six-feet-and-a-half beam,
and was two feet six inches deep. Her build was the
characteristic one of the American whaleboats, too flat-
bottomed for ordinary use, but much improved by a
false keel, which Ohlsen had given her throughout her
entire length. After all, she was a mere cockle-shell.

Her great fault was her knife-like bow, which cut
into the short seas most cruelly. To remedy this in
some degree, and to make up for her want of height,
I devised a sort of half-deck of canvas and gum-elastic
cloth, extending back beyond the foremast, and continued along the gunwale; a sort of weather-cloth,
which might possibly add to her safety, and would
certainly make her more comfortable in heavy weather.

I left her rig altogether to McGary. She carried what any one but a New London whaler would call an inordinate spread of canvas, a light cotton foresail of twelve-feet lift, a stouter mainsail of fourteen-feet lift with a spreet eighteen feet long, and a snug little jib. Her masts were of course selected very carefully, for we could not carry extra sticks: and we trusted to the good old-fashioned steering-oar rather than a rudder.

Morton, who was in my confidence from the first, had all our stores ready. We had no game, and no meat but pork, of which we took some hundred and fifty pounds. I wanted pemmican, and sent the men out in search of the cases which were left on the floe by the frozen depôt-party during the rescue of last March; but they could not find a trace of them, or indeed of any thing else we abandoned at that time: a proof, if we wanted one, how blurred all our faculties must have been by suffering, for we marked them as we thought with marvellous care.

We lifted our boat over the side in the afternoon, and floated her to the crack at the Observatory Island; mounted her there on our large sledge "The Faith," by an arrangement of cradles of Mr. Ohlsen's devising; stowed in every thing but the provisions, and carried her on to the bluff of Sylvia Headland: and the next morning a party consisting of all but the sick was detailed to transport her to open water; while McGary, Hans and myself followed with our St. John's sledge, carrying our stores.

The surface of the ice was very irregular and covered

with water-pools. Our sledge broke down with repeated strainings, and we had a fatiguing walk of thirty-
six miles to get another. We passed the first night
wet and supperless on the rocks; a bad beginning, for
the next day found us stiff and out of sorts.

The ice continued troublesome, the land-ices swaying
hither and thither with the tide. The second day's
progress, little as it was, cost us very hard labor. But
another night of repose on the rocks refreshed us; so
that, the day after, we were able to make about seven
miles along the ice-belt. Two days more, and we had
carried the boat across twenty miles of heavy ice-floe,
and launched her in open water. It was not far from
the hut on Esquimaux Point.

The straits were much clogged with drift, but I
followed the coast southward without difficulty. We
travelled at night, resting when the sun was hottest.
I had every reason to be pleased with the performance
of the whaleboat, and the men kept up their spirits
well. We landed at the point where we left our life-
boat a year ago, and to our great joy found it un-
touched: the cove and inlet were still fast in ice.

We now neared the Littleton Island of Captain
Inglefield, where a piece of good fortune awaited us.
We saw a number of ducks, both eiders and hareldas;
and it occurred to me that by tracking their flight we
should reach their breeding-grounds. There was no
trouble in doing so, for they flew in a bee-line to a
group of rocky islets, above which the whole horizon was
studded with birds. A rugged little ledge, which I

named Eider Island, was so thickly colonized that we could hardly walk without treading on a nest. We killed with guns and stones over two hundred birds in a few hours.

EIDER ISLAND.

It was near the close of the breeding-season. The nests were still occupied by the mother-birds, but many of the young had burst the shell, and were nestling under the wing, or taking their first lessons in the water-pools. Some, more advanced, were already in the ice-sheltered channels, greedily waiting for the shell-fish and sea-urchins, which the old bird busied herself in procuring for them.

Near by was a low and isolated rock-ledge, which we called Hans Island. The glaucous gulls, those cormorants of the Arctic seas, had made it their peculiar homestead. Their progeny, already full-fledged and voracious, crowded the guano-whitened rocks; and the

GLAUCOUS AND TRIDACTYL GULLS.

mothers, with long necks and gaping yellow bills, swooped above the peaceful shallows of the eiders, carrying off the young birds, seemingly just as their wants required. A more domineering and insatiable rapacity I have never witnessed. The gull would gobble up and swallow a young eider in less time than it takes me to describe the act. For a moment you would see the paddling feet of the poor little wretch protruding from the mouth; then came a distension of the neck as it descended into the stomach; a few moments more, and the young gulls were feeding on the ejected morsel.

The mother-duck, of course nearly distracted, battles, and battles well; but she cannot always reassemble her brood; and in her efforts to defend one, uncovering the others, I have seen her left as destitute as Niobe. Hans tells me that in such cases she adopts a new progeny; and, as he is well versed in the habits of the bird, I see no reason to doubt his assertion.

The glaucous is not the only predatory gull of Smith's Strait. In fact, all the Arctic species, without including their cousins the jagers, have the propensity strongly marked. I have seen the ivory gull, the most beautiful and snowy St. Agnes of the ice-fields, seize our wounded awks, and, after a sharp battle, carry them off in her talons. A novel use of a palmated foot.

I could sentimentalize on these bereavements of the ducks and their companions in diet: it would be only the every-day sermonizing of the world. But while the gulls were fattening their young on the eiders, the eiders were fattening theirs on the lesser life of the sea, and we were as busily engaged upon both in true predatory sympathy. The squab-gull of Hans Island has a well-earned reputation in South Greenland for its delicious juices, and the eggs of Eider Island can well

afford to suffer from the occasional visits of gulls and
other bipeds; for a locust-swarm of foragers might
fatten without stint on their surplus abundance.

We camped at this nursery of wild-fowl, and laid in
four large India-rubber bags full, cleaned and rudely
boned.   Our boat was hauled up and refitted; and, the
trial having shown us that she was too heavily laden
for safety, I made a general reduction of our stores,
and cached the surplus under the rocks.

On Wednesday, the 19th, we left Flagstaff Point,
where we fixed our beacon last year; and stood W. 10° S.
under full canvas.   My aim was to take the channel
obliquely at Littleton Island; and, making the drift-ice
or the land to the southwest in the neighborhood of
Cape Combermere, push on for Kent Island and leave
a cairn there.

I had the good fortune to get satisfactory meridian
observations, as well as angular bearings between Cape
Alexander and Flagstaff Point, and found, as our
operations by theodolite had already indicated, that the
entire coast-line upon the Admiralty Charts of my predecessor would have to be altered.

Cape Isabella, the western headland of the strait,
whose discovery, by-the-way, is due rather to old Baffin
than his follower Sir John Ross, bears W. 22° N. (solar)
from Cape Alexander; its former location being some
20° to the south of west.   The narrowest part of
Smith's Straits is not, as has been considered, between
these two capes, but upon the parallel of 78° 24′, where
Cape Isabella bears due west of Littleton Island, and

the diameter of the channel is reduced to thirty-seven miles.

The difference between our projection of this coast and Captain Inglefield's, refers itself naturally to the

CAPE ISABELLA.

differing circumstances under which the two were framed. The sluggishness of the compass, and the eccentricities of refraction in the Arctic seas, are well fitted to embarrass and mislead a navigator. I might hesitate to assert the greater certainty for our results, had not the position of our observatory at Fern Rock, to which our survey is referred, been determined by a careful series of astronomical observations.[54]

Captain Inglefield gives the mean trend of the east coast about 20° too much to the north; in consequence

of which the capes and indentations sighted by him
are too high in latitude.

Cape Frederick VII., his highest northern point,
is placed in lat. 79° 30', while no land—the glacier
not being considered as such—is found on that coast
beyond 79° 13'. The same cape as laid down in
the Admiralty Chart of 1852 is about eighty miles
from the farthest position reached by Captain Inglefield. To see land upon the horizon at this distance,
even from a mast-head eighty feet high, would require
it to be a mountain whose altitude exceeded three
thousand five hundred feet. An island similar in position to that designated by Captain Inglefield as Louis
Napoleon does not exist. The land sighted in that
direction may have been the top of a high mountain
on the north side of Franklin Pierce Bay, though this
supposition requires us to assume an error in the bearing; for, as given in the chart, no land could be within
the range of sight. In deference to Captain Inglefield,
I have continued for this promontory the name which
he had impressed upon it as an island.

Toward night the wind freshened from the northward, and we passed beyond the protection of the
straits into the open seaway. My journal gives no
picture of the life we now entered on. The oldest
sailor, who treads the deck of his ship with the familiar
confidence of a man at home, has a distrust of open-
boat navigation which a landsman hardly shares. The
feeling grew upon us as we lost the land. McGary

was an old Behring's Straits whaler, and there is no
better boatman in the world than he; but I know
that he shared my doubts, as the boat buried herself
again and again in the trough of a short chopping
sea, which it taxed all his dexterity in steering to
meet.

Baffin passed around this gulf in 1616 with two
small vessels; but they were giants beside ours. I
thought of them as we crossed his track steering for
Cape Combermere, then about sixty miles distant, with
every prospect of a heavy gale.

We were in the centre of this large area of open
water when the gale broke upon us from the north.
We were near foundering. Our false bow of India-
rubber cloth was beaten in, and our frail weather-
boarding soon followed it. With the utmost exertion
we could hardly keep our boat from broaching to: a
broken oar or an accidental twitch would have been
fatal to us at any time. But McGary handled that
whaler's marvel, the long steering-oar, with admirable
skill. None of us could pretend to take his place. For
twenty-two unbroken hours he stuck to his post without relaxing his attention or his efforts.

I was not prepared for such a storm. I do not think
I have seen a worse sea raised by the northers of the
Gulf of Mexico. At last the wind hauled to the eastward, and we were glad to drive before it for the
in-shore floes. We had passed several bergs; but
the sea dashed against their sides so furiously as to

negative all hope of protection at their base: the pack or floe, so much feared before, was now looked to for a refuge.

I remember well our anxiety as we entered the loose streams of drift after four hours' scudding, and our relief when we felt their influence upon the sea. We fastened to an old floe, not fifty yards in diameter, and, with the weather-surf breaking over our heads, rode out the storm under a warp and grapnel.

CHAPTER XXV.

WORKING ON—A BOAT NIP—ICE-BARRIER—THE BARRIER PACK—
PROGRESS HOPELESS—NORTHUMBERLAND ISLAND—NORTHUMBER-
LAND GLACIER—ICE-CASCADES—NEVE.

THE obstacle we had now to encounter was the pack
that stretched between us and the south.

When the storm abated, we commenced boring into
it,—slow work at the best of times; but my companions encountered it with a persevering activity
quite as admirable as their fortitude in danger. It
had its own hazards too; and more than once it
looked as if we were permanently beset. I myself
knew that we might rely on the southerly wind to
liberate us from such an imprisonment; but I saw
that the men thought otherwise, as the ice-fields closed
around us and the horizon showed an unchanging circle
of ice.

We were still laboring on, hardly past the middle
of the bay, when the floes began to relax. On Sunday,
the 23d of July, the whole aspect around us changed.
The sun came out cheeringly, the leads opened more
and more, and, as we pulled through them to the

south, each ice-tongue that we doubled brought us
nearer to the Greenland shore. A slackening of the
ice to the east enabled us after a while to lay our
course for Hakluyt Island. We spread our canvas
again, and reached the in-shore fields by one in the
afternoon. We made our camp, dried our buffalo-
skins, and sunned and slept away our fatigue.

We renewed our labors in the morning. Keeping
inside the pack, we coasted along for the Cary Islands,
encountering now and then a projecting floe, and
either boring or passing around it, but making a satisfactory progress on the whole toward Lancaster Sound.
But at the south point of Northumberland Island the
pack arrested us once more. The seam by which we
had come east lay between Whale Sound and Murchison
Inlet, and the ice-drift from the southern of these had
now piled itself in our way.

I was confident that I should find the "Eastern
Water" if I could only reach Cape Parry, and that this
would give me a free track to Cary Islands. I therefore looked anxiously for a fissure in the pack, and
pressed our little craft into the first one that seemed at
all practicable.

For the next three days we worked painfully through
the half-open leads, making in all some fifteen miles to
the south. We had very seldom room enough to row;
but, as we tracked along, it was not difficult to escape
nippings, by hauling up the boat on the ice. Still she
received some hard knocks, and a twist or two that did
not help her sea-worthiness; for she began to leak; and

this, with the rain which fell heavily, forced us to bale her out every other hour. Of course, we could not sleep, and one of our little party fell sick with the unmitigated fatigue.

On the twenty-ninth, it came on to blow, the wind

SOUTH POINT OF NORTHUMBERLAND ISLAND.

still keeping from the southwest, but cold and almost rising to a gale. We had had another wet and sleepless night, for the floes still baffled us by their capricious movements. But at three in the afternoon we had the sun again, and the ice opened just enough to tempt us. It was uncomfortable toil. We pushed forward our little weather-worn craft, her gunwales touching on both sides, till the toppling ice began to break down on us, and sometimes, critically suspended, met above our heads.

One of these passages I am sure we all of us remember. We were in an alley of pounded ice-masses, such as the receding floes leave when they have crushed the tables that were between them, and had pushed our way far enough to make retreat impossible, when the fields began to close in. There was no escaping a nip, for every thing was loose and rolling around us, and the floes broke into hummock-ridges as they came together. They met just ahead of us, and gradually swayed in toward our boat. The fragments were already splitting off and spinning over us, when we found ourselves borne up by the accumulating rubbish, like the Advance in her winter drift; and, after resting for twenty minutes high out of water, quietly lowered again as the fields relaxed their pressure.

Generally, however, the ice-fields came together directly, and so gradually as to enable us to anticipate their contact. In such cases, as we were short-handed and our boat heavily laden, we were glad to avail ourselves of the motion of the floes to assist in lifting her upon them. We threw her across the lead by a small pull of the steering-oar, and let her meet the approaching ice upon her bow. The effect, as we found in every instance, was to press her down forward as the floe advanced against her, and to raise her stern above the

level of the other field.   We held ourselves ready for
the spring as she began to rise.

It was a time of almost unbroken excitement; yet I
am not surprised, as I turn over the notes of my
meagre diary, to find how little of stirring incident it
records.   The story of one day's strife with the ice-floes
might almost serve for those which followed it: I
remember that we were four times nipped before we
succeeded in releasing ourselves, and that we were glad
to haul upon the floes as often as a dozen times a day.
We attempted to drag forward on the occasional fields;
but we had to give it up, for it strained the boat so
much that she was barely sea-worthy: it kept one man
busy the last six days baling her out.

On the 31st, at the distance of ten miles from Cape
Parry, we came to a dead halt.   A solid mass lay
directly across our path, extending onward to our
farthest horizon.   There were bergs in sight to the
westward, and by walking for some four miles over
the moving floe in that direction, McGary and myself
succeeded in reaching one.   We climbed it to the height
of a hundred and twenty feet, and, looking out from it
with my excellent spy-glass to the south and west, we
saw that all within a radius of thirty miles was a motionless, unbroken, and impenetrable sea.

I had not counted on this.   Captain Inglefield found
open water two years before at this very point.   I
myself met no ice here only seven days later in 1853.
Yet it was plain, that from Cape Combermere on the
west side, and an unnamed bay immediately to the

north of it, across to Hackluyt Island, there extended
a continuous barrier of ice. We had scarcely penetrated beyond its margin.

We had, in fact, reached the dividing pack of the
two great open waters of Baffin's Bay. The experience of the whalers and of the expedition-ships that
have traversed this region have made all of us familiar with that great expanse of open sea, to the north
of Cape Dudley Diggs, which has received the name
of the North Water. Combining the observations of
Baffin, Ross, and Inglefield, we know that this sometimes extends as far north as Littleton Island, em-
bracing an area of ninety thousand square miles. The
voyagers I have named could not, of course, be aware
of the interesting fact that this water is divided, at
least occasionally, into two distinct bodies; the one
comprehended between Lancaster and Jones's Sounds,
the other extending from the point we had now
reached to the upper pack of Smith's Straits. But it
was evident to all of our party that the barrier which
now arrested us was made up of the ices which Jones's
Sound on the west and Murchison's on the east had
discharged and driven together.

I may mention, as bearing on the physical geography of the region, that south of Cape Isabella the
western shore is invested by a zone of unbroken ice.
We encountered it when we were about twenty miles
from the land. It followed the curves of three great
indentations, whose bases were lined with glaciers
rivalling those of Melville Bay. The bergs from them

were numerous and large, entangling the floating floes,
and contributing as much as the currents to the ice-
clad character of this most dreary coast.   The currents
alone would not explain it.   Yet when we recur to
the observations of Graah, who describes a similar belt
on the eastern coast of Greenland, and to the observations of the same character that have been made on
the coasts of Arctic America to the southeast, it is not
easy to escape the thought that this accumulation of
ice on the western shores must be due, in part at
least, to the rotary movements of the earth, whose
increasing radius as we recede from the Pole gives
increased velocity to the southern ice-pack.

To return to our narrative.   It was obvious that a
further attempt to penetrate to the south must be
hopeless till the ice-barrier before us should undergo
a change.   I had observed, when passing Northumberland Island, that some of its glacier-slopes were mar-
gined with verdure, an almost unfailing indication of
animal life; and, as my men were much wasted by
diarrhœa, and our supplies of food had become scanty,
I resolved to work my way to the island and recruit
there for another effort.

Tracking and sometimes rowing through a heavy
rain, we traversed the leads for two days, working
eastward; and on the morning of the third gained the
open water near the shore.   Here a breeze came to our
aid, and in a couple of hours more we passed with now
unwonted facility to the southern face of the island.
We met several flocks of little auks as we approached

it, and found on landing that it was one enormous
homestead of the auks, dovekies, and gulls.

We encamped on the 31st, on a low beach at the foot
of a moraine that came down between precipitous cliffs
of surpassing wildness. It had evidently been selected
by the Esquimaux for a winter settlement: five well-

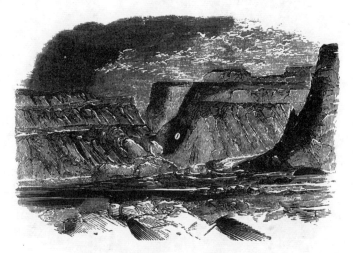

NORTHUMBERLAND ISLAND.

built huts of stone attested this. Three of them were
still tolerably perfect, and bore marks of recent habitation. The droppings of the birds had fertilized the
soil, and it abounded in grasses, sorrel, and cochlearia,
to the water's edge. The foxes were about in great
numbers, attracted, of course, by the abundance of
birds. They were all of them of the lead-colored
variety, without a white one among them. The young

ones, as yet lean and seemingly unskilled in hospitable courtesies, barked at us as we walked about.

I was greatly interested by a glacier that occupied the head of the moraine. It came down abruptly from

GLACIER OF NORTHUMBERLAND ISLAND.

the central plateau of the island, with an angle of descent of more than seventy degrees. I have never seen one that illustrated more beautifully the viscous or semi-solid movement of these masses. Like a well-known glacier of the Alps, it had two planes of descent; the upper nearly precipitous for about four hundred feet from the summit; the lower of about the same height, but with an angle of some fifty degrees; the two communicating by a slightly-inclined platform perhaps half a mile long. This ice was unbroken through its entire extent. It came down from the level of the upper country, a vast icicle, with the folds or waves impressed upon it by its onward motion undisturbed by any apparent fracture or crevasse. Thus it rolled onward over the rugged and contracting platform below, and thence poured its semi-solid mass down upon the plain. Where it encountered occasional knobs of rock it passed round them, bearing still the distinctive marks of an imperfect fluid obstructed in its descent; and its lower fall described a dome, or, to use the more accurate simile of Forbes, a great outspread clam-shell of ice.

It seemed as if an interior ice-lake was rising above the brink of the cliffs that confined it. In many places it could be seen exuding or forcing its way over the very crest of the rocks, and hanging down in huge icy stalactites seventy and a hundred feet long. These were still lengthening out by the continuous overflow, some of them breaking off as their weight became too great for their tenacity, others swelling by constant supplies from the interior, but spitting off fragmentary masses with an unremitting clamor. The plain below these cataractine glaciers was piling up with the debris, while torrents of the melted rubbish found their way, foaming and muddy, to the sea, carrying gravel and rocks along with them.

These ice-cascades, as we called them, kept up their din the whole night, sometimes startling us with a heavy booming sound, as the larger masses fell, but more generally rattling away like the random fires of a militia parade.   On examining the ice of which they were made up, I found grains of *neve* larger than a walnut; so large, indeed, that it was hard to realize that they could be formed by the ordinary granulating processes of the winter snows.   My impression is, that the surface of the plateau-ice, the *mer de glace* of the island, is made up of these agglomerated nodules, and that they are forced out and discarded by the advance of the more compact ice from higher levels.[65]

CHAPTER XXVI.

It was with mingled feelings that we neared the brig. Our little party had grown fat and strong upon the auks and eiders and scurvy-grass; and surmises were rife among us as to the condition of our comrades and the prospects of our ice-bound little ship.

The tide-leads, which one year ago had afforded a precarious passage to the vessel, now barely admitted our whaleboat; and, as we forced her through the broken ice, she showed such signs of hard usage, that I had her hauled up upon the land-belt and housed under the cliffs at Six-mile Ravine. We crossed the rocks on foot, aided by our jumping-poles, and startled our shipmates by our sudden appearance.

In the midst of the greeting which always met our returning parties, and which gave to our little vessel the endearing associations of a homestead, our thoughts reverted to the feeble chances of our liberation, and the failure of our recent effort to secure the means of a retreat.

The brig had been imprisoned by closely-cementing ice for eleven months, during which period she had not budged an inch from her icy cradle. My journal will show the efforts and the hopes which engrossed our few remaining days of uncertainty and suspense:—

"August 8, Tuesday.—This morning two saw-lines were passed from the open-water pools at the sides of our sternpost, and the ice was bored for blasting. In the course of our operations the brig surged and righted, rising two and a half feet. We are now trying to warp her a few yards toward Butler Island, where we again go to work with our powder-canisters.

"August 11, Friday.—Returned yesterday from an inspection of the ice toward the Esquimaux settlements; but, absorbing as was my errand, I managed to take geognostical sections and profiles of the coast as far south as Peter Force Bay, beyond which the ice was impenetrable.

"I have often referred to the massive character of the ice in that neighborhood. The ice-foot, by our winter measurement twenty-seven feet in mean thickness by forty yards in width, is now of dimensions still more formidable. Large masses, released like land-slides by the action of torrents from the coast, form here and there a belt or reef, which clogs the shoal water near the shore and prevents a passage. Such ice I have seen thirty-six feet in height; and when subjected, as it often is, to hummock-squeezing, sixty and seventy feet. It requires experience to distinguish it from the true iceberg.

"When I passed up the Sound on the 6th of August, after my long southern journey, I found the ice-foot comparatively unbroken, and a fine interval of open water between it and the large floes of the pack. Since then, this pack has been broken up, and the comminuted fragments, forming a great drift, move with tides and currents in such a way as to obliterate the 'land-water' at high tide, and under some circumstances at other times. This broken rubbish occasionally expands enough to permit a boat to pass through; but, as we found it, a passage could only be effected by heavy labor, and at great expense to our boat, nearly unseaworthy now from her former trials. We hauled her up near Bedevilled Headland, and returned to the brig on foot.

"As I travelled back along the coast, I observed the wonderful changes brought about by the disruption of the pack. It was my hope to have extricated the brig, if she was ever to be liberated, before the drift had choked the land-leads; but now they are closely jammed with stupendous ice-fragments, records of inconceivable pressures. The bergs, released from their winter cement, have driven down in crowds, grounding on the shallows, and extending in reefs or chains out to seaward, where they have caught and retained the floating ices. The prospect was really desolation itself. One floe measured nine feet in mean elevation above the water-level; thus implying a tabular thickness by

direct congelation of sixty-three feet. It had so closed
in with the shore, too, as to rear up a barricade of
crushed ice which it was futile to attempt to pass. All
prospect of forcing a passage ceased north of Six-mile
Ravine.

APPROACH TO OBSERVATORY.

"On reaching the brig, I found that the blasting had
succeeded: one canister cracked and uplifted two
hundred square yards of ice with but five pounds of
powder. A prospect showed itself of getting inside the
island at high-water; and I determined to attempt it at
the highest spring-tide, which takes place on the 12th.

"August 12, Saturday.—The brig bore the strain of

her new position very well. The tide fell fifteen feet, leaving her high and dry; but, as the water rose, every thing was replaced, and the deck put in order for warping again. Every one in the little vessel turned to; and after much excitement, at the very top of the tide, she passed 'by the skin of her teeth.' She was then warped into a bight of the floe, near Fox-Trap Point, and there she now lies.

"We congratulate ourselves upon effecting this crossing. Had we failed, we should have had to remain fast probably for the high tides a fortnight hence. The young ice is already making, and our hopes rest mainly upon the gales of late August and September.

"August 13, Sunday.—Still fast to the old floe near Fox-Trap Point, waiting a heavy wind as our only means of liberation. The land-trash is cemented by young ice, which is already an inch and a half thick. The thermometer has been as low as 29°; but the fog and mist which prevail to-day are in our favor. The perfect clearness of the past five days hastened the growth of young ice, and it has been forming without intermission.

"I took a long walk to inspect the ice toward Six-mile Ravine. This ice has never been moved either by wind or water since its formation. I found that it lined the entire shore with long ridges of detached fragments : a discouraging obstacle, if it should remain, in the way of our future liberation. It is in direct contact with the big floe that we are now fast to, and is the remnant of the triple lines of 'land-ices' which I have described already.   I attribute its permanency to the almost constant shadow of the mountains near it.

"August 15, Tuesday.—To-day I made another ice-inspection to the N.E.   The floe on which I have trudged so often, the big bay-floe of our former mooring, is nearly the same as when we left it.   I recognised the holes and cracks, through the fog, by a sort of instinct.   McGary and myself had little difficulty in reaching the Fiord Water by our jumping-poles.

"I have my eye on this water; for it may connect with the Northeast Headland and hereafter give us a passage.

"The season travels on: the young ice grows thicker, and my messmates' faces grow longer, every day.   I have again to play buffoon to keep up the spirits of the party.

"A raven!   The snow-birds begin to fly to the south in groups, coming at night to our brig to hover on the rigging.   Winter is hurrying upon us.   The poppies are quite wilted.

"Examined ice with Mr. Bonsall, and determined to enter the broken land-ices by warping; not that there is the slightest probability of getting through, but it affords moral aid and comfort to the men and officers: it looks as if we were doing something.

"August 17, Thursday.—Warped about one hundred yards into the trash, and, after a long day of labor, have turned in, hoping to recommence at 5 A.M. tomorrow.

"In five days the spring-tides come back: should

we fail in passing with them, I think our fortunes are fixed. The young ice bore a man this morning: it had a bad look, this man-supporting August ice! The temperature never falls below 28°; but it is cold o' nights with no fire.

"August 18, Friday.—Reduced our allowance of wood to six pounds a meal. This, among eighteen mouths, is one-third of a pound of fuel for each. It allows us coffee twice a day, and soup once. Our fare besides this is cold pork boiled in quantity and eaten as required. This sort of thing works badly; but I must save coal for other emergencies. I see 'darkness ahead.'

"I inspected the ice again to-day. Bad! bad!—I must look another winter in the face. I do not shrink from the thought; but, while we have a chance ahead, it is my first duty to have all things in readiness to meet it. It is *horrible*—yes, that is the word—to look forward to another year of disease and darkness to be met without fresh food and without fuel. I should meet it with a more tempered sadness if I had no comrades to think for and protect.

"August 20, Sunday.—Rest for all hands. The daily prayer is no longer 'Lord, accept our gratitude and bless our undertaking,' but 'Lord, accept our gratitude and restore us to our homes.' The ice shows no change: after a boat and foot journey around the entire southeastern curve of the bay, no signs!

"I was out in the Red Eric with Bonsall, McGary, Hans, Riley, and John. We tracked her over the ice

to the Burgomaster Cove, the flanking cape of Charlotte Wood Fiord and its river. Here we launched
her, and went all round the long canal which the
running waters have eaten into the otherwise unchanged ice. Charlotte Wood Fiord is a commanding
sheet of water, nearly as wide as the Delaware : in the
midst of the extreme solidity around us, it looked de-
ceitfully gladdening. After getting to the other side,
near Little Willie's Monument, we ascended a high
bluff, and saw every thing weary and discouraging
beyond. Our party returned quite crestfallen."

My attempt to reach Beechy Island had disclosed,
as I thought it would, the impossibility of reaching
the settlements of Greenland. Between the American
and the opposite side of the bay was one continuous
pack of ice, which, after I had travelled on it for many
miles to the south, was still of undefined extent before
me. The birds had left their colonies. The water-
streams from the bergs and of the shore were freezing
up rapidly. The young ice made the water-surface
impassable even to a whaleboat. It was clear to me
that without an absolute change of circumstances, such
as it was vain to look for any longer, to leave the ship
would be to enter upon a wilderness destitute of resources, and from which it would be difficult, if not
impracticable, to return.

Every thing before us was involved in gloomy doubt.
Hopeful as I had been, it was impossible not to feel
that we were near the climax of the expedition.

I determined to place upon Observatory Island a

large signal-beacon or cairn, and to bury under it documents which, in case of disaster to our party, would convey to any who might seek us intelligence of our proceedings and our fate. The memory of the first winter quarters of Sir John Franklin, and the painful feelings with which, while standing by the graves of his dead, I had five years before sought for written signs pointing to the fate of the living, made me careful to avoid a similar neglect.

A conspicuous spot was selected upon a cliff looking out upon the icy desert, and on a broad face of rock the words

ADVANCE,

A. D. 1853-54,

were painted in letters which could be read at a distance. A pyramid of heavy stones, perched above it, was marked with the Christian symbol of the cross. It was not without a holier sentiment than that of mere utility that I placed under this the coffins of our two poor comrades. It was our beacon and their gravestone.

Near this a hole was worked into the rock, and a paper, enclosed in glass, sealed in with melted lead. It read as follows :—

"BRIG ADVANCE, August 14, 1854.

"E. K. Kane, with his comrades Henry Brooks, John Wall Wilson, James McGary, J. J. Hayes, Christian Ohlsen, Amos Bonsall, Henry Goodfellow, August Sontag, William Morton, J. Carl Petersen, George

Stephenson, Jefferson Temple Baker, George Riley,
Peter Schubert, George Whipple, John Blake, Thomas
Hickey, William Godfrey, and Hans Cristian, members of the Second Grinnell Expedition in search of
Sir John Franklin and the missing crews of the Erebus
and Terror, were forced into this harbor while endeavoring to bore the ice to the north and east.

"They were frozen in on the 8th of September,
1853, and liberated ———

"During this period the labors of the expedition
have delineated nine hundred and sixty miles of coast-
line, without developing any traces of the missing ships
or the slightest information bearing upon their fate.
The amount of travel to effect this exploration exceeded two thousand miles, all of which was upon foot
or by the aid of dogs.

"Greenland has been traced to its northern face,
whence it is connected with the farther north of the
opposite coast by a great glacier. This coast has been
charted as high as lat. 82° 27'. Smith's Sound expands into a capacious bay: it has been surveyed
throughout its entire extent. From its northern and
eastern corner, in lat. 80° 10', long. 66°, a channel has
been discovered and followed until farther progress
was checked by water free from ice. This channel
trended nearly due north, and expanded into an apparently open sea, which abounded with birds and bears
and marine life.

"The death of the dogs during the winter threw
the travel essential to the above discoveries upon the

personal efforts of the officers and men. The summer finds them much broken in health and strength.

"Jefferson Temple Baker and Peter Schubert died from injuries received from cold while in manly performance of their duty. Their remains are deposited under a cairn at the north point of Observatory Island.

"The site of the observatory is seventy-six English feet from the northernmost salient point of this island, in a direction S. 14° E. Its position is in lat. 78° 37' 10", long. 70° 40'. The mean tidal level is twenty-nine feet below the highest point upon this island. Both of these sites are further designated by copper bolts sealed with melted lead into holes upon the rocks.

"On the 12th of August, 1854, the brig warped from her position, and, after passing inside the group of islands, fastened to the outer floe about a mile to the northwest, where she is now awaiting further changes in the ice.

"Signed,   "E. K. KANE,

"Commanding Expedition.

"Fox-Trap Point, August 14, 1854."

Some hours later, the following note was added.

"The young ice having formed between the brig and this island, and prospects of a gale showing themselves, the date of departure is left unfilled. If possible, a second visit will be made to insert our dates, our final escape being still dependent upon the course of the season.   E. K. KANE."

And now came the question of the second winter: how to look our enemy in the face, and how to meet him. Any thing was better than inaction; and, in spite of the uncertainty which yet attended our plans, a host of expedients were to be resorted to, and much Robinson Crusoe labor ahead. Moss was to be gathered for eking out our winter fuel, and willow-stems and stonecrops and sorrel, as antiscorbutics, collected and buried in the snow. But while all these were in progress came other and graver questions.

Some of my party had entertained the idea that an escape to the south was still practicable; and this opinion was supported by Mr. Petersen, our Danish interpreter, who had accompanied the Searching Expedition of Captain Penny, and had a matured experience in the changes of Arctic ice. They even thought that the safety of all would be promoted by a withdrawal from the brig.

"August 21, Monday.—The question of detaching a party was in my mind some time ago; but the more I thought it over, the more I was convinced that it would be neither right in itself nor practically safe. For myself personally, it is a simple duty of honor to remain by the brig: I could not think of leaving her till I had proved the effect of the later tides; and after that, as I have known all along, it would be too late.—Come what may, I share her fortunes.

"But it is a different question with my associates. I cannot expect them to adopt my impulses; and I am by no means sure that I ought to hold them bound by my conclusions. Have I the *moral right?* for, as to nautical rules, they do not fit the circumstances: among the whalers, when a ship is hopelessly beset, the master's authority gives way, and the crew take counsel for themselves whether to go or stay by her. My party is subordinate and well disposed; but if the restlessness of suffering makes some of them anxious to brave the chances, they may certainly plead that a second winter in the ice was no part of the cruise they bargained for.

"But what presses on me is of another character. I cannot disguise it from myself that we are wretchedly prepared for another winter on board. We are a set of scurvy-riddled, broken-down men; our provisions are sorely reduced in quantity, and are altogether unsuited to our condition. My only hope of maintaining or restoring such a degree of health among us as is indispensable to our escape in the spring has been and must be in a wholesome elastic tone of feeling among the men: a reluctant, brooding, disheartened spirit would sweep our decks like a pestilence. I fear the bane of depressing example.

"I know all this as a medical man and an officer; and I feel that we might be wearing away the hearts and energies, if not the lives of all, by forcing those who were reluctant to remain. With half a dozen confiding resolute men, I have no fears of ultimate safety.

"I will make a thorough inspection of the ice tomorrow, and decide finally the prospects of our liberation.

"August 23, Wednesday.—The brig cannot escape. I got an eligible position with my sledge to review the floes, and returned this morning at two o'clock. There is no possibility of our release, unless by some extreme intervention of the coming tides. I doubt whether a boat could be forced as far as the Southern Water. When I think of the extraordinary way in which the ice was impacted last winter, how very little it has yielded through the summer, and how early another winter is making its onset upon us, I am very doubtful, indeed, whether our brig can get away at all. It would be inexpedient to attempt leaving her now in boats; the water-streams closing, the pack nearly fast again, and the young ice almost impenetrable.

"I shall call the officers and crew together, and make known to them very fully how things look, and what hazards must attend such an effort as has been proposed among them. They shall have my views unequivocally expressed. I will then give them twenty-four hours to deliberate; and at the end of that time all who determine to go shall say so in writing, with a full exposition of the circumstances of the case. They shall have the best outfit I can give, an abundant share of our remaining stores, and my good-bye blessing.

"August 24, Thursday.—At noon to-day I had all hands called, and explained to them frankly the considerations which have determined me to remain where we are. I endeavored to show them that an escape to open water could not succeed, and that the effort must be exceedingly hazardous: I alluded to our

duties to the ship: in a word, I advised them strenuously
to forego the project. I then told them that I should
freely give my permission to such as were desirous of
making the attempt, but that I should require them to
place themselves under the command of officers selected
by them before setting out, and to renounce in writing
all claims upon myself and the rest who were resolved
to stay by the vessel. Having done this, I directed the
roll to be called, and each man to answer for himself."

In the result, eight out of the seventeen survivors of
my party resolved to stand by the brig. It is just that
I should record their names. They were Henry Brooks,
James McGary, J. W. Wilson, Henry Goodfellow, Wil-
liam Morton, Christian Ohlsen, Thomas Hickey, Hàns
Cristian.

I divided to the others their portion of our resources
justly and even liberally; and they left us on Monday,
the 28th, with every appliance our narrow circumstances could furnish to speed and guard them. One
of them, George Riley, returned a few days afterward;
but weary months went by before we saw the rest
again. They carried with them a written assurance of
a brother's welcome should they be driven back; and
this assurance was redeemed when hard trials had prepared them to share again our fortunes.

CHAPTER XXVII.

THE party moved off with the elastic step of men
confident in their purpose, and were out of sight in a
few hours.   As we lost them among the hummocks, the
stern realities of our condition pressed themselves upon
us anew.   The reduced numbers of our party, the helplessness of many, the waning efficiency of all, the impending winter with its cold, dark night, our penury
of resources, the dreary sense of increased isolation,—
these made the staple of our thoughts.   For a time, Sir
John Franklin and his party, our daily topic through
so many months, gave place to the question of our own
fortunes,—how we were to escape, how to live.   The
summer had gone, the harvest was ended, and——
We did not care to finish the sentence.

Following close on this gloomy train, and in fact
blending with it, came the more important discussion
of our duties.   We were like men driven to the wall,
quickened, not depressed.   Our plans were formed at

352

once : there is nothing like emergency to speed, if not to instruct, the energies.

It was my first definite resolve that, come what might, our organization and its routine of observances should be adhered to strictly. It is the experience of every man who has either combated difficulties himself or attempted to guide others through them, that the controlling law shall be systematic action. Nothing depresses and demoralizes so much as a surrender of the approved and habitual forms of life. I resolved that every thing should go on as it had done. The arrangement of hours, the distribution and details of duty, the religious exercises, the ceremonials of the table, the fires, the lights, the watch, even the labors of the observatory and the notation of the tides and the sky,—nothing should be intermitted that had contributed to make up the day.

My next was to practise on the lessons we had learned from the Esquimaux. I had studied them carefully, and determined that their form of habitations and their peculiarities of diet, without their unthrift and filth, were the safest and best to which the necessity of our circumstances invited us.

My journal tells how these resolves were carried out :—

"September 6, Wednesday.—We are at it, all hands, sick and well, each man according to his measure, working at our winter's home. We are none of us in condition to brave the frost, and our fuel is nearly out. I have determined to borrow a lesson from our Esquimaux neighbors, and am turning the brig into an *igloë*.

"The sledge is to bring us moss and turf from wherever the men can scrape it. This is an excellent non-conductor; and when we get the quarter-deck

GATHERING MOSS.

well padded with it we shall have a nearly cold-proof covering. Down below we will enclose a space some eighteen feet square, and pack it from floor to ceiling with inner walls of the same material. The floor itself we are calking carefully with plaster of Paris and common paste, and will cover it when we have done with Manilla oakum a couple of inches deep, and a canvas carpet. The entrance is to be from the hold, by a low moss-lined tunnel, the *tossut* of the native huts, with as many doors and curtains to close it up as our ingenuity can devise. This is to be our apartment of all uses,—not a very large one; but we are only ten to stow away, and the closer the warmer.

"September 9, Saturday.—All hands but the carpenter and Morton are out 'mossing.' This mossing, though it has a very May-day sound, is a frightfully wintry operation. The mixed turf of willows, heaths, grasses, and moss, is frozen solid. We cannot cut it out from the beds of the snow-streams any longer, and are obliged to seek for it on the ledges of the rocks, quarrying it with crowbars and carrying it to the ship like so much stone. I would escape this labor if I could, for our party have all of them more or less scurvy in their systems, and the thermometer is often below zero. But there is no help for it. I have some eight sledge-loads more to collect before our little home can be called wind-proof: and then, if we only have snow enough to bank up against the brig's sides, I shall have no fear either for height or uniformity of temperature.

"September 10, Sunday.—'The work goes bravely on.' We have got moss enough for our roof, and something to spare for below. To-morrow we begin to strip off the outer-deck planking of the brig, and to stack it for firewood. It is cold work, hatches open and no fires going; but we saved time enough for our Sunday's exercises, though we forego its rest.

"It is twelve months to-day since I returned from

the weary foot-tramp that determined me to try the
winter search.   Things have changed since then, and
the prospect ahead is less cheery.   But I close my
pilgrim-experience of the year with devout gratitude
for the blessings it has registered, and an earnest faith
in the support it pledges for the times to come.

"September 11, Monday.—Our stock of game is
down to a mere mouthful,—six long-tailed ducks not
larger than a partridge, and three ptarmigan.   The
rabbits have not yet come to us, and the foxes seem
tired of touching our trap-baits.

"I determined last Saturday to try a novel expedient
for catching seal.   Not more than ten miles to seaward
the icebergs keep up a rude stream of broken ice and
water, and the seals resort there in scanty numbers to
breathe.   I drove out with my dogs, taking Hans
along; but we found the spot so hemmed in by loose
and fragile ice that there was no approaching it.   The
thermometer was 8°, and a light breeze increased my
difficulties.

"*Deo volente*, I will be more lucky to-morrow.   I am
going to take my long Kentucky rifle, the kayack, an
Esquimaux harpoon with its attached line and bladder,
naligeit and *awahtok*, and a pair of large snow-shoes to
boot.   My plan this time is to kneel where the ice is
unsafe, resting my weight on the broad surface of the
snow-shoes, Hans following astride of his kayack, as a
sort of life-preserver in case of breaking in.   If I am
fortunate enough to stalk within gun-range, Hans will
take to the water and secure the game before it sinks.

We will be gone for some days probably, tenting it in the open air; but our sick men—that is to say, all of us—are languishing for fresh meat."

I started with Hans and five dogs, all we could muster from our disabled pack, and reached the "Pinnacly Berg" in a single hour's run. But where was the water? where were the seal? The floes had closed,

STARTING TO HUNT.

and the crushed ice was all that told of our intended hunting-ground.

Ascending a berg, however, we could see to the north and west the dark cloud-stratus which betokens water. It ran through our old battle-ground, the "Bergy Belt,"—the labyrinth of our wanderings after the frozen party of last winter. I had not been over it since, and the feeling it gave me was any thing but joyous.

But in a couple of hours we emerged upon a plain unlimited to the eye and smooth as a billiard-table. Feathers of young frosting gave a plush-like nap to its surface, and toward the horizon dark columns of frost-smoke pointed clearly to the open water. This ice was firm enough: our experience satisfied us that it was not a very recent freezing. We pushed on without

THE ICE-PLAIN.

hesitation, cheering ourselves with the expectation of coming every minute to the seals. We passed a second ice-growth: it was not so strong as the one we had just come over, but still safe for a party like ours. On we went, at a brisker gallop, maybe for another mile, when Hans sang out, at the top of his voice, "Pusey! puseymut! seal, seal!" At the same instant the dogs bounded forward, and, as I looked up, I saw crowds of gray netsik, the rough or hispid seal of the whalers, disporting in an open sea of water.

I had hardly welcomed the spectacle when I saw that we had passed upon a new belt of ice that was obviously unsafe. To the right and left and front was one great expanse of snow-flowered ice. The nearest solid floe was a mere lump, which stood like an island in the white level. To turn was impossible: we had to keep up our gait. We urged on the dogs with whip

SEALS SPORTING.

and voice, the ice rolling like leather beneath the sledge-runners: it was more than a mile to the lump of solid ice. Fear gave to the poor beasts their utmost speed, and our voices were soon hushed to silence.

The suspense, unrelieved by action or effort, was intolerable: we knew that there was no remedy but to reach the floe, and that every thing depended upon our dogs, and our dogs alone. A moment's check would plunge the whole concern into the rapid tideway: no presence of mind or resource bodily or mental could avail us. The seals—for we were now near enough to see their expressive faces—were looking at us with that strange curiosity which seems to be their characteristic expression: we must have passed some fifty of them, breast-high out of water, mocking us by their self-complacency.

This desperate race against fate could not last: the rolling of the tough salt-water ice terrified our dogs; and when within fifty paces from the floe they paused. The left-hand runner went through: our leader "Toodlamick" followed, and in one second the entire left of the sledge was submerged. My first thought was to liberate the dogs. I leaned forward to cut poor Tood's traces, and the next minute was swimming in a little circle of pasty ice and water alongside him. Hans, dear good fellow, drew near to help me, uttering piteous expressions in broken English; but I ordered him to throw himself on his belly, with his hands and legs extended, and to make for the island by cogging himself forward with his jack-knife. In the mean time—a mere instant—I was floundering about with sledge, dogs, and lines, in confused puddle around me.

I succeeded in cutting poor Tood's lines and letting him scramble to the ice, for the poor fellow was drowning me with his piteous caresses, and made my way for the sledge; but I found that it would not buoy me, and that I had no resource but to try the circumference of the hole. Around this I paddled faithfully, the miserable ice always yielding when my hopes of a lodgement were greatest. During this process I enlarged my circle of operations to a very uncomfortable diameter, and was beginning to feel weaker after every effort. Hans meanwhile had reached the firm ice, and was on his knees, like a good Moravian, praying incoherently in English and Esquimaux; at every fresh crushing-in of the ice he would ejaculate "God!" and when I recommenced my paddling he recommenced his prayers.

I was nearly gone. My knife had been lost in cutting out the dogs; and a spare one which I carried in my trousers-pocket was so enveloped in the wet skins that I could not reach it. I owed my extrication at last to a newly-broken team-dog, who was still fast to the sledge and in struggling carried one of the runners chock against the edge of the circle. All my previous attempts to use the sledge as a bridge had failed, for it broke through, to the much greater injury of the ice. I felt that it was a last chance. I threw myself on my back, so as to lessen as much as possible my weight, and placed the nape of my neck against the rim or edge of the ice; then with caution slowly bent my leg, and, placing the ball of my moccasined foot against the sledge, I pressed steadily against the runner, listening to the half-yielding crunch of the ice beneath.

Presently I felt that my head was pillowed by the ice, and that my wet fur jumper was sliding up the surface. Next came my shoulders; they were fairly on. One more decided push, and I was launched up on the ice and safe. I reached the ice-floe, and was frictioned

by Hans with frightful zeal. We saved all the dogs;
but the sledge, kayack, tent, guns, snow-shoes, and
every thing besides, were left behind. The thermometer at 8° will keep them frozen fast in the sledge
till we can come and cut them out.

On reaching the ship, after a twelve-mile trot, I
found so much of comfort and warm welcome that I
forgot my failure. The fire was lit up, and one of our
few birds slaughtered forthwith. It is with real gratitude that I look back upon my escape, and bless the
great presiding Goodness for the very many resources
which remain to us.

"September 14, Thursday.—Tiger, our best remaining dog, the partner of poor Bruiser, was seized with a
fit, ominously resembling the last winter's curse. In
the delirium which followed his seizure, he ran into the
water and drowned himself, like a sailor with the hor-
rors. The other dogs are all doing well."

CHAPTER XXVIII.

THE ESQUIMAUX — LARCENY — THE ARREST — THE PUNISHMENT —
THE TREATY — "UNBROKEN FAITH" — MY BROTHER — RETURN
FROM A HUNT — OUR LIFE — ANOATOK — A WELCOME — TREATY
CONFIRMED.

It is, I suppose, the fortune of every one who affects
to register the story of an active life, that his record
becomes briefer and more imperfect in proportion as
the incidents press upon each other more rapidly and
with increasing excitement. The narrative is arrested
as soon as the faculties are claimed for action, and the
memory brings back reluctantly afterward those details
which, though interesting at the moment, have not reflected themselves in the result. I find that my journal
is exceedingly meagre for the period of our anxious
preparations to meet the winter, and that I have
omitted to mention the course of circumstances which
led us step by step into familiar communication with
the Esquimaux.

My last notice of this strange people, whose fortunes became afterward so closely connected with our
own, was at the time of Myouk's escape from imprison-

ment on board the brig. Although during my absence
on the attempted visit to Beechy Island, the men I had
left behind had frequent and unrestrained intercourse
with them, I myself saw no natives in Rensselaer Bay
till immediately after the departure of Petersen and his
companions. Just then, by a coincidence which convinced me how closely we had been under surveillance,
a party of three made their appearance, as if to note
for themselves our condition and resources.

Times had indeed altered with us. We had parted
with half our provisions, half our boats and sledges,
and more than half our able-bodied men. It looked
very much as if we were to lie ensconced in our ice-
battered citadel, rarely venturing to sally out for exploration or supplies. We feared nothing of course but
the want of fresh meat, and it was much less important
that our neighbors should fear us than that we should
secure from them offices of kindness. They were over-
bearing sometimes, and needed the instruction of
rebuke; but I treated them with carefully-regulated
hospitality.

When the three visitors came to us near the end
of August, I established them in a tent below deck,
with a copper lamp, a cooking-basin, and a liberal supply of slush for fuel. I left them under guard when I
went to bed at two in the morning, contentedly eating
and cooking and eating again without the promise of
an intermission. An American or a European would
have slept after such a debauch till the recognised hour
for hock and seltzer-water. But our guests managed

to elude the officer of the deck and escape unsearched. They repaid my liberality by stealing not only the lamp, boiler, and cooking-pot they had used for the feast, but Nannook also, my best dog. If the rest of my team had not been worn down by over-travel, no doubt they would have taken them all. Besides this, we discovered the next morning that they had found the buffalo-robes and India-rubber cloth which McGary had left a few days before on the ice-foot near Six-mile Ravine, and had added the whole to the spoils of their visit.

The theft of these articles embarrassed me. I was indisposed to take it as an act of hostility. Their pilferings before this had been conducted with such a superb simplicity, the detection followed by such honest explosions of laughter, that I could not help thinking they had some law of general appropriation, less removed from the Lycurgan than the Mosaic code. But it was plain at least that we were now too few to watch our property as we had done, and that our gentleness was to some extent misunderstood.

I was puzzled how to inflict punishment, but saw that I must act vigorously, even at a venture. I despatched my two best walkers, Morton and Riley, as soon as I heard of the theft of the stores, with orders to make all speed to Anoatok, and overtake the thieves, who, I thought, would probably halt there to rest. They found young Myouk making himself quite comfortable in the hut, in company with Sievu, the wife of Metek, and Aningna, the wife of Marsinga, and my buffalo-robes already tailored into kapetahs on their backs.

A continued search of the premises recovered the cooking-utensils, and a number of other things of

ANINGNA.

greater or less value that we had not missed from the brig. With the prompt ceremonial which outraged law delights in among the officials of the police everywhere, the women were stripped and tied; and then, laden with their stolen goods and as much walrus-beef besides from their own stores as would pay for their board, they were marched on the instant back to the brig.

The thirty miles was a hard walk for them; but they did not complain, nor did their constabulary guardians, who had marched thirty miles already to apprehend them. It was hardly twenty-four hours since they left the brig with their booty before they were prisoners in the hold, with a dreadful white man for keeper, who never addressed to them a word that had not all the terrors of an unintelligible reproof, and whose scowl, I flatter myself, exhibited a well-arranged variety of menacing and demoniacal expressions.

They had not even the companionship of Myouk. Him I had despatched to Metek, "head-man of Etah, and others," with the message of a melo-dramatic tyrant, to negotiate for their ransom. For five long days the women had to sigh and sing and cry in solitary converse,—their appetite continuing excellent, it should be remarked, though mourning the while a rightfully-impending doom. At last the great Metek arrived. He brought with him Ootuniah, another man of elevated social position, and quite a sledge-load of knives, tin cups, and other stolen goods, refuse of wood and scraps of iron, the sinful prizes of many covetings.

I may pass over our peace conferences and the indirect advantages which I of course derived from having the opposing powers represented in my own capital. But the splendors of our Arctic centre of civilization, with its wonders of art and science,—our "fire-death"

ordnance included,—could not all of them impress
Metek so much as the intimations he had received
of our superior physical endowments. Nomads as
they are, these people know better than all the world
besides what endurance and energy it requires to
brave the moving ice and snow-drifts. Metek thought,
no doubt, that our strength was gone with the withdrawing party : but the fact that within ten hours
after the loss of our buffalo-skins we had marched to
their hut, seized three of their culprits, and marched
them back to the brig as prisoners,—such a sixty miles'
achievement as this they thoroughly understood. It
confirmed them in the faith that the whites are and
of right ought to be everywhere the dominant tribe.

The protocol was arranged without difficulty, though
not without the accustomed number of adjournments
for festivity and repose. It abounded in protestations
of power, fearlessness, and good-will by each of the
contracting parties, which meant as much as such protestations usually do on both sides the Arctic circle.
I could give a summary of it without invading the
privacy of a diplomatic bureau, for I have notes of it
that were taken by a subordinate ; but I prefer passing
at once to the reciprocal engagements in which it
resulted.

On the part of the *Inuit*, the Esquimaux, they were
after this fashion :—

"We promise that we will not steal. We promise
we will bring you fresh meat. We promise we will
sell or lend you dogs. We will keep you company

whenever you want us, and show you where to find the game."

On the part of the *Kablunah*, the white men, the stipulation was of this ample equivalent :—

" We promise that we will not visit you with death or sorcery, nor do you any hurt or mischief whatsoever. We will shoot for you on our hunts. You shall be made welcome aboard ship. We will give you presents of needles, pins, two kinds of knife, a hoop, three bits of hard wood, some fat, an awl, and some sewing-thread; and we will trade with you of these and every thing else you want for walrus and seal-meat of the first quality."

And the closing formula might have read, if the Esquimaux political system had included reading among its qualifications for diplomacy, in this time-consecrated and, in civilized regions, veracious assurance :—

" We, the high contracting parties, pledge ourselves now and forever brothers and friends.

This treaty—which, though I have spoken of it jocosely, was really an affair of much interest to us—was ratified, with Hans and Morton as my accredited representatives, by a full assembly of the people at Etah. All our future intercourse was conducted under it. It was not solemnized by an oath; but it was never broken. We went to and fro between the villages and the brig, paid our visits of courtesy and necessity on both sides, met each other in hunting parties on the floe and the ice-foot, organized a general community of interests, and really, I believe, established some personal attachments deserving of the name. As long as we remained prisoners of the ice, we were indebted to them for invaluable counsel in relation to our hunting expeditions; and in the joint hunt we shared alike, according to their own laws.

HANGING GLACIER.

Our dogs were in one sense common property; and often have they robbed themselves to offer supplies of food to our starving teams. They gave us supplies of meat at critical periods: we were able to do as much for them. They learned to look on us only as benefactors; and, I know, mourned our departure bitterly. The greeting which they gave my brother John, when he came out after me to Etah with the

Rescue Expedition, should be of itself enough to satisfy me of this. I should be glad to borrow from his ingenuous narrative the story of his meeting with Myouk and Metek and Ootuniah, and of the almost affectionate confidence with which the maimed and sick invited his professional succor, as the representative of the elder "Docto Kayen."

"September 16, Saturday.—Back last night from a walrus-hunt. I brought in the spoil with my dogs, leaving Hans and Ohlsen to follow afoot. This Marston rifle is an admirable substitute for the primitive lance-head. It killed at the first fire. Five nights' camping out in the snow, with hard-working days between, have made me ache a little in the joints; but, strange to say, I feel better than when I left the vessel. This climate exacts heavy feeding, but it invites to muscular energy. McGary and Morton are off at Anoatok. From what I gathered on the hunt, they will find the council very willing to ratify our alliance. But they should have been at home before this.

"September 17, Sunday.—Writing by this miserable flicker of my pork-fat lamp, I can hardly steady pen, paper, or thought. All hands have rested after a heavy week's work, which has advanced us nobly in our arrangements for the winter. The season is by our tables at least three weeks earlier than the last, and every thing indicates a severe ordeal ahead of us.

"Just as we were finishing our chapter this morning in the 'Book of Ruth,' McGary and Morton came in triumphantly, pretty well worn down by their fifty miles' travel, but with good news, and a flipper of walrus that must weigh some forty pounds. Ohlsen and Hans are in too. They arrived as we were sitting down to celebrate the Anoatok ratification of our treaty of the 6th.

"It is a strange life we are leading. We are absolutely nomads, so far as there can be any thing of pastoral life in this region; and our wild encounter with the elements seems to agree with us all. Our table-talk at supper was as merry as a marriage-bell. One party was just in from a seventy-four miles' trip with the dogs; another from a foot-journey of a hundred and sixty, with five nights on the floe. Each had his story to tell; and while the story was telling some at least were projecting new expeditions. I have one myself in my mind's eye, that may peradventure cover some lines of my journal before the winter ends.

"McGary and Morton sledged it along the ice-foot completely round the Reach, and made the huts by ten o'clock the night after they left us. They found only three men, Ootuniah, our elfish rogue Myouk, and a stranger who has not been with us that we know of. It looked at first a little doubtful whether the visit was not to be misunderstood. Myouk particularly was an awkward party to negotiate with. He had been our prisoner for stealing only a little while before, and at this very moment is an escaped hostage. He was in pawn to us for a lot of walrus-beef, as indemnity for our boat. He thought naturally enough that the visit might have something more than a representative bearing on his interests. Both our men had been his jailers on board the brig, and he was the first person they met as they came upon the village.

"But when he found, by McGary's expressive pantomime, that the visit was not specially to him, and that the first appeal was to his hospitality and his fellows', his entire demeanor underwent a change. He seemed to take a new character, as if, said Morton, he had dropped a mask. He gave them welcome with unmixed cordiality, carried them to his hut, cleared away the end farthest from the opening for their reception, and filled up the fire of moss and blubber.

"The others joined him, and the attention of the whole settlement was directed at once to the wants of the visitors. Their wet boots were turned toward the fire, their woollen socks wrung out and placed on a heated stone, dry grass was padded round their feet, and the choicest cuts of walrus-liver were put into the cooking-pot. Whatever might be the infirmity of their notions of honesty, it was plain that we had no lessons to give them in the virtues of hospitable welcome. Indeed, there was a frankness and cordiality in the mode of receiving their guests, that explained the unreserve and conscious security which they showed when they first visited us.

"I could hardly guess at that time, when we saw them practising antics and grimaces among the rocks, what was the meaning of their harlequin gestures, and how they could venture afterward so fearlessly on board. I have understood the riddle since. It was a display of their powers of entertainment, intended to solicit from us a reception; and the invitation once given, all their experience and impulses assured them of safety.

"Every thing they had, cooking-utensils, snow-melting stone, scanty weapons of the chase, personal service, pledges of grateful welcome,—they gave them all.

KOTLIK, WITH OUR OWN KOLUP SOOT.

They confirmed all Metek's engagements, as if the whole favor was for them; and when our party was coming away they placed on the sledge, seemingly as a matter of course, all the meat that was left.

"September 20, Wednesday.—The natives are really acting up to contract. They are on board to-day, and I have been off with a party of them on a hunt inland. We had no great luck; the weather was against us, and there are signs of a gale. The thermometer has been two degrees below zero for the entire twenty-four hours. This is September with a vengeance!

"September 22, Friday.—I am off for the walrus-grounds with our wild allies. It will be my sixth trip. I know the country and its landmarks now as well as any of them, and can name every rock and chasm and watercourse, in night or fog, just as I could the familiar spots about the dear Old Mills where I passed my childhood.

"The weather does not promise well; but the state of our larder makes the jaunt necessary."

SECTION OF WINTER APARTMENT.

CHAPTER XXIX.

"SEPTEMBER 29, Friday.—I returned last night from
Anoatok, after a journey of much risk and exposure,
that I should have avoided but for the insuperable
obstinacy of our savage friends.

"I set out for the walrus-grounds at noon, by the
track of the 'Wind Point' of Anoatok, known to us as
Esquimaux Point. I took the light sledge, and, in
addition to the five of my available team, harnessed in
two animals belonging to the Esquimaux. Ootuniah,
Myouk, and the dark stranger accompanied me, with
Morton and Hans.

"Our sledge was overladen: I could not persuade
the Esquimaux to reduce its weight; and the consequence was that we failed to reach Force Bay in time

for a daylight crossing. To follow the indentations of the land was to make the travel long and dangerous. We trusted to the tracks of our former journeys, and pushed out on the ice. But the darkness came on us rapidly, and the snow began to drift before a heavy north wind.

"At about 10 P.M. we had lost the land, and, while driving the dogs rapidly, all of us running alongside of them, we took a wrong direction, and travelled out toward the floating ice of the Sound. There was no guide to the points of the compass; our Esquimaux were completely at fault; and the alarm of the dogs, which became every moment more manifest, extended itself to our party. The instinct of a sledge-dog makes him perfectly aware of unsafe ice, and I know nothing more subduing to a man than the warnings of an unseen peril conveyed by the instinctive fears of the lower animals.

"We had to keep moving, for we could not camp in the gale, that blew around us so fiercely that we could scarcely hold down the sledge. But we moved with caution, feeling our way with the tent-poles, which I distributed among the party for the purpose. A murmur had reached my ear for some time in the cadences of the storm, steadier and deeper, I thought, than the tone of the wind: on a sudden it struck me that I heard the noise of waves, and that we must be coming close on the open water. I had hardly time for the hurried order, 'Turn the dogs,' before a wreath of wet frost-smoke swept over us, and the sea showed itself, with a great fringe of foam, hardly a quarter of a mile ahead. We could now guess our position and its dangers. The ice was breaking up before the storm, and it was not certain that even a direct retreat in the face of the gale would extricate us. I determined to run to the south for Godsend Island. The floes were heavy in that direction, and less likely to give way in a northerly gale. It was at best a dreary venture.

"The surf-line kept encroaching on us till we could feel the ice undulating under our feet. Very soon it began to give way. Lines of hummocks rose before us, and we had to run the gauntlet between them as they closed. Escaping these, we toiled over the crushed fragments that lay between them and the shore, stumbling over the projecting crags, or sinking in the water that rose among them. It was too dark to see the island which we were steering for; but the black loom of a lofty cape broke the line of the horizon and served as a landmark. The dogs, relieved from the burden of carrying us, moved with more spirit. We began to draw near the shore, the ice-storm still raging behind us. But our difficulties were only reaching their climax. We knew as icemen that the access to the land-ice from the floe was, under the most favoring circumstances, both toilsome and dangerous. The rise and fall of the tides always breaks up the ice at the margin of the ice-belt in a tangle of irregular, half-floating masses; and these were now surging under the energies of the gale. It was pitchy dark. I per-

suaded Ootuniah, the eldest of the Esquimaux, to
have a tent-pole lashed horizontally across his shoulders. I gave him the end of a line, which I had fastened at the other end round my waist. The rest of
the party followed him.

"As I moved ahead, feeling round me for a practicable way, Ootuniah followed; and when a table of
ice was found large enough, the others would urge
forward the dogs, pushing the sledge themselves, or
clinging to it, as the moment prompted. We had acci-
dents of course, some of them menacing for the time,
but none to be remembered for their consequences;
and at last one after another succeeded in clambering
after me upon the ice-foot, driving the dogs before
them.

"Providence had been our guide. The shore on
which we landed was Anoatok, not four hundred yards
from the familiar Esquimaux homestead. With a
shout of joy, each man in his own dialect, we hastened
to the 'wind-loved spot;' and in less than an hour, our
lamps burning cheerfully, we were discussing a famous
stew of walrus-steaks, none the less relished for an
unbroken ice-walk of forty-eight miles and twenty halt-
less hours.

"When I reached the hut, our stranger Esquimaux,
whose name we found to be Awahtok, or 'Seal-bladder
float,' was striking a fire from two stones, one a plain
piece of angular milky quartz, held in the right hand,
the other apparently an oxide of iron. He struck
them together after the true tinder-box fashion, throw-

ing a scanty supply of sparks on a tinder composed of
the silky down of the willow-catkins, (*S. lanata*,) which
he held on a lump of dried moss.

"The hut or igloë at Anoatok was a single rude
elliptical apartment, built not unskilfully of stone, the
outside lined with sods. At its farther end a rude
platform, also of stone, was lifted about a foot above
the entering floor. The roof formed something of a
curve: it was composed of flat stones, remarkably large
and heavy, arranged so as to overlap each other, but
apparently without any intelligent application of the
principle of the arch. The height of this cave-like
abode barely permitted one to sit upright. Its length
was eight feet, its breadth seven feet, and an expansion
of the tunnelled entrance made an appendage of perhaps two feet more.

"The true winter entrance is called the *tossut*. It
is a walled tunnel, ten feet long, and so narrow that a
man can hardly crawl along it. It opens outside below
the level of the igloë, into which it leads by a gradual
ascent.

"Time had done its work on the igloë of Anoatok,
as among the palatial structures of more southern de-
serts. The entire front of the dome had fallen in,
closing up the tossut, and forcing us to enter at the solitary window above it. The breach was large enough
to admit a sledge-team; but our Arctic comrades showed
no anxiety to close it up. Their clothes saturated with
the freezing water of the floes, these iron men gathered
themselves round the blubber-fire and steamed away

in apparent comfort. The only departure from their practised routine, which the bleak night and open roof seemed to suggest to them, was that they did not strip themselves naked before coming into the hut, and hang up their vestments in the air to dry, like a votive offering to the god of the sea.

"Their kitchen-implements were even more simple than our own. A rude saucer-shaped cup of seal-skin, to gather and hold water in, was

SEAL-SKIN CUP.

the solitary utensil that could be dignified as table-furniture. A flat stone, a fixture of the hut, supported by other stones just above the shoulder-blade of a wal-

SNOW-MELTER, ANOATOK.

rus,—the stone slightly inclined, the cavity of the bone large enough to hold a moss-wick and some blubber;— a square block of snow was placed on the stone, and, as the hot smoke circled round it, the seal-skin saucer caught the water that dripped from the edge. They had no vessel for boiling; what they did not eat raw they baked upon a hot stone. A solitary coil of walrus-line, fastened to a movable lance-head, (noon-ghak,) with the well-worn and well-soaked clothes on their backs, completed the inventory of their effects.

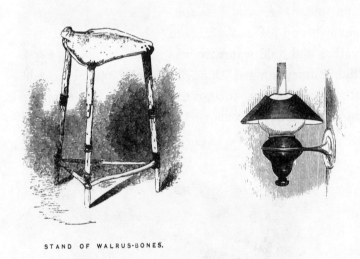

STAND OF WALRUS-BONES.

"We felt that we were more civilized than our poor cousins, as we fell to work making ourselves comfortable after our own fashion. The dais was scraped, and its accumulated filth of years removed; a canvas tent was folded double over the dry, frozen stones, our buffalo-bag spread over this, and dry socks and moccasins were drawn from under our wet overclothes. My copper lamp, a true Berzelius Argand, invaluable for short journeys, soon flamed with a cheerful fire. The soup-pot, the walrus-steak, and the hot coffee were the next things to be thought of; and, while these were getting ready, an India-rubber floor-cloth was fastened over the gaping entrance of the cave.

"During our long march and its series of ice-fights we had taken care to manifest no weariness, and had, indeed, borne both Ootuniah and Myouk at times upon our shoulders. We showed no signs either of cold; so that all this preparation and rich store of appliances could not be attributed by the Esquimaux to effeminacy or inferior power. I could see that they were profoundly impressed with a conviction of our superiority, the last feeling which the egotistical self-conceit of savage life admits.

"I felt sure now that they were our more than sworn friends. They sang 'Amna Ayah' for us, their rude, monotonous song, till our ears cracked with the discord; and improvised a special eulogistic chant,

Am - na - yah, Am - na - yah, Am - na - yah, Am - na - yah,

which they repeated over and over again with laughable gravity of utterance, subsiding always into the *refrain* of '*Nalegak! nalegak! nalegak-soak!*' 'Captain! captain! great captain!' They nicknamed and adopted all of us as members of their fraternity, with grave and abundant form; reminding me through all their

mummery, solemn and ludicrous at once, of the analogous ceremonies of our North American Indians.

"The chant and the feed and the ceremony all completed, Hans, Morton, and myself crawled feet-foremost
into our buffalo-bag, and Ootuniah, Awahtok, and

PARHELIA, DRAWN BY MR. SONTAG.

Myouk flung themselves outside the skin between us.
The last I heard of them or any thing else was the
renewed chorus of 'Nalegak! nalegak! nalegak-soak!'
mingling itself sleepily in my dreams with school-boy
memories of Aristophanes and The Frogs. I slept
eleven hours.

"They were up long before us, and had breakfasted

on raw meat cut from a large joint, which lay, without regard to cleanliness, among the deposits on the floor of the igloë. Their mode of eating was ingeniously active. They cut the meat in long strips, introduced one end into the mouth, swallowed it as far as the powers of deglutition would allow, and then, cutting off the protruding portion close to the lips, prepared themselves for a second mouthful. It was really a feat of address: those of us who tried it failed awkwardly; and yet I have seen infants in the mother's hood, not two years old, who managed to perform it without accident."

I pass over the story of the hunt that followed. It had nothing to distinguish it from many others, and I find in my journal of a few days later the fresh narrative of Morton, after he had seen one for the first time.

My next extracts show the progress of our winter arrangements.

"September 30, Saturday.—We have been clearing up on the ice. Our system for the winter has not the dignity of a year ago. We have no Butler Storehouse, no Medary, no Fern Rock, with their appliances. We are ten men in a casemate, with all our energies concentrated against the enemy outside.

"Our beef-house is now a pile of barrels holding our water-soaked beef and pork. Flour, beans, and dried apples make a quadrangular blockhouse on the floe: from one corner of it rises our flagstaff, lighting up the dusky gray with its red and white ensign, only on

Sunday giving place to the Henry Grinnell flag, of happy memories.

"From this, along an avenue that opens abeam of the brig,—New London Avenue, named after McGary's town at home,—are our boats and square cordage. Outside of all these is a magnificent hut of barrel-frames and snow, to accommodate our Esquimaux visitors; the only thing about it exposed to hazard being the tempting woodwork. What remains to complete our camp-plot is the rope barrier that is to mark out our little curtilage around the vessel: this, when finished, is to be the dividing-line between us and the rest of mankind.

"There is something in the simplicity of all this, 'simplex munditiis,' which might commend itself to the most rigorous taste. Nothing is wasted on ornament.

"October 4, Wednesday.—I sent Hans and Hickey two days ago out to the hunting-ice, to see if the natives have had any luck with the walrus. They are back to night with bad news,—no meat, no Esquimaux. These strange children of the snow have made a mysterious flitting. Where or how, it is hard to guess, for they have no sledges. They cannot have travelled very far; and yet they have such unquiet impulses, that, once on the track, no civilized man can say where they will bring up.

"Ohlsen had just completed a sledge, fashioned like the Smith Sound *kommetik*, with an improved curvature of the runners. It weighs only twenty-four

J. White.

Engraved at J.M.Butler's establishment 84 Chestnut S^t

J.C.McRae.

BEAR HUNT.

pounds, and, though I think it too short for light draught, it is just the article our Etah neighbors would delight in for their land-portages. I intended it for them, as a great price for a great stock of walrus-meat: but the other parties to the bargain have flown.

"October 5, Thursday.—We are nearly out of fresh meat again, one rabbit and three ducks being our sum total. We have been on short allowance for several days. What vegetables we have—the dried apples and peaches, and pickled cabbage—have lost much of their anti-scorbutic virtue by constant use. Our spices are all gone. Except four small bottles of horse-radish, our carte is comprised in three lines—bread, beef, pork.

"I must be off after these Esquimaux. They certainly have meat, and wherever they have gone we can follow. Once upon their trail, our hungry instincts will not risk being baffled. I will stay only long enough to complete my latest root-beer brewage. Its basis is the big crawling willow, the miniature giant of our Arctic forests, of which we laid in a stock some weeks ago. It is quite pleasantly bitter, and I hope to get it fermenting in the deck-house without extra fuel, by heat from below.

"October 7, Saturday.—Lively sensation, as they say in the land of olives and champagne. 'Nannook, nannook!'—'A bear, a bear!'—Hans and Morton in a breath!

"To the scandal of our domestic regulations, the guns were all impracticable. While the men were loading and capping anew, I seized my pillow-companion six-shooter, and ran on deck. A medium-sized bear, with a four months' cub, was in active warfare with our dogs. They were hanging on her skirts, and she with wonderful alertness was picking out one victim after another, snatching him by the nape of the neck, and flinging him many feet or rather yards, by a barely perceptible movement of her head.

"Tudla, our master dog, was already *hors de combat:* he had been tossed twice. Jenny, just as I emerged from the hatch, was making an extraordinary somerset of some eight fathoms, and alighted senseless. Old Whitey, stanch but not bear-wise, had been the first in the battle: he was yelping in helplessness on the snow.

"It seemed as if the controversy was adjourned: and Nannook evidently thought so; for she turned off to our beef-barrels, and began in the most unconcerned manner to turn them over and nose out their fatness. She was apparently as devoid of fear as any of the bears in the stories of old Barentz and the Spitzbergen voyagers.

"I lodged a pistol-ball in the side of the cub. At once the mother placed her little one between her hind-legs, and, shoving it along, made her way behind the beef-house. Mr. Ohlsen wounded her as she went with my Webster rifle; but she scarcely noticed it. She tore down by single efforts of her forearms the barrels of frozen beef which made the triple walls of the storehouse, mounted the rubbish, and, snatching up a half-barrel of herrings, carried it down by her teeth, and was making off. It was time to close, I thought. Going up within half pistol-range, I gave her six buckshot. She dropped, but instantly rose, and, getting her cub into its former position, moved off once more.

"This time she would really have escaped but for the admirable tactics of our new recruits from the Esquimaux. The dogs of Smith's Sound are educated more thoroughly than any of their more southern brethren. Next to the walrus, the bear is the staple of diet to the north, and, except the fox, supplies the most important element of the wardrobe. Unlike the dogs we had brought with us from Baffin's Bay, these were trained not to attack, but to embarrass. They ran in circles round the bear, and when pursued would keep ahead with regulated gait, their comrades effecting a diversion at the critical moment by a nip at her hind-quarters. This was done so systematically and with so little seeming excitement as to strike every one on board. I have seen bear-dogs elsewhere that had been drilled to relieve each other in the *melée* and avoid the direct assault; but here, two dogs without even a demonstration of attack would put themselves before the path of the animal, and, retreating right and left, lead him into a profitless pursuit that checked his advance completely.

"The poor animal was still backing out, yet still fighting, carrying along her wounded cub, embarrassed by the dogs yet gaining distance from the brig, when Hans and myself threw in the odds in the shape of a couple of rifle-balls. She staggered in front of her young one, faced us in deathlike defiance, and only sank when pierced by six more bullets.

"We found nine balls in skinning her body. She was of medium size, very lean, and without a particle of food in her stomach. Hunger must have caused her boldness. The net weight of the cleansed carcass was three hundred pounds; that of the entire animal, six hundred and fifty; her length, but seven feet eight inches.

"Bears in this lean condition are much the most palatable food. The impregnation of fatty oil through the cellular tissue makes a well-fed bear nearly uneatable. The flesh of a famished beast, although less nutritious as a fuel diet, is rather sweet and tender than otherwise.

"The little cub is larger than the adjective implies. She was taller than a dog, and weighs one hundred and fourteen pounds. Like Morton's bear in Kennedy's Channel, she sprang upon the corpse of her mother, and raised a woful lamentation over her wounds. She repelled my efforts to noose her with great ferocity; but at last, completely muzzled with a line fastened by a running knot between her jaws and the back of her head, she moved off to the brig amid the clamor of the dogs. We have her now chained alongside, but snarling and snapping constantly, evidently suffering from her wound.

"Of the eight dogs who took part in this passage of arms, only one—'Sneak,' as the men call him, 'Young

Whitey,' as he figures in this journal—lost a flower from his chaplet. But two of the rest escaped without a grip.

"Strange to say, in spite of the powerful flings which they were subjected to in the fight, not a dog suffers seriously. I expected, from my knowledge of the hugging propensity of the plantigrades, that the animal would rear, or at least use her forearm; but she invariably seized the dogs with her teeth, and, after disposing of them for the time, abstained from following up the advantage. The Esquimaux assert that this is the habit of the hunted bear. One of our Smith Sound dogs, 'Jack,' made no struggle when he was seized, but was flung, with all his muscles relaxed, I hardly dare to say how far: the next instant he rose and renewed the attack. The Esquimaux both of Proven and of this country say that the dogs soon learn this 'possum-playing' habit. Jack was an old bear-dog.

"The bear seems to be more ferocious as he increases his latitude, or more probably as he recedes from the hunting-fields.

"At Oominak, last winter, (1852,) an Esquimaux and his son were nearly killed by a bear that had housed himself in an iceberg. They attacked him with the lance, but he turned on them and worsted them badly before making his escape.

"But the continued pursuit of man seems to have exerted already a modifying influence upon the ursine character in South Greenland; at all events, the bears there never attack, and even in self-defence seldom inflict injury upon the hunter. Many instances have occurred where they have defended themselves and even charged after being wounded, but in none of them was life lost. I have myself shot as many as a dozen bears near at hand, and never but once received a charge in return.

"I heard another adventure from the Danes as occurring in 1834 :—

"A stout Esquimaux, an assistant to the cooper of Upernavik,—not a Christian, but a stout, manly savage,—fired at a she-bear, and the animal closed on the instant of receiving the ball. The man flung himself on the ground, putting forward his arm to protect his head, but lying afterward perfectly motionless. The beast was taken in. She gave the arm a bite or two, but, finding her enemy did not move, she retired a few paces and sat upon her haunches to watch. But she did not watch as carefully as she should have done, for the hunter adroitly reloaded his rifle and killed her with the second shot.

"October 8, Sunday.—When I was out in the Advance, with Captain De Haven, I satisfied myself that it was a vulgar prejudice to regard the liver of the bear as poisonous. I ate of it freely myself, and succeeded in making it a favorite dish with the mess. But I find to my cost that it may sometimes be more savory than safe. The cub's liver was my supper last night, and to-day I have the symptoms of poison in full measure—vertigo, diarrhœa, and their concomitants."

I may mention, in connection with the fact which I have given from my journal, that I repeated the experiment several times afterward, and sometimes, but not always, with the same result. I remember once, near the Great Glacier, all our party sickened after feeding on the liver of a bear that we had killed; and a few weeks afterward, when we were tempted into a similar indulgence, we were forced to undergo the same penance. The animal in both cases was old and fat. The dogs ate to repletion, without injury.

Another article of diet, less inviting at first, but which I found more innocuous, was the rat. We had failed to exterminate this animal by our varied and perilous efforts of the year before, and a well-justified fear forbade our renewing the crusade. It was marvellous, in a region apparently so unfavorable to reproduction, what a perfect warren we soon had on board. Their impudence and address increased with their numbers. It became impossible to stow any thing below decks. Furs, woollens, shoes, specimens of natural history, every thing we disliked to lose, however little valuable to them, was gnawed into and destroyed. They harbored among the men's bedding in the forecastle, and showed such boldness in fight and such dexterity in dodging missiles that they were tolerated at last as inevitable nuisances. Before the winter ended, I avenged our griefs by decimating them for my private table. I find in my journal of the 10th of October an anecdote that illustrates their boldness:—

"We have moved every thing movable out upon the

ice, and, besides our dividing moss wall between our
sanctum and the forecastle, we have built up a rude
barrier of our iron sheathing to prevent these abomi-
nable rats from gnawing through. It is all in vain.
They are everywhere already, under the stove, in the
steward's lockers, in our cushions, about our beds. If I
was asked what, after darkness and cold and scurvy,
are the three besetting curses of our Arctic sojourn, I
should say, RATS, RATS, RATS. A mother-rat bit my
finger to the bone last Friday, as I was intruding my
hand into a bear-skin mitten which she had chosen as
a homestead for her little family. I withdrew it of
course with instinctive courtesy; but among them they
carried off the mitten before I could suck the finger.

"Last week, I sent down Rhina, the most intelligent
dog of our whole pack, to bivouac in their citadel forward: I thought she might at least be able to defend
herself against them, for she had distinguished herself
in the bear-hunt. She slept very well for a couple of
hours on a bed she had chosen for herself on the top
of some iron spikes. But the rats could not or would
not forego the horny skin about her paws; and they
gnawed her feet and nails so ferociously that we drew
her up yelping and vanquished."

Before I pass from these intrepid and pertinacious
visitors, let me add that on the whole I am personally
much their debtor. Through the long winter night,
Hans used to beguile his lonely hours of watch by
shooting them with the bow and arrow. The repug-
nance of my associates to share with me the table

luxury of "such small deer" gave me the frequent
advantage of a fresh-meat soup, which contributed no
doubt to my comparative immunity from scurvy.   I
had only one competitor in the dispensation of this
entremet, or rather one companion; for there was an
abundance for both.   It was a fox:—we caught and
domesticated him late in the winter; but the scantiness
of our resources, and of course his own, soon instructed
him in all the antipathies of a terrier.   He had only
one fault as a rat-catcher: he would never catch a
second till he had eaten the first.

At the date of these entries the Arctic hares had
not ceased to be numerous about our harbor.   They
were very beautiful, as white as swans' down, with a
crescent of black marking the ear-tips.   They feed on
the bark and catkins of the willow, and affect the
stony sides of the worn-down rocks, where they find
protection from the wind and snow-drifts.   They do not
burrow like our hares at home, but squat in crevices or
under large stones.   Their average weight is about
nine pounds.   They would have entered largely into
our diet-list but for our Esquimaux dogs, who regarded
them with relishing appetite.   Parry found the hare at
Melville Island, in latitude 75°; but we have traced it
from Littleton Island as far north as 79° 08', and its
range probably extends still farther toward the Pole.
Its structure and habits enable it to penetrate the
snow-crusts, and obtain food where the reindeer and
the musk-ox perish in consequence of the glazed covering of their feeding-grounds.

"October 11, Wednesday.—There is no need of looking at the thermometer and comparing registers, to
show how far this season has advanced beyond its
fellow of last year. The ice-foot is more easily read,
and quite as certain.

THE ICE-FOOT CANOPY.

"The under part of it is covered now with long sta-
lactitic columns of ice, unlike the ordinary icicle in
shape, for they have the characteristic bulge of the
carbonate-of-lime stalactite. They look like the fantastic columns hanging from the roof of a frozen
temple, the dark recess behind them giving all the

effect of a grotto.   There is one that brings back to me saddened memories of Elephanta and the merry friends that bore me company under its rock-chiselled portico.   The fig-trees and the palms, and the gallant major's curries and his old India ale, are wanting in the picture.   Sometimes again it is a canopy fringed with gems in the moonlight.   Nothing can be purer or more beautiful.

"The ice has begun to fasten on our brig: I have called a consultation of officers to determine how she may be best secured.

"October 13, Friday.—The Esquimaux have not been near us, and it is a puzzle of some interest where they have retreated to.   Wherever they are, there must be our hunting-grounds, for they certainly have not changed their quarters to a more destitute region. I have sent Morton and Hans to-day to track them out if they can.   They carry a hand-sledge with them, Ohlsen's last manufacture, ride with the dog-sledge as far as Anoatok, and leave the old dogs of our team there.   From that point they are to try a device of my own.   We have a couple of dogs that we got from these same Esquimaux, who are at least as instinctive as their former masters.   One of these they are to let run, holding the other by a long leash.   I feel confident that the free dog will find the camping-ground, and I think it probable the other will follow.   I thought of tying the two together; but it would embarrass their movements, and give them something to occupy their minds besides the leading object of their mission.

"October 14, Saturday.—Mr. Wilson and Hickey reported last night a wolf at the meat-house. Now, the meat-house is a thing of too much worth to be left to casualty, and a wolf might incidentally add some freshness of flavor to its contents. So I went out in all haste with the Marston rifle, but without my mittens and with only a single cartridge. The metal burnt my hands, as metal is apt to do at fifty degrees below the point of freezing; but I got a somewhat rapid shot. I hit—— one of our dogs, a truant from Morton's team; luckily a flesh-wound only, for he is too good a beast to lose. I could have sworn he was a wolf."

There is so much of identical character between our Arctic dogs and wolves, that I am inclined to agree with Mr. Broderip, who in the "Zoological Recreations" assigns to them a family origin. The oblique position of the wolf's eye is not uncommon among the dogs of my team. I have a slut, one of the tamest and most affectionate of the whole of them, who has the long legs, and compact body, and drooping tail, and wild, scared expression of the eye, which some naturalists have supposed to characterize the wolf alone. When domesticated early,—and it is easy to domesticate him,—the wolf follows and loves you like a dog. That they are fond of a loose foot proves nothing: many of our pack will run away for weeks into the wilderness of ice; yet they cannot be persuaded when they come back to inhabit the kennel we have built for them only a hundred yards off. They

crouch around for the companionship of men. Both
animals howl in unison alike: the bell at the settlements of South Greenland always starts them. Their
footprint is the same, at least in Smith's Sound. Dr.
Richardson's remark to the contrary made me observe
the fact that our northern dogs leave the same "spread
track" of the toes when running, though not perhaps
as well marked as the wolf's.

The old proverb, and the circumstance of the wolf
having sometimes carried off an Esquimaux dog, has
been alluded to by the editors of the "Diffusion of
Knowledge Library." But this too is inconclusive, for
the proverb is false. It is not quite a month ago since
I found five of our dogs gluttonizing on the carcasses
of their dead companions who had been thrown out
on a rubbish-heap; and I have seen pups only two
months old risk an indigestion by overfeeding on their
twin brethren who had preceded them in a like im-
prudence.

Nor is there any thing in the supposed difference of
strength. The Esquimaux dog of Smith's Sound encounters the wolf fearlessly and with success. The
wolves of Northern America never venture near the
huts; but it is well known that when they have been
chasing the deer or the moose, the dogs have come up
as rivals in the hunt, beaten them off, and appropriated
the prey to themselves.

"October 16, Monday.—I have been wearied and
vexed for half a day by a vain chase after some

bear-tracks. There was a fox evidently following them, (*C. lagopus.*)"

There are fables about the relation between these two animals which I once thought my observations had confirmed. They are very often found together: the bear striding on ahead with his prey; the fox behind gathering in the crumbs as they fall; and I have often seen the parasite licking at the traces of a wounded seal which his champion had borne off over the snow. The story is that the two hunt in couples. I doubt this now, though it is certain that the inferior animal rejoices in his association with the superior, at least for the profits, if not the sympathy it brings to him. I once wounded a bear when I was out with Morton during our former voyage, and followed him for twelve miles over the ice. A miserable little fox travelled close behind his patron, and licked up the blood wherever he lay down. The bear at last made the water; and, as we returned from our fruitless chase, we saw the fox running at full speed along the edge of the thin ice, as if to rejoin him. It is a mistake to suppose he cannot swim: he does, and that boldly.

"October 19, Thursday.—Our black dog Erebus has come back to the brig. Morton has perhaps released him, but he has more probably broken loose.

"I have no doubt Morton is making the best of his way after the Esquimaux. These trips are valuable to us, even when they fail of their immediate object. They keep the natives in wholesome respect for us.

We are careful to impress them with our physical
prowess, and avoid showing either fatigue or cold when
we are travelling together. I could not help being
amused some ten days ago with the complacent manner
of Myouk, as he hooked himself to me for support after
I had been walking for thirty miles ahead of the sledge.
The fellow was worth four of me; but he let me carry
him almost as far as the land-ice.

THE BRIG IN HER SECOND WINTER.

"We have been completing our arrangements for
raising the brig. The heavy masses of ice that adhere
to her in the winter make her condition dangerous at
seasons of low tide. Her frame could not sustain the
pressure of such a weight. Our object, therefore, has
been to lift her mechanically above her line of flotation,
and let her freeze in on a sort of ice-dock; so that the

ice around her as it sinks may take the bottom and hold her up clear of the danger. We have detached four of the massive beams that were intended to resist the lateral pressure of nips, and have placed them as shores, two on each side of the vessel, opposite the channels. Brooks has rigged a crab or capstan on the floe, and has passed the chain cable under the keel at four bearing-points. As these are hauled in by the crab and the vessel rises, the shores are made to take hold under heavy cleats spiked below the bulwarks, and in this manner to sustain her weight.

"We made our first trial of the apparatus to-day. The chains held perfectly, and had raised the brig nearly three feet, when away went one of our chain-slings, and she fell back of course to her more familiar bearings. We will repeat the experiment to-morrow, using six chains, two at each line of stress.

"October 21, Saturday.—Hard at it still, slinging chains and planting shores. The thermometer is too near zero for work like this. We swaddle our feet in old cloth, and guard our hands with fur mits; but the cold iron bites through them all.

"6.30 P.M.—Morton and Hans are in, after tracking the Esquimaux to the lower settlement of Etah. I cannot give their report to-night: the poor fellows are completely knocked up by the hardships of their march. Hans, who is always careless of powder and fire-arms,— a trait which I have observed among both the American and the Oriental savages,—exploded his powder-flask while attempting to kindle a tinder-fire. The explosion has risked his hand. I have dressed it, extracting several pieces of foreign matter and poulticing it in yeast and charcoal. Morton has frostbitten both his heels; I hope not too severely, for the indurated skin of the heel makes it a bad region for suppuration. But they bring us two hundred and seventy pounds of walrus-meat and a couple of foxes. This supply, with what we have remaining of our two bears, must last us till the return of daylight allows us to join the natives in their hunts.

"The light is fast leaving us. The sun has ceased to reach the vessel. The northeastern headlands or their southern faces up the fiords have still a warm yellow tint, and the pinnacles of the icebergs far out on the floes are lighted up at noonday: but all else is dark shadow."

OUR GREENLAND SLEDGES.

CHAPTER XXX.

Journey of Morton and Hans.

MORTON reached the huts beyond Anoatok upon the
fourth day after leaving the brig.

The little settlement is inside the northeastern
islands of Hartstene Bay, about five miles from Gray's
Fiord, and some sixty-five or seventy from our brig.
The slope on which it stands fronts the southwest, and
is protected from the north and northeast by a rocky
island and the hills of the mainland.

There were four huts; but two of them are in ruins.
They were all of them the homes of families only four
winters ago. Of the two which are still habitable,
Myouk, his father, mother, brother, and sister occupied
one; and Awahtok and Ootuniah, with their wives and
three young ones, the other. The little community
had lost two of its members by death since the spring.

They received Morton and his companion with
404

much kindness, giving them water to drink, rubbing their feet, drying their moccasins, and the like. The women, who did this with something of the good-wife's air of prerogative, seemed to have toned down much of

PORTRAIT OF OOTUNIAH.

the rudeness which characterized the bachelor settlement at Anoatok. The lamps were cheerful and smokeless, and the huts much less filthy. Each had its two lamp-fires constantly burning, with a framework of bone hooks and walrus-line above them for drying the wet clothes of the household. Except a few dog-skins,

which are used as a support to the small of the back,
the dais was destitute of sleeping-accommodations
altogether: a single walrus-hide was spread out for
Morton and Hans. The hut had the usual tossut, at
least twelve feet long,—very low, straight, and level,
until it reached the inner part of the chamber, when
it rose abruptly by a small hole, through which with

ETAH, AWAHTOK'S HUT.

some squeezing was the entrance into the true apartment. Over this entrance was the rude window, with
its scraped seal-intestine instead of glass, heavily coated
with frost of course; but a small eye-hole commanding
the bay enabled the in-dwellers to peep out and speak
or call to any who were outside. A smoke-hole passed
through the roof.

When all the family, with Morton and Hans, were
gathered together, the two lamps in full blaze and the

narrow hole of entrance covered by a flat stone, the
heat became insupportable. Outside, the thermometer
stood at 30° below zero; within, 90° above: a difference of one hundred and twenty degrees.

The vermin were not as troublesome as in the
Anoatok dormitory, the natives hanging their clothing
over the lamp-frames, and lying down to sleep perfectly naked, with the exception of a sort of T bandage,
as surgeons call it, of seal-skin, three inches wide, worn
by the women as a badge of their sex, and supported
by a mere strip around the hips.

After sharing the supper of their hosts,—that is to
say, after disposing of six frozen auks apiece,—the
visitors stretched themselves out and passed the night
in unbroken perspiration and slumber. It was evident
from the meagreness of the larder that the hunters of
the family had work to do; and from some signs, which
did not escape the sagacity of Morton, it was plain that
Myouk and his father had determined to seek their
next dinner upon the floes. They were going upon a
walrus-hunt; and Morton, true to the mission with
which I had charged him, invited himself and Hans to
be of the party.

I have not yet described one of these exciting incidents of Esquimaux life. Morton was full of the one
he witnessed; and his account of it when he came back
was so graphic that I should be glad to escape from
the egotism of personal narrative by giving it in his
own words. Let me first, however, endeavor to describe the animal.

His portrait on a neighboring page is truer to nature
than any I have seen in the books: the specimens in
the museums of collectors are imperfect, on account of
the drying of the skin of the face against the skull.
The head of the walrus has not the characteristic oval
of the seal: on the contrary, the frontal bone is so
covered as to present a steep descent to the eyes and
a square, blocked-out aspect to the upper face. The
muzzle is less protruding than the seal's, and the cheeks
and lips are completely masked by the heavy quill-like

ESQUIMAUX SLEDGE.

bristles. Add to this the tusks as a garniture to the
lower face; and you have for the walrus a grim, ferocious aspect peculiarly his own. I have seen him with
tusks nearly thirty inches long; his body not less than
eighteen feet. When of this size he certainly reminds
you of the elephant more than any other living
monster.

The resemblance of the walrus to man has been
greatly overrated. The notion occurs in our systematic
treatises, accompanied with the suggestion that this
animal may have represented the merman and mer-

maid. The square, blocked-out head which I have noticed, effectually destroys the resemblance to humanity when distant, and the colossal size does the same when near. Some of the seals deserve the distinction much more: the size of the head, the regularity of the facial oval, the droop of the shoulders, even the movements of this animal, whether singly or in group, remind you strikingly of man.

The party which Morton attended upon their walrus-hunt had three sledges. One was to be taken to a cache in the neighborhood; the other two dragged at a quick run toward the open water, about ten miles off to the southwest. They had but nine dogs to these two sledges, one man only riding, the others running by turns. As they neared the new ice, and where the black wastes of mingled cloud and water betokened the open sea, they would from time to time remove their hoods and listen intently for the animal's voice.

ESQUIMAUX WHIP,
WOOD AND BONE PIECED.

After a while Myouk became convinced, from signs

or sounds, or both,—for they were inappreciable by
Morton,—that the walrus were waiting for him in a
small space of recently-open water that was glazed over
with a few days' growth of ice; and, moving gently
on, they soon heard the characteristic bellow of a bull
awuk. The walrus, like some of the higher order of
beings to which he has been compared, is fond of his
own music, and will lie for hours listening to himself.
His vocalization is something between the mooing of a

WATCHING AT THE WALRUS-HOLE.

cow and the deepest baying of a mastiff: very round
and full, with its barks or detached notes repeated
rather quickly seven to nine times in succession.

The party now formed in single file, following in
each other's steps; and, guided by an admirable knowledge of ice-topography, wound behind hummocks and
ridges in a serpentine approach toward a group of
pond-like discolorations, recently-frozen ice-spots, but
surrounded by firmer and older ice.

When within half a mile of these, the line broke,
and each man crawled toward a separate pool; Morton

on his hands and knees following Myouk. In a few
minutes the walrus were in sight. They were five in
number, rising at intervals through the ice in a body,
and breaking it up with an explosive puff that might
have been heard for miles. Two large grim-looking
males were conspicuous as the leaders of the group.

MYOUK

Now for the marvel of the craft. When the walrus
is above water, the hunter is flat and motionless; as he
begins to sink, alert and ready for a spring. The animal's head is hardly below the water-line before every
man is in a rapid run; and again, as if by instinct,
before the beast returns, all are motionless behind protecting knolls of ice. They seem to know beforehand

not only the time he will be absent, but the very spot
at which he will reappear.   In this way, hiding and
advancing by turns, Myouk, with Morton at his heels,
has reached a plate of thin ice, hardly strong enough
to bear them, at the very brink of the water-pool the
walrus are curvetting in.

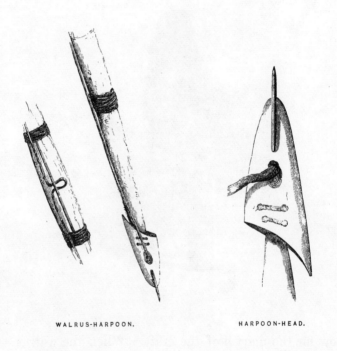

WALRUS-HARPOON.   HARPOON-HEAD.

Myouk, till now phlegmatic, seems to waken with
excitement.   His coil of walrus-hide, a well-trimmed
line of many fathoms' length, is lying at his side.   He
fixes one end of it in an iron barb, and fastens this
loosely by a socket upon a shaft of unicorn's horn: the
other end is already looped, or, as sailors would say,

"doubled in a bight." It is the work of a moment.
He has grasped the harpoon: the water is in motion. Puffing with pent-up respiration, the walrus is
within a couple of fathoms, close before him. Myouk
rises slowly; his right arm thrown back, the left flat
at his side. The walrus looks about him, shaking the
water from his crest: Myouk throws up his left arm;

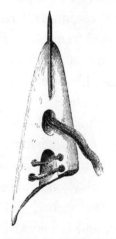

NOZZLE OF HARPOON-HEAD.   HARPOON-HEAD, FREE.

and the animal, rising breast-high, fixes one look before
he plunges. It has cost him all that curiosity can
cost: the harpoon is buried under his left flipper.

Though the awuk is down in a moment, Myouk is
running at desperate speed from the scene of his victory, paying off his coil freely, but clutching the end
by its loop. He seizes as he runs a small stick of
bone, rudely pointed with iron, and by a sudden

movement drives it into the ice: to this he secures his line, pressing it down close to the ice-surface with his feet.

Now comes the struggle. The hole is dashed in mad commotion with the struggles of the wounded beast; the line is drawn tight at one moment, the next relaxed: the hunter has not left his station. There is a crash of the ice; and rearing up through it are two walruses, not many yards from where he stands. One of them, the male, is excited and seemingly terrified: the other, the female, collected and vengeful. Down they go again, after one grim survey of the field; and on the instant Myouk has changed his position, carrying his coil with him and fixing it anew.

He has hardly fixed it before the pair have again risen, breaking up an area of ten feet diameter about the very spot he left. As they sink once more he again changes his place. And so the conflict goes on between address and force, till the victim, half exhausted, receives a second wound, and is played like a trout by the angler's reel.

The instinct of attack which characterizes the walrus is interesting to the naturalist, as it is characteristic also of the land animals, the pachyderms, with which he is classed. When wounded, he rises high out of the water, plunges heavily against the ice, and strives to raise himself with his fore-flippers upon its surface. As it breaks under his weight, his countenance assumes a still more vindictive expression, his bark changes to a roar, and the foam pours out from his jaws till it froths his beard.

Even when not excited, he manages his tusks bravely. They are so strong that he uses them to grapple the rocks with, and climbs steeps of ice and land which would be inaccessible to him without their aid. He ascends in this way rocky islands that are sixty and a hundred feet above the level of the sea; and I have myself seen him in these elevated positions basking with his young in the cool sunshine of August and September.

He can strike a fearful blow; but prefers charging with his tusks in a soldierly manner. I do not doubt the old stories of the Spitzbergen fisheries and Cherie Island, where the walrus put to flight the crowds of European boats. Awuk is the lion of the Danish Esquimaux, and they always speak of him with the highest respect.

I have heard of oomiaks being detained for days at a time at the crossings of straits and passages which he infested. Governor Flaischer told me that, in 1830, a brown walrus, which, according to the Esquimaux, is the fiercest, after being lanced and maimed near Upernavik, routed his numerous assailants, and drove them in fear to seek for help from the settlement. His movements were so violent as to jerk out the harpoons that were stuck into him. The governor slew him with great difficulty after several rifle-shots and lance-wounds from his whaleboat.

On another occasion, a young and adventurous Inuit

plunged his nalegeit into a brown walrus; but, startled
by the savage demeanor of the beast, called for help
before using the lance. The older men in vain cau-
tioned him to desist. "It is a brown walrus," said
they: "*Aúvek-Kaiok!*" "Hold back!" Finding the cau-

LANCE-HEAD, FROM MARSHALL BAY.

LANCE-HEAD, FROM SUNNY GORGE.

tion disregarded, his only brother rowed forward and
plunged the second harpoon. Almost in an instant the
animal charged upon the kayacker, ripping him up, as
the description went, after the fashion of his sylvan

ESQUIMAUX LANCE-HEAD, "AKBAH."

brother, the wild boar. The story was told to me with
much animation; how the brother remaining rescued
the corpse of the brother dead; and how, as they
hauled it up on the ice-floes, the ferocious beast plunged

in foaming circles, seeking fresh victims in that part of the sea which was discolored by his blood.

Some idea may be formed of the ferocity of the walrus, from the fact that the battle which Morton witnessed, not without sharing some of its danger, lasted four hours; during which the animal rushed continually at the Esquimaux as they approached, tearing off great tables of ice with his tusks, and showing no indications of fear whatever. He received upward of seventy lance-wounds,—Morton counted over sixty; and even then he remained hooked by his tusks to the margin of the ice, unable or unwilling to retire. His female fought in the same manner, but fled on receiving a lance-wound.

The Esquimaux seemed to be fully aware of the danger of venturing too near; for at the first onset of the walrus they jumped back far enough to be clear of the broken ice. Morton described the last three hours as wearing, on both sides, the aspect of an unbroken and seemingly doubtful combat.

The method of landing the beast upon the ice, too, showed a great deal of clever contrivance. They made two pair of incisions in the neck, where the hide is very thick, about six inches apart and parallel to each other, so as to form a couple of bands. A line of cut hide, about a quarter of an inch in diameter, was passed under one of these bands and carried up on the ice to a firm stick well secured in the floe, where it went through a loop, and was then taken back to the animal, made to pass under the second band, and led off to the

Esquimaux. This formed a sort of "double purchase,"
the blubber so lubricating the cord as to admit of a
free movement. By this contrivance the beast, weigh-
ing some seven hundred pounds, was hauled up and
butchered at leisure.

The two sledges now journeyed homeward, carrying
the more valued parts of their prize. The intestines
and a large share of the carcass were buried up in the
cavities of a berg: Lucullus himself could not have
dreamed of a grander icehouse.

As they doubled the little island which stood in

SOUTHERN KNIFE, "AWAYU."   FROM GRAVE, BUSHNALL ISLAND.

front of their settlement, the women ran down the
rocks to meet them. A long hail carried the good
news; and, as the party alighted on the beach, knives
were quickly at work, the allotment of the meat being
determined by well-understood hunter laws. The
Esquimaux, however gluttonously they may eat, evidently bear hunger with as little difficulty as excess.
None of the morning party had breakfasted; yet it
was after ten o'clock at night before they sat down
to dinner. "Sat down to dinner!" This is the only
expression of our own gastrology which is applicable
to an Esquimaux feast. They truly sit down, man,

woman, and child, knife in hand, squatting cross-legged around a formidable joint,—say forty pounds,—and, without waiting for the tardy coction of the lamp, falling to like college commoners after grace. I have seen many such feeds. Hans's account, however, of the glutton-festival at Etah is too characteristic to be omitted.

"Why, Cappen Ken, sir, even the children ate all night:—you know the little two-year-old that Awiu carried in her hood—the one that bit you, when you tickled it?—yes. Well, Cappen Ken, sir, that baby cut for herself, with a knife made out of an iron hoop and so heavy that it could barely lift it, and cut and ate, and ate and cut, as long as I looked at it."

"Well, Hans, try now and think; for I want an accurate answer: how much as to weight or quantity would you say that child ate?" Hans is an exact and truthful man: he pondered a little and said that he could not answer my question. "But I know this, sir, that it ate a *sipak*"—the Esquimaux name for the lump which is cut off close to the lips—"as large as its own head; and three hours afterward, when I went to bed, it was cutting off another lump and eating still."—A sipak, like the Dutch governor's foot, is, however, a varying unit of weight.

CHAPTER XXXI.

AN AURORA—WOOD-CUTTING—FUEL ESTIMATE—THE STOVE-PIPES
—THE ARCTIC FIRMAMENT—ESQUIMAUX ASTRONOMY—HEATING
APPARATUS—METEORIC SHOWER—A BEAR—HASTY RETREAT—
THE CABIN BY NIGHT—SICKNESS INCREASING—CUTTING INTO
THE BRIG—THE NIGHT-WATCH.

"OCTOBER 24, Tuesday.—We are at work that makes us realize how short-handed we are. The brig was lifted for the third time to day, with double chains passed under her at low tide, both astern and amidships. Her bows were already raised three feet above the water, and nothing seemed wanting to our complete success, when at the critical moment one of the aftershores parted, and she fell over about five streaks to starboard. The slings were hove to by the crab, and luckily held her from going farther, so that she now stands about three feet above her flotation-line, drawing four feet forward, but four and a half aft. She has righted a little with the return of tide, and now awaits the freezing-in of her winter cradle. She is well out of water; and, if the chains only hold, we shall have

420

the spectacle of a brig, high and dry, spending an Arctic winter over an Arctic ice-bed.

"We shall be engaged now at the hold and with the housing on deck. From our lodge-room to the forward timbers every thing is clear already. We have moved the carpenter's bench into our little dormitorium: everywhere else it is too cold for handling tools.

"9 P.M.—A true and unbroken auroral arch: the first we have seen in Smith's Sound. It was colorless, but

THE BRIG CRADLED.

extremely bright. There was no pendant from the lower curve of the arc; but from its outer, an active wavy movement, dissipating itself into barely-perceptible cirrhus, was broken here and there by rays nearly perpendicular, with a slight inclination to the east. The atmosphere was beautifully clear.

"October 26, Thursday.—The thermometer at 34° below zero, but fortunately no wind blowing. We go on with the out-door work. The gangway of ice is finished, and we have passed wooden steam-tubes through the deck-house to carry off the vapors of our cooking-stove and the lighter impurities of the crowded cabin.

"We burn but seventy pounds of fuel a day, most of it in the galley; the fire being allowed to go out between meals. We go without fire altogether for four hours of the night; yet such is the excellence of our moss walls, and the air-proof of our tossut, that the thermometer in-doors never indicates less than 45° above zero, with the outside air at 30° below. When our housing is arranged and the main hatch secured with a proper weather-tight screen of canvas, we shall be able, I hope, to meet the extreme cold of February and March without fear.

"Darkness is the worst enemy we have to face; but we will strive against the scurvy in spite of him, till the light days of sun and vegetation. The spring hunt will open in March, though it will avail us very little till late in April.

"Wilson and Brooks are my principal subjects of anxiety; for, although Morton and Hans are on their backs, making four of our ten, I can see strength of system in their cheerfulness of heart. The best prophylactic is a hopeful, sanguine temperament; the best cure, moral resistance, that spirit of combat against every trial which is alone true bravery.

"October 27, Friday.—The work is going on: we are ripping off the extra planking of our deck for fuel during the winter. The cold increases fast, verging now upon 40° below zero; and in spite of all my efforts we will have to burn largely into the brig. I prepared for this two months ago, and satisfied myself, after a consultation with the carpenter, that we may cut away some seven or eight tons of fuel without absolutely destroying her sea-worthiness. Ohlsen's report marked out the order in which her timbers should be appropriated to uses of necessity:—1, The monkey-rail; 2, the bulwarks; 3, the upper ceiling of the deck; 4, eight extra cross-beams; 5, the flooring and remaining wood-work of the forecastle; 6, the square girders of the forepeak; 7, the main topsail-yard and topmast; 8, the outside trebling or oak sheathing.

"We had then but thirty buckets of coal remaining, and had already burnt up the bulkheads. Since then we have made some additional inroads on our stock; but, unless there is an error in the estimate, we can go on at the rate of seventy pounds a day. Close house-keeping this; but we cannot do better. We must remodel our heating-arrangements. The scurvy exacts a comfortable temperature and a drying one. Our mean thus far has been 47°,—decidedly too low; and by the clogging of our worn-out pipe it is now reduced to 42°.

"The ice-belt, sorry chronicler of winter progress, has begun to widen with the rise and fall of the sludgy water.

"October 31, Tuesday.—We have had a scene on board. We play many parts on this Arctic stage of ours, and can hardly be expected to be at home in all of them.

"To-day was appropriated to the reformation of the

stoves, and there was demand, of course, for all our
ingenuity both as tinkers and chimney-sweeps. Of my
company of nine, Hans had the good luck to be out on
the hunt, and Brooks, Morton, Wilson, and Goodfellow
were scurvy-ridden in their bunks. The other four
and the commanding officer made up the detail of
duty. First, we were to give the smoke-tubes of the
stove a thorough cleansing, the first they have had
for now seventeen months; next, to reduce our effete
snow-melter to its elements of imperfect pipes and
pans; and, last, to combine the practicable remains
of the two into one efficient system for warming and
melting.

"Of these, the first has been executed most gallantly. 'Glory enough for one day!' The work with
the scrapers on the heated pipes—for the accumulation inside of them was as hard as the iron itself till
we melted it down—was decidedly unpleasant to our
gentle senses; and we were glad when it had advanced
far enough to authorize a resort to the good old-
fashioned country custom of firing. But we had not
calculated the quantity of the gases, combustible and
incombustible, which this process was to evolve, with
duly scientific reference to the size of their outlet. In
a word, they were smothering us, and, in a fit of despe-
ration, we threw open our apartment to the atmosphere
outside. This made short work of the smoky flocculi;
the dormitory decked itself on the instant with a frosty
forest of feathers, and it now rejoices in a drapery as
gray as a cygnet's breast.

"It was cold work reorganizing the stove for the nonce; but we have got it going again, as red as a cherry, and my well-worn dog-skin suit is drying before it. The blackened water is just beginning to drip, drip, drop, from the walls and ceiling, and the bed-clothes and the table on which I write."

My narrative has reached a period at which every thing like progress was suspended. The increasing cold and brightening stars, the labors and anxieties and sickness that pressed upon us,—these almost engross the pages of my journal. Now and then I find some marvel of Petersen's about the fox's dexterity as a hunter; and Hans tells me of domestic life in South Greenland, or of a seal-hunt and a wrecked kayack; or perhaps McGary repeats his thrice-told tale of humor; but the night has closed down upon us, and we are hibernating through it.

Yet some of these were topics of interest. The intense beauty of the Arctic firmament can hardly be imagined. It looked close above our heads, with its stars magnified in glory and the very planets twinkling so much as to baffle the observations of our astronomer. I am afraid to speak of some of these night-scenes. I have trodden the deck and the floes, when the life of earth seemed suspended, its movements, its sounds, its coloring, its companionships; and as I looked on the radiant hemisphere, circling above me as if rendering worship to the unseen Centre of light, I have ejaculated in humility of spirit, "Lord, what is man that

thou art mindful of him?" And then I have thought
of the kindly world we had left, with its revolving sunshine and shadow, and the other stars that gladden it
in their changes, and the hearts that warmed to us
there; till I lost myself in memories of those who are
not;—and they bore me back to the stars again.

The Esquimaux, like other nomads, are careful
observers of the heavenly bodies. An illustration of
the confidence with which they avail themselves of
this knowledge occurred while Petersen's party were
at Tessieusak. I copy it from my journal of November 6.

"A number of Esquimaux sought sleeping-quarters
in the hut, much to the annoyance of the earlier visitors. The night was clear; and Petersen, anxious to
hasten their departure, pointed to the horizon, saying
it would soon be daylight. 'No,' said the savage; 'when
that star there gets round to that point,' indicating the
quarter of the heavens, 'and is no higher than this star,'
naming it, 'will be the time to harness up my dogs.'
Petersen was astounded; but he went out the next
morning and verified the sidereal fact.

"I have been shooting a hare to-day up the ravine
pointed out by Ootuniah. It has been quite a pleasant
incident. I can hardly say how valuable the advice
of our Esquimaux friends has been to us upon our
hunts. This desert homestead of theirs is as thoroughly
travelled over as a sheepwalk. Every movement of
the ice or wind or season is noted; and they predict
its influence upon the course of the birds of passage

with the same sagacity that has taught them the habits of the resident animals.

"They foretold to me the exact range of the water off Cape Alexander during September, October, November and December, and anticipated the excessive fall of snow which has taken place this winter, by reference to this mysterious water.

"In the darkest weather of October, when every thing around is apparently congealed and solid, they discover water by means as inscrutable as the divining-rod. I was once journeying to Anoatok, and completely enveloped in darkness among the rolled-ice off Godsend Island. My dogs were suffering for water. September was half gone, and the water-streams both on shore and on the bergs had been solid for nearly a fortnight. Myouk, my companion, began climbing the dune-like summits of the ice-hills, tapping with his ice-pole and occasionally applying his ear to parts of the surface. He did so to three hills without any result, but at the fourth he called out, 'Water!' I examined the spot by hand and tongue, for it was too dark to see; but I could detect no liquid. Lying down and listening, I first perceived the metallic tinkle of a rivulet. A few minutes' digging brought us down to a scanty infiltration of drinkable water.

"November 8, Wednesday.—Still tinkering at our stove and ice-melter; at last successful. Old iron pipes, and tin kettles, and all the refuse kitchen-ware of the brig figure now in picturesque association and rejoice in the title of our heating-apparatus. It is a great result. We have burnt from 6 A. M. to 10 P. M. but seventy-five pounds, and will finish the twenty-four hours with fifteen pounds more. It has been a mild day, the thermometer keeping some tenths above 13° below zero; but then we have maintained a temperature inside of 55° above. With our old contrivances we could never get higher than 47°, and that without any certainty, though it cost us a hundred and fifty-four pounds a day. A vast increase of comfort, and still greater saving of fuel. This last is a most important consideration. Not a stick of wood comes below without my eyes following it through the scales to the wood-stack. I weigh it to the very ounce.

"The tide-register, with its new wheel-and-axle arrangements, has given us out-door work for the day. Inside, after rigging the stove, we have been busy chopping wood. The ice is already three feet thick at our tide-hole.

"November 15, Wednesday.—The last forty-eight hours should have given us the annual meteoric shower. We were fully prepared to observe it; but it would not come off. It would have been a godsend variety. In eight hours that I helped to watch, from nine of last night until five this morning, there were only fifty-one shooting stars. I have seen as many between the same hours in December and February of last winter.

"Our traps have been empty for ten days past: but for the pittance of excitement which the visit to them gives, we might as well be without them.

"The men are getting nervous and depressed. Mc-

Gary paced the deck all last Sunday in a fit of home-sickness, without eating a meal. I do my best to cheer them; but it is hard work to hide one's own trials for the sake of others who have not as many. I am glad of my professional drill and its companion influence over the sick and toil-worn. I could not get along at all unless I combined the offices of physician and com-mander. You cannot punish sick men.

"November 20, Monday.—I was out to-day looking over the empty traps with Hans, and when about two miles off the brig—luckily not more—I heard what I thought was the bellow of a walrus on the floe-ice. 'Hark there, Hans!' The words were scarcely uttered before we had a second roar, altogether unmistakable. No walrus at all: a bear, a bear! We had jumped to the ice-foot already. The day was just thirty minutes past the hour of noon; but, practised as we all are to see through the darkness, it was impossible to make out an object two hundred yards off. What to do?—we had no arms.

"We were both of us afraid to run, for we knew that the sight of a runner would be the signal for a chase; and, besides, it went to our hearts to lose such a provi-dential accession to our means of life. A second roar, well pitched and abundant in volume, assured us that the game was coming nearer, and that he was large and of no doubt corresponding flavor. 'Run for the brig, Hans,'—he is a noble runner,—'and I will play decoy.' Off went Hans like a deer. Another roar; but he was already out of sight.

"I may confess it to these well-worn pages: there was something not altogether pleasant in the silent communings of the next few minutes; but they were silent ones.

"I had no stimulus to loquacity, and the bear had ceased to be communicative. The floe was about three-quarters of a tide; some ten feet it may be, lower than the ice-foot on which I lay. The bear was of course below my horizon. I began after a while to think over the reality of what I had heard, and to doubt whether it might not be after all a creature of the brain. It was very cold on that ice-foot. I resolved to crawl to the edge of it and peer under my hands into the dark shadow of the hummock-ridges.

"I did so. One look: nothing. A second: no bear after all. A third: what is that long rounded shade? Stained ice? Yes: stained ice. The stained ice gave a gross menagerie roar, and charged on the instant for my position. I had not even a knife, and did not wait to think what would have been appropriate if I had had one. I ran,—ran as I never expect these scurvy-stiffened knees to run again,—throwing off first one mitten and then its fellow to avoid pursuit. I gained the brig, and the bear my mittens. I got back one of them an hour afterward, but the other was carried off as a trophy in spite of all the rifles we could bring to the rescue.[56]

"November 24, Friday.—The weather still mild. I attempted to work to-day at charting. I placed a large board on our stove, and pasted my paper to it.

My lamp reposed on the lid of the coffee-kettle, my instruments in the slush-boiler, my feet in the ash-pan; and thus I drew the first coast-line of Grinnell Land. The stove, by close watching and niggard feeding, has burnt only sixty-five pounds in the last twenty-four hours. Of course, working by night I work without fire. In the daytime our little company take every man his share of duty as he is able. Poor Wilson, just able to stump about after his late attack of scurvy, helps to wash the dishes. Morton and Brooks sew at sledge-clothing, while Riley, McGary, and Ohlsen, our only really able-bodied men, cut the ice and firewood.

"December 1, Friday.—I am writing at midnight. I have the watch from eight to two. It is day in the moonlight on deck, the thermometer getting up again to 36° below zero. As I come down to the cabin—for so we still call this little moss-lined igloë of ours—every one is asleep, snoring, gritting his teeth, or talking in his dreams. This is pathognomonic; it tells of Arctic winter and its companion scurvy. Tom Hickey, our good-humored, blundering cabin-boy, decorated since poor Schubert's death with the dignities of cook, is in that little dirty cot on the starboard side; the rest are bedded in rows, Mr. Brooks and myself chock aft. Our bunks are close against the frozen moss wall, where we can take in the entire family at a glance. The apartment measures twenty feet by eighteen; its height six feet four inches at one place, but diversified elsewhere by beams crossing at different distances from the floor. The avenue by which it is approached is barely to be seen in the moss wall forward:—twenty feet of air-tight space make misty distance, for the puff of outside-temperature that came in with me has filled our atmosphere with vesicles of vapor. The avenue—Ben-Djerback is our poetic name for it—closes on the inside with a door well patched with flannel, from which, stooping upon all-fours, you back down a descent of four feet in twelve through a tunnel three feet high and two feet six inches broad. It would have been a tight squeeze for a man like Mr. Brooks when he was better fed and fatter. Arrived at the bottom, you straighten yourself, and a second door admits you into the dark and sorrowing hold, empty of stores and stripped to its naked ceiling for firewood. From this we grope our way to the main hatch, and mount by a rude stairway of boxes into the open air.

"December 2, Saturday.—Had to put Mr. McGary and Riley under active treatment for scurvy. Gums retracted, ankles swollen, and bad lumbago. Mr. Wilson's case, a still worse one, has been brought under. Morton's is a saddening one: I cannot afford to lose him. He is not only one of my most intelligent men, but he is daring, cool, and everyway trustworthy. His tendon Achilles has been completely perforated, and the surface of the heel-bone exposed. An operation in cold, darkness, and privation, would probably bring on locked-jaw. Brooks grows discouraged: the poor fellow has scurvy in his stump, and his leg is drawn up by the contraction of the flexors at the knee-joint. This is the third case on board,—the fourth if I include my own,—of contracted tendons.

"December 3, Sunday.—I have now on hand twenty-four hundred pounds of chopped wood, a store collected with great difficulty; and yet how inadequate a provision for the sickness and accident we must look for through the rest of the dark days! It requires the most vigorous effort of what we call a healthy man to tear from the oak ribs of our stout little vessel a single day's firewood. We have but three left who can manage even this; and we cannot spare more than one for the daily duty. Two thousand pounds will barely carry us to the end of January, and the two severest months of the Arctic year, February and March, will still be ahead of us.

"To carry us over these, our days of greatest anticipated trial, we have the outside oak sheathing,—or trebling, as the carpenters call it,—a sort of extra skin to protect the brig against the shocks of the ice. Although nearly three inches thick, it is only spiked to her sides, and carpenter Ohlsen is sure that its removal will not interfere with her sea-worthiness. Cut the trebling only to the water-line, and it will give me at least two and a half tons; and with this— God willing—I may get through this awful winter, *and save the brig besides!*

"December 4, Monday.—That stove is smoking so that three of our party are down with acute inflammation of the eyes. I fear I must increase the diameter of our smoke-pipes, for the pitch-pine which we burn, to save up our oak for the greater cold, is redundantly charged with turpentine. Yet we do not want an increased draught to consume our seventy pounds; the fiat 'No more wood' comes soon enough.

"Then for the night-watch. I have generally something on hand to occupy me, and can volunteer for the hours before my regular term. Every thing is closed tight; I muffle myself in furs, and write; or, if the cold denies me that pleasure, I read, or at least think. Thank heaven, even an Arctic temperature leaves the mind unchilled. But in truth, though our hourly observations in the air range between —46° and —30°, we seldom register less than +36° below.

"December 5, Tuesday.—McGary is no better, but happily has no notion how bad he is. I have to give him a grating of our treasured potatoes. He and Brooks will doubtless finish the two I have got out, and then there will be left twelve. They are now three years old, poor old frozen memorials of the dear land they grew in. They are worth more than their weight in gold."

CHAPTER XXXII.

ESQUIMAUX SLEDGES—BONSALL'S RETURN—RESULTS OF THE HUNT
—RETURN OF WITHDRAWING PARTY—THEIR RECEPTION—THE
ESQUIMAUX ESCORT—CONFERENCE—CONCILIATION—ON FIRE—
CASUALTY—CHRISTMAS—OLE BEN—A JOURNEY AHEAD—SET-
TING OUT—A DREARY NIGHT—STRIKING A LIGHT—END OF
1854.

I WAS asleep in the forenoon of the 7th, after the
fatigue of an extra night-watch, when I was called to
the deck by the report of " Esquimaux sledges." They
came on rapidly, five sledges, with teams of six dogs
each, most of the drivers strangers to us; and in a
few minutes were at the brig. Their errand was of
charity: they were bringing back to us Bonsall and
Petersen, two of the party that left us on the 28th of
August.

The party had many adventures and much suffering
to tell of. They had verified by painful and perilous
experience all I had anticipated for them. But the
most stirring of their announcements was the condition
they had left their associates in, two hundred miles off,
divided in their counsels, their energies broken, and

435

their provisions nearly gone. I reserve for another page the history of their wanderings. My first thought was of the means of rescuing and relieving them.

I resolved to despatch the Esquimaux escort at once with such supplies as our miserably-imperfect stores allowed, they giving their pledge to carry them with all speed, and, what I felt to be much less certain, with all honesty. But neither of the gentlemen who had come with them felt himself in condition to repeat the journey. Mr. Bonsall was evidently broken down, and Petersen, never too reliable in emergency, was for postponing the time of setting out. Of our own party— those who had remained with the brig—McGary, Hans, and myself were the only ones able to move, and of these McGary was now fairly on the sick list. We could not be absent for a single day without jeoparding the lives of the rest.

"December 8, Friday.—I am much afraid these provisions will never reach the wanderers. We were busy every hour since Bonsall arrived getting them ready. We cleaned and boiled and packed a hundred pounds of pork, and sewed up smaller packages of meat-biscuit, bread-dust, and tea; and despatched the whole, some three hundred and fifty pounds, by the returning convoy. But I have no faith in an Esquimaux under temptation, and I almost regret that I did not accompany them myself. It might have been wiser. But I will set Hans on the track in the morning; and, if I do not hear within four days that the stores are fairly on their way, *coûte qui coûte*, I will be

off to the lower bay and hold the whole tribe as host-
ages for the absent party.

"Brooks is wasting with night-sweats; and my iron
man, McGary, has been suffering for two days with
anomalous cramps from exposure.

"These Esquimaux have left us some walrus-beef;
and poor little Myouk, who is unabated in his affection for me, made me a special present of half a liver.
These go of course to the hospital. God knows they
are needed there!

"December 9, Saturday.—The superabundant life
of Northumberland Island has impressed Petersen as
much as it did me. I cannot think of it without
recurring to the fortunes of Franklin's party. Our
own sickness I attribute to our civilized diet; had we
plenty of frozen walrus I would laugh at the scurvy.
And it was only because I was looking to other objects—
summer researches, and explorations in the fall with
the single view to escape—that I failed to secure an
abundance of fresh food. Even in August I could
have gathered a winter's supply of birds and cochlearia.

"From May to August we lived on seal, twenty-five
before the middle of July, all brought in by one man:
a more assiduous and better-organized hunt would
have swelled the number without a limit. A few boat-
parties in June would have stocked us with eider-eggs
for winter use, three thousand to the trip; and the
snowdrifts would have kept them fresh for the break-
fast-table. I loaded my boat with ducks in three
hours, as late as the middle of July and not more than

thirty-five miles from our anchorage. And even now, here are these Esquimaux, sleek and oily with their walrus-blubber, only seventy miles off. It is not a region for starvation, nor ought it to be for scurvy.

CLIFFS, NORTHUMBERLAND ISLAND.

"December 12, Tuesday.—Brooks awoke me at three this morning with the cry of 'Esquimaux again!' I dressed hastily, and, groping my way over the pile of boxes that leads up from the hold into the darkness above, made out a group of human figures, masked by the hooded jumpers of the natives. They stopped at

the gangway, and, as I was about to challenge, one of
them sprang forward and grasped my hand. It was
Doctor Hayes. A few words, dictated by suffering,
certainly not by any anxiety as to his reception, and
at his bidding the whole party came upon deck. Poor
fellows! I could only grasp their hands and give them
a brother's welcome.

"The thermometer was at minus 50°; they were
covered with rime and snow, and were fainting with
hunger. It was necessary to use caution in taking
them below; for, after an exposure of such fearful
intensity and duration as they had gone through, the
warmth of the cabin would have prostrated them completely. They had journeyed three hundred and fifty
miles; and their last run from the bay near Etah, some
seventy miles in a right line, was through the hummocks at this appalling temperature.

"One by one they all came in and were housed.
Poor fellows! as they threw open their Esquimaux
garments by the stove, how they relished the scanty
luxuries which we had to offer them! The coffee and
the meat-biscuit soup, and the molasses and the wheat
bread, even the salt pork which our scurvy forbade the
rest of us to touch,—how they relished it all! For
more than two months they had lived on frozen seal
and walrus-meat.

"They are almost all of them in danger of collapse,
but I have no apprehension of life unless from tetanus.
Stephenson is prostrate with pericarditis. I resigned
my own bunk to Dr. Hayes, who is much prostrated:

he will probably lose two of his toes, perhaps a third. The rest have no special injury.

"I cannot crowd the details of their journey into my diary. I have noted some of them from Dr. Hayes's words; but he has promised me a written report, and I wait for it. It was providential that they did not stop for Petersen's return or rely on the engagements which his Esquimaux attendants had made to them as well as to us. The sledges that carried our relief of provisions passed through the Etah settlement empty, on some furtive project, we know not what.

"December 13, Wednesday.—The Esquimaux who accompanied the returning party are nearly all of them well-known friends. They were engaged from different settlements, but, as they neared the brig, volunteers added themselves to the escort till they numbered six drivers and as many as forty-two dogs. Whatever may have been their motive, their conduct to our poor friends was certainly full of humanity. They drove at flying speed; every hut gave its welcome as they halted; the women were ready without invitation to dry and chafe their worn-out guests.

"I found, however, that there were other objects connected with their visit to the brig. Suffering and a sense of necessity had involved some of our foot-worn absentees in a breach of hospitality. While resting at Kalutunah's hut, they had found opportunity of appropriating to their own use certain articles of clothing, fox-skins and the like, under circumstances which admitted of justification only by the law of the more sagacious and the stronger. It was apparent that our savage friends had their plaint to make, or, it might be, to avenge.

"My first attention, after ministering to the immediate wants of all, was turned to the office of conciliating our Esquimaux benefactors. Though they wore their habitual faces of smiling satisfaction, I could read them too well to be deceived. Policy as well as moral duty have made me anxious always to deserve their respect; but I had seen enough of mankind in its varied relations not to know that respect is little else than a tribute to superiority either real or supposed,—and that among the rude at least, one of its elements is fear.

"I therefore called them together in stern and cheerless conference on the deck, as if to inquire into the truth of transactions that I had heard of, leaving it doubtful from my manner which was the party I proposed to implicate. Then, by the intervention of Petersen, I called on Kalutunah for his story, and went through a full train of questionings on both sides. It was not difficult to satisfy them that it was my purpose to do justice all round. The subject of controversy was set out fully, and in such a manner as to convince me that an appeal to kind feeling might have been substituted with all effect for the resort to artifice or force. I therefore, to the immense satisfaction of our stranger guests, assured them of my approval, and pulled their hair all around.

"They were introduced into the oriental recess of

our dormitory,—hitherto an unsolved mystery. There, seated on a red blanket, with four pork-fat lamps, throwing an illumination over old worsted damask curtains, hunting-knives, rifles, beer-barrels, galley-stove and chronometers, I dealt out to each man five needles, a file, and a stick of wood. To Kalutunah and Shunghu

SHUNGHU.

I gave knives and other extras; and in conclusion spread out our one remaining buffalo close to the stove, built a roaring fire, cooked a hearty supper, and by noonday they were sleeping away in a state of thorough content. I explained to them further that my people did not steal; that the fox-jumpers and boots and

C. Schuessele   Engraved at J M Butler's establishment. 84 Chestnu.. St   J Mc Goffin.

BONSALL.   BROOKS   DR KANE   DR. HAYES   MORTON

LIFE IN THE BRIG

sledges were only taken to save their lives; and I there-upon returned them.

"The party took a sound sleep, and a second or rather a continuous feed, and left again on their return through the hummocks with apparent confidence and good-humor. Of course they prigged a few knives and forks;—but that refers itself to a national trait.

"December 23, Saturday.—This uncalculated acces-sion of numbers makes our little room too crowded to be wholesome: I have to guard its ventilation with all the severity that would befit a surgical ward of our Blockley Hospital. We are using the Esquimaux lamp as an accessory to our stove: it helps out the cooking and water-making, without encroaching upon our rigorously-meted allowance of wood. But the odor of pork-fat, our only oil, we have found to be injurious; and our lamps are there-fore placed outside the *tossut*, in a small room bulk-headed off for their use.

"This new arrangement gave rise yesterday to a nearly fatal disaster. A watch had been stationed in charge of the lamp, with the usual order of 'No un-covered lights.' He deserted his post. Soon afterward, Hans found the cooking-room on fire. It was a hor-rible crisis; for no less than eight of our party were absolutely nailed to their beds, and there was nothing but a bulkhead between them and the fire. I gave short but instant orders, stationing a line between the tide-hole and the main hatch, detailing two men to work with me, and ordering all the rest who could move to their quarters. Dr. Hayes with his maimed foot, Mr. Brooks with his contracted legs, and poor Morton, otherwise among our best men, could do nothing.

"Before we reached the fire, the entire bulkhead was in a blaze, as well as the dry timbers and skin of the brig. Our moss walls, with their own tinder-like material and their light casing of inflammable wood, were entirely hidden by the flames. Fortunately the furs of the recently-returned party were at hand, and with them I succeeded in smothering the fire. But I was obliged to push through the blaze of our sailcloth bulk-head in order to defend the wall; and, in my anxiety to save time, I had left the cabin without either cap or mittens. I got through somehow or other, and tore down the canvas which hung against that dangerous locality. Our rifles were in this corner, and their muzzles pointing in all directions.

"The water now began to pass down; but with the discharge of the first bucketful the smoke overcame me. As I found myself going, I pushed for the hatch-way, knowing that the bucket-line would *feel* me. Seeing was impossible; but, striking Ohlsen's legs as I fell, I was passed up to the deck, *minus* beard, eye-brows, and forelock, *plus* two burns on the forehead and one on each palm.

"In about three minutes after making way with the canvas, the fire was got under, and in less than half an hour all was safe again. But the transition, for even the shortest time, from the fiery Shadrachian furnace-temperature below, to 46° below zero above, was intolerably trying. Every man suffered, and few escaped without frost-bitten fingers.

"The remembrance of the danger and its horrible results almost miraculously averted shocks us all. Had we lost our brig, not a man could have survived: without shelter, clothing, or food, the thermometer almost eighty degrees below the freezing point, and a brisk wind stirring, what hope could we have on the open ice-field?

"December 25, Christmas, Monday.—All together again, the returned and the steadfast, we sat down to our Christmas dinner. There was more love than with the stalled ox of former times; but of herbs none. We forgot our discomforts in the blessings which adhered to us still; and when we thought of the long road ahead of us, we thought of it hopefully. I pledged myself to give them their next Christmas with their homes; and each of us drank his 'absent friends' with ferocious zest over one-eighteenth part of a bottle of sillery,—the last of its hamper, and, alas! no longer *mousseux*.

"But if this solitary relic of festival days had lost its sparkle, we had not. We passed around merrily our turkeys roast and boiled, roast-beef, onions, potatoes and cucumbers, watermelons, and God knows what other cravings of the scurvy-sickened palate, with entire exclusion of the fact that each one of these was variously represented by pork and beans. Lord Peter himself was not more cordial in his dispensa-

tion of plum-pudding, mutton, and custard to his
unbelieving brothers.

"McGary, of course, told us his story: we hear it
every day, and laugh at it almost as heartily as he
does himself. Cæsar Johnson is the guest of 'Ole
Ben,' colored gentlemen both, who do occasional white-
washing. The worthies have dined stanchly on the
dish of beans, browned and relished by its surmount-
ing cube of pork. A hospitable pause, and, with a
complacent wave of the hand, Ole Ben addresses the
lady hostess:—'Ole woman! bring on de resarve.'
'Ha'n't got no resarve.' 'Well, den,'—with a placid
smile,—'bring on de beans!'

"So much for the Merrie Christmas. What portion
of its mirth was genuine with the rest I cannot tell,
for we are practised actors some of us; but there was
no heart in my share of it. My thoughts were with
those far off, who are thinking, I know, of me. I
could bear my own troubles as I do my eider-down
coverlet; for I can see myself as I am, and feel sustained by the knowledge that I have fought my battle
well. But there is no one to tell of this at the home-
table. Pertinacity, unwise daring, calamity,—any of
these may come up unbidden, as my name circles
round, to explain why I am still away."

For some days before Christmas I had been medi-
tating a sledge-journey to our Esquimaux neighbors.
The condition of the little party under my charge left
me no alternative, uncomfortable and hazardous as I
knew that it must be. I failed in the first effort; but

there were incidents connected with it which may deserve a place in this volume. I recur to my journal for a succinct record of my motives in setting out :—

"December 26, Tuesday.—The moon is nearly above the cliffs; the thermometer —57° to —45°, the mean of the past four days. In the midst of this cheering conjunction, I have ahead of me a journey of a hundred miles; to say nothing of the return. Worse than this, I have no landmarks to guide me, and must be my own pioneer.

"But there is a duty in the case. McGary and Brooks are sinking, and that rapidly. Walrus-beef alone can sustain them, and it is to be got from the natives and nowhere else. It is a merciful change of conditions that I am the strongest now of the whole party, as last winter I was the weakest. The duty of collecting food is on me. I shall go first to the lower Bay Esquimaux, and thence, if the hunt has failed there, to Cape Robertson.

"My misgivings are mostly on account of the dogs; for it is a rugged, hummocked drive of twenty-two hours, even with strong teams and Esquimaux drivers. We have been feeding them on salt meat, for we have had nothing else to give them; and they are out of health; and there are hardly enough of them at best to carry our lightest load. If one of these tetanoids should attack them on the road, it may be *game up* for all of us.

"But it is to be tried at last: Petersen will go with

me, and we will club our wits. I do not fear the cold: we are impregnable in our furs while under exercise, though if we should be forced to walk, and give out, it might be a different matter. We shall have, I imagine, a temperature not much above —54°, and I do not see how we are to carry heating-apparatus. We have load enough without it. Our only diet will be a stock of meat-biscuit, to which I shall add for myself—Petersen's taste is less educated—a few rats, chopped up and frozen into the tallow-balls.

"December 28, Thursday.—I have fed the dogs the last two days on their dead brethren. Spite of all proverbs, *dog will eat dog*, if properly cooked. I have been saving up some who died of fits, intending to use their skins, and these have come in very opportunely. I boil them into a sort of bloody soup, and deal them out twice a day in chunks and solid jelly; for of course they are frozen like quartz rock. These salt meats are absolutely poisonous to the Northern Esquimaux dog. We have now lost fifty odd, and one died yesterday in the very act of eating his reformed diet.

"The moon to-morrow will be for twelve hours above the horizon, and so nearly circumpolar afterward as to justify me in the attempt to reach the Esquimaux hunting-ground about Cape Alexander. Every thing is ready; and, God willing, I start to-morrow, and pass the four-hours' dog-halt in the untenanted hut of Anoatok. Then we have, as it may be, a fifteen, eighteen, or twenty hours' march, run and drive, before we reach a shelter among the heathen of the Bay.

"January 2, Tuesday.—The dogs began to show signs of that accursed tetanoid spasm of theirs before we passed Ten-mile Ravine. When we reached Basalt Camp, six out of eight were nearly useless. Our thermometer was at —44°, and the wind was blowing sharply out of the gorge from the glacier. Petersen wanted to return, but was persuaded by me to walk on to the huts at Anoatok, in the hope that a halt might restore the animals. We reached them after a thirty miles' march.

"The sinuosities of this bay gave fearful travel: the broken ice clung to the rocks; and we could only advance by climbing up the ice-foot and down again upon the floe, as one or the other gave us the chance of passing. It was eleven hours and over before we were at the huts, having made by sledge and foot-tramp forty-five miles. We took to the best hut, filled in its broken front with snow, housed our dogs, and crawled in among them.

"It was too cold to sleep. Next morning we broke down our door and tried the dogs again: they could hardly stand. A gale now set in from the southwest, obscuring the moon and blowing very hard. We were forced back into the hut; but, after corking up all openings with snow and making a fire with our Esquimaux lamp, we got up the temperature to 30° below zero, cooked coffee, and fed the dogs freely. This done, both Petersen and myself, our clothing frozen stiff, fell asleep through sheer exhaustion; the wind outside blowing death to all that might be exposed to its influence.

"I do not know how long we slept, but my admirable clothing kept me up. I was cold, but far from dangerously so; and was in a fair way of sleeping out a refreshing night, when Petersen waked me with— 'Captain Kane, the lamp's out.' I heard him with a thrill of horror. The gale had increased; the cold was piercing, the darkness intense; our tinder had become moist, and was now like an icicle. All our fire-arms were stacked outside, for no Arctic man will trust powder in a condensing temperature. We did not dare to break down our doorway, for that would admit the gale; our only hope of heat was in re-lighting our lamp. Petersen, acting by my directions, made several attempts to obtain fire from a pocket-pistol; but his only tinder was moss, and our heavily stone-roofed hut or cave would not bear the concussion of a rammed wad.

"By good luck I found a bit of tolerably dry paper in my jumper; and, becoming apprehensive that Petersen would waste our few percussion-caps with his ineffectual snappings, I determined to take the pistol myself. It was so intensely dark that I had to grope for it, and in doing so touched his hand. At that instant the pistol became distinctly visible. A pale bluish light, slightly tremulous but not broken, covered the metallic parts of it, the barrel, lock, and trigger. The stock too, was clearly discernible as if by the reflected light, and, to the amazement of both of us, the thumb and two fingers with which Petersen was holding it, the creases, wrinkles, and circuit of the nails clearly defined upon the skin. The phosphorescence was not unlike the ineffectual fire of the glowworm. As I took the pistol my hand became illuminated also, and so did the powder-rubbed paper when I raised it against the muzzle.

"The paper did not ignite at the first trial, but, the light from it continuing, I was able to charge the pistol without difficulty, rolled up my paper into a cone, filled it with moss sprinkled over with powder, and held it in my hand while I fired. This time I succeeded in producing flame, and we saw no more of the phosphorescence. I do not stop for theory or argument to explain this opportune phenomenon; our fur clothing and the state of the atmosphere may refer it plausibly enough to our electrical condition.

"As soon as the wind had partially subsided, we broke out of the hut and tried the dogs toward Refuge Inlet; but the poor broken-down animals could not surmount the hummocks; and, as a forced necessity to save their lives and ours, we resolved to push for the brig on foot, driving them before us. We made the walk of forty-four miles in sixteen hours, almost scudding before the gale, and arrived safely at 7 P. M. of Sunday; the temperature —40°."

With this fruitless adventure closed the year 1854.

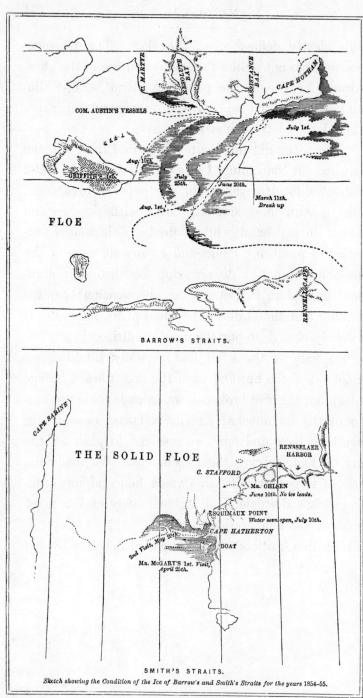

C. MARTYR

RESOLUTE BAY

ASSISTANCE BAY

CAPE HOTHAM

COM. AUSTIN'S VESSELS

July 1st.

Aug. 10th.

GRIFFITH'S ISd.

July 25th.

June 20th.

March 11th.
Break up

Aug. 1st.

FLOE

RENNEL CAPE

BARROW'S STRAITS.

CAPE SABINE

THE SOLID FLOE

RENSSELAER
HARBOR

C. STAFFORD

Mr. OHLSEN
June 10th. No ice leads.

ESQUIMAUX POINT
Water seen open, July 10th.

CAPE HATHERTON
BOAT

2nd Visit, May 20th.

Mr. McGARY'S 1st. Visit,
April 25th.

SMITH'S STRAITS.

Sketch showing the Condition of the Ice of Barrow's and Smith's Straits for the years 1854–55.

SEE PAGE 314 &c.

NOTES.

NOTE 1, p. 21.

SPRINGS, properly speaking, as outlets of subterranean drainage, are almost unknown in North Greenland. At Godhavn, Disco, at the line of junction of the greenstones and the basis-granites, there is a permanent spring, with a winter temperature of 33·5° Fahr.; but the so-called springs of the Danish settlements, as far north as 73°, are derived from a surface-drainage which is suspended during the colder months of the year.

NOTE 2, p. 23.

The shark-oil trade is of recent growth in North Greenland. It has lately been extended as far north as Proven. At Neorkanek, the seat of greatest yield, about three hundred fish are taken annually. The oil is expressed from the liver of the Arctic shark, (*S. borealis*,) the Hvowcalder of the Icelanders: it is extremely pure, resisting cold, and well adapted to lubrication. It brings a higher price in the Copenhagen market than the best seal-oils.

NOTE 3, p. 25.

There are no Moravian missions in North Greenland, and but three of their settlements in the south. Named in the order of their date of colonization, they are New Hernhut, Lichtenfels, and Frederickstahl. With these exceptions, the entire coast is Lutheran. The Lutheran missions, although distinct in organization from the Royal Greenland Company, are nevertheless under the direct patronage of government, and administered by a board appointed by the crown. The Moravians have no special facilities, and are dependent for their supplies upon private negotiations and the courtesy of the Danish trading-vessels.

NOTE 4, p. 29.

There are four sizes of reindeer-skins, of distinct qualities and marked values among the Esquimaux:—1. Bennesoak: the largest males, generally without antlers. 2. Nersutok: males of lesser size, retaining their antlers during the

453

winter. 3. Koluak: females still smaller, but not materially so. 4. Nohkak: the yearlings or younger animals. These last are prized for children's clothing. It is the Bennesoak which is so useful as an Arctic sleeping-bag in the sledge-journeys.

NOTE 5, p. 32.

Within comparatively recent periods the Esquimaux had summer settlements around Wilcox Point and the Melville Glacier; but in 1826 the small-pox so reduced them that they were concentrated about Upernavik. Except occasional parties for the chase of the white bear or the collection of eider-down, there are no natives north of Yotlik. Cape Shackleton and Horse's Head are, however, visited annually for eggs and down. By the tortuous route of the Colonial Itinerary, the latter is rated at twenty-eight Danish, or about one hundred and thirty-five statute, miles from Upernavik.

NOTE 6, p. 43.

The North Water, although its position varies with the character and period of the season, may be found, under ordinary conditions, in the month of August off Cape York. The local name given to it by the whalers is the Cape York Water.

NOTE 7, p. 46.

This moss—an unrecognised sphagnum—was studded with the pale-yellow flowers of the Ranunculus sabinii. No less than four species of Draba were afterward found on the island.

NOTE 8, p. 46.

Poa and alopecurus, with their accompanying bird-life, are abundant on the southern faces of Cape Alexander; but all the headlands to the north are utterly destitute of apparent vegetation. On Sutherland's Island a scanty supply of scurvy-grass (*Cochlearia fenestrata*) may be found.

NOTE 9, p. 49.

This ice was not distinguishable from aloft at the time of leaving the brig.

NOTE 10, p. 55.

My survey of this harbor shows forty fathoms water to within a biscuit-toss of its northern headland,—a square face of gneiss rock; thence E. by S., (true,) heading for a small glacier, you may carry seven fathoms to within two hundred yards of land. The southern side is shoal and rocky. The holding-ground is good, and the cove completely landlocked, except a small channel from the westward; but, owing to the prevalence of fogs as well as wind-eddies from the cliffs and persistence of local ice, I cannot recommend it for a winter harbor.

NOTE 11, p. 56.

This animal presented one of those rare cases of a well-developed second process protruding about six inches. I was unable to preserve the specimen.

NOTE 12, p. 58.

These were the results of direct pressure,—more properly, "crushed ice." The ice-hills of Von Wrangell and American authorities are grounded ices upreared by wave and tidal actions.

NOTE 13, p. 63.

These are arranged in lines not unlike those described by Captain Bayfield on the Labrador coast. They are undoubtedly the result of ice-transportation, the process being still going on. At the head of Force Bay are traces of an ancient moraine.

NOTE 14, p. 65.

My note-books contain many instances of the facility with which the Esquimaux dog relapses into a savage state. There is an island near the Holsteinberg fiords where such animals hunt the reindeer in packs, and are habitually shot by the natives.

NOTE 15, p. 68.

See page 323 and Appendix No. VI. For comparisons of difference of longitude between my own and Captain Inglefield's surveys, consult any point on Admiralty charts north of 78° 37′,—the latitude of Rensselaer Harbor, which was regarded as our prime meridian.

NOTE 16, p. 71.

This valley is flanked by terraced beach-lines: its background is the seat of an ancient moraine worthy of study.

NOTE 17, p. 77.

A case of similar peril is reported by Captain Cator, of H. B. M. steamer Intrepid. His vessel was carried bodily up the inclined face of an iceberg, and, after being high and dry out of water, launched again without injury. See "Nautical Magazine."

Note 18, p. 81.

The observations of our parties extended the range of the musk-ox (*Ovibos moschatus*) to the Greenland coast. None of us saw a living specimen; but the great number of skeletons, their state of preservation and probable foot-tracks, when taken in conjunction with the information of the Esquimaux, leave me no room to doubt but that these animals have been recent visitors.

Note 19, p. 82.

See "Examination of Plants," by Elias Durand, Esq., in Appendix No. XVIII.

Note 20, p. 87.

Except for cases of sudden effort and not calling for continued exertion or exposure, grog was not looked upon as advisable. Hot coffee was a frequent and valuable stimulus.

Note 21, p. 93.

The tenacity with which the ice-belt adheres to the rocks is well shown by its ability to resist the overflow of the tides. The displacement thus occasioned is sometimes, however, so excessive that the entire mass is floated away, carrying with it the fragments which had been luted to it from below, as well as those incorporated with its mass by deposits from above.

Note 22, p. 95.

A reindeer-skull found in the same gorge was completely fossilized. That the snow-waters around Rensselaer Harbor held large quantities of carbonate of lime in solution was proved not only by the tufaceous deposit which incrusted the masses, but by actual tests. The broken-down magnesian limestones of the upper plateaux readily explain this.

Note 23, p. 97.

The several minor streams which make up Mary Minturn River run nearly parallel with the axis of the interior glacier from which they take their origin, and unite in a single canal without intermediate lakes.

Note 24, p. 99.

The flower-growth of the valley of Mary Minturn River proves that certain favoring influences—especially those of reverberation of heat from the rocks and continued distillation of water through protecting mosses—give a local richness to the Arctic flora which seems to render it independent of arbitrary zones. No less than five Crucifers were collected at this favored spot, two species of Draba, the Cochlearia fenestrata, Hesperis pallasii, and Vesicaria arctica. The poppy grew at a little distance from the stream; and, still further shaded by the rocks, was the Oxyria digyna in such quantities as to afford bountiful salads to our party. The immediate neighborhood of the water-course presented a beautiful carpet of Lychnis and Ranunculus, varied by Dryas octopetala and Potentilla pulchella growing from beds of richest moss. For the determination of the species of these plants I am indebted to Mr. Durand: it was not until my return and my plants had been subjected to his able analysis that I was aware that Vesicaria was upon my list. I had never seen it north of Egedesminde, latitude 68°; yet both it and Hesperis are also among Dr. Hayes's collections.

NOTE 25, p. 101.

The lines of junction of floes serve rudely as an index to the direction of drift. The hummocks are generally at right angles to the axis of drift.

NOTE 26, p. 110.

The dimensions and general structure of the sledge are of vital importance for a successful journey. Very slight, almost imperceptible, differences cause an increase of friction more than equal to the draught of an additional man or dog. The curvature of the runners—that of minimum resistance—depends upon elements not easily computed: it is best determined experimentally. The "Faith"—which for the heavy and snow-covered ice of Smith's Straits was the best sledge I ever saw—differed somewhat from the excellent model of Captain McClintock, furnished me by the British Admiralty: its increased breadth of runner kept it from burying in the snow; while its lesser height made it stronger and diminished the strain upon the lashings. I subjoin the dimensions of two nearly similar sledges,—Mr. McClintock's and my own :—

McClintock's.	ft.	in.	*The Faith.*	ft.	in.
Length of runner	13	0	Length of runner	13	0
Height of do.	0	11½	Height of do.	0	8
Horizontal width of all parts	0	2¾	Horizontal width of rail	0	2¼
			" " base of runner	0	3¼
			" " other parts	0	2
Thickness of all parts	0	1¼	Thickness of all parts	0	1¼
Length, resting on a plane surface	5	0	Length, resting on a plane surface	6	0
Cross-bars, six in number, making a width of	3	0	Cross-bars, five in number, making a width of	3	8

The shoeing of the large sledges of English expeditions was of burnished one-eighth-inch iron; our own were of annealed three-sixteenths-inch steel, as light as possible, to admit of slightly countersunk rivets. Seal-skin lashings were used for the cross-bars, applied wet; the wood was hickory and oak, not the Canada elm used by the Lancaster Sound parties.

A sledge thus constructed, with a canvas cover on which to place and confine the cargo, would readily load, according to the state of the travel, from one hundred and fifty to two hundred pounds per man. The "Faith" has carried sixteen hundred pounds.

NOTE 27, p. 113.

These boats were not well adapted to their purpose, their bulk being too great for portability. The casing of basket-willow I regard as better than a wooden frame or distension by simple inflation with air. No sledge, however, should be without the India-rubber floats or portable boat of Lieutenant Halkett.

NOTE 28, p. 114.

This is quoted from the original report of the party. There are no syenites upon this plain: the rocks are entirely destitute of hornblende. They are of the same bottom-series as the fiords about our harbor, highly feldspathic and sometimes porphyritic granites passing into coarse gneisses.

NOTE 29, p. 117.

One end of the cord represented a fixed point, by being anchored to the bottom; the free end, with an attached weight, rose and fell with the brig, and recorded its motion on the grooved circumference of a wheel. This method was liable to objections; but it was corrected by daily soundings. The movements of our vessel partook of those of the floe in which she was imbedded, and were unaccompanied by any lateral deviation.

NOTE 30, p. 118.

For methods of observation, see Appendix No. XI. Vol. II.

NOTE 31, p. 122.

The almost incomprehensible use of these small kennels as dormitories was afterward satisfactorily ascertained from the Esquimaux themselves. They are spoken of as far south as Karsuk, (near Upernavik,) and are at this moment resorted to in case of arrivals of hunting-parties, &c. Unlike the Siberian pologs, they are not enclosed by a second chamber. The hardy tenant, muffled in furs, at a temperature of —60° is dependent for warmth upon his own powers and the slow conduction of the thick walls.

NOTE 32, p. 126.

Hair evidently from the musk-ox was found near Refuge Inlet. The last of these animals seen by the Esquimaux was in the late spring of 1850, near Cape George Russell. Here Metek saw a group of six.

NOTE 33, p. 138.

For an account of the destruction of provision-depôts by bears, see the reports of the singularly efficient sledge-operations of Commodore Austin, (Parliamentary Blue-Book.) The wolverine, (*Gulo luscus,*) the most destructive animal to Arctic caches, is not found north of Lancaster Sound. So ·destructive are the bears about Peabody Bay, that nothing but a metallic cylinder with conical terminations gave any protection against their assaults.

NOTE 34, p. 155.

The liquids subjected to these low temperatures were for the most part the ethers and volatile oils. The results will be published elsewhere.

PAGE 158.

Hydrophobia. The caption at the head of the page is not intended to affirm the existence of this disease in this high North. Some of the tetanoid symptoms attendant upon tonic spasm closely simulated it; but the disease, strictly speaking, is unknown there.

NOTE 35, p. 220.

There is a local reservoir of interior ice around Cape Alexander and toward Cape Saumaurez, which may be, however, a process from the great *mer de glace* of the interior.

NOTES 36 to 41 inclusive, pp. 221, 222.

I intended to refer by these numerals to a somewhat enlarged summary of the geognostic characters of this coast; but I find it impracticable to condense my observations into the narrow limits which have been reserved for these notes. Like many other topics of more scientific than popular interest, they may find a place in the Official Reports upon which I am now engaged under the orders of the Navy Department.

NOTE 42, p. 222

Where this face came in contact with opposing masses of rocks,—as at islands or at the sides of its issuing-trough,—abrupt fractures and excessive crevassing indicated the resistance to the passage of the ice-stream. I think I have mentioned a small island near the cache that was already partially buried by the advance of the glacier and the discharged fragments at its base.

NOTE 43, p. 225.

Our surveys give four points for the determination of the trend of this interior *mer de glace*:—1. Up the fiord of Marshall Bay; 2. In the interior, about lat. 78° 32′, as observed by Dr. Hayes; 3. South of Force Bay; 4. Near Etah. These give the axis of the stream nearly due north and south.

NOTE 44, p. 226.

Australia, between Bass and Torres Straits, measures about sixteen hundred miles.

NOTE 45, p. 227.

Looking upon the glaciers of Greenland as canals of exudation, for the most part at right angles to the general axis of the interior ice, we have a system of discharge, both on the east and west coasts, coincident in direction with the fiords, which themselves bear a fixed relation to the coast-line. This coast-line, however, having now been traced to its northern face, analogy would sustain the view of the central *mer de glace* finding its exit into an unknown Polar space.

I have spoken of Humboldt Glacier as connecting the two continents of America and Greenland. The expression requires explanation:—

All of Arctic America north of Dolphin and Union Straits is broken up into large insular masses, and may be considered as a vast archipelago. While, therefore, a liberal definition would assign these land-masses to the American continent, Grinnell Land cannot strictly be regarded as part of the continent of America. Washington Land seems, in physical characters and position, to be a sort of middle ground, which, according to the different views of geographers, may be assigned indifferently to either of the two great divisions. From the American land-masses it is separated by a channel of but thirty-five miles in width; and, at this point, Greenland, losing its peninsular character, partakes in general character with the land-masses of the West. A water-channel not wider than Lancaster Sound or Murchison's, which have heretofore not been regarded as breaking a geographical continuity, is all that intervenes.

NOTE 46, p. 232.

Extract from Report of I. I. Hayes, M.D., Surgeon to Expedition.

"You were carried to the brig nearly insensible by the more able men of the party, and so swollen from scurvy as to be hardly recognisable. I believe that a few hours' more exposure would have terminated your life, and at the time regarded your ultimate recovery as nearly hopeless."

NOTE 47, p. 242.

This term is applied to the circular hole which the fetid seal (*P. hispida*) constructs in the younger floes, and through which it finds access to the air and sun. The term *atluk* is applied also to the seal itself when killed beside its retreat. I find I have sometimes written the word as *attuk*. He who has attempted the orthography of an unwritten language will excuse the variation.

NOTE 48, p. 290.

The dovekie (*Uria grylle*) not unfrequently winters among the open ice to the southward. I killed a specimen in full winter plumage, in the middle pack of Baffin's Bay, late in February.

NOTE 49, p. 299.

The immediate appearance of drifting ice under the influence of winds is well known to Arctic navigators; and this entire absence of it during a continued gale from the north seems to indicate either a far-extended open water, or ice so solid and unbroken as to be incapable of motion.

NOTE 50, p. 304.

The frequency with which the seal—both the hispid and bearded species—occurred in the open channel may explain why it is so favorite a resort of the white bear. No less than five of these animals were counted, and two were killed. They seemed, however, generally to seek the inland ravines which were the breeding-grounds of fowl. No marine life was reported, unless a small fish—probably a cottus—which was caught by the kittiwake gull; yet, from the bones of cetaceans found on the beach, I do not doubt but that both the sea-unicorn (*Monodon monoceros*) and white whale frequent the channel.

The bird-life was more extended. I throw into tabular form a list of the

Birds seen about the Open Water.

Brent goose	Anas bernicla	Flying diagonally across channel to N. and E.
Eider-duck	S. mollissima	In great numbers in southern part of Kennedy Channel.
King-duck	S. spectabilis	Flying inland up Morris Bay; probably breeding.
Dovekie	Uria grylle	Breeding in rock N. of Cape Jackson; very numerous.
Arctic petrel	Procellaria glacialis	North of Cape Jefferson and out to seaward.
Ivory-gull	Larus eburneus	Same.
An ash-backed gull, (unrecognised)	L. argentalus?	Same.
Burgomaster	L. glaucus	Southern parts of channel.
Kittiwake	L. trydactylus	Same.
Sea-swallow	Sterna arctica	Breeding in great numbers S. of Cape Jefferson.

The season was not sufficiently advanced to allow me to judge of the characters of the flora; but both Morton and Hans think that the growth was much more forward than that of our own harbor. They describe the recesses of Lafayette Bay as rivalling in richness the growths of Minturn River. They brought back no collections; and it was only by carefully comparing known specimens found about Rensselaer Bay with those seen and recognised to the north by Hans that I was able to determine upon a certain number of plants. Some others—after availing myself of the advice of my friend Mr. Durand, to whose courtesy as well as patient skill I am glad to bear tribute—I have not felt myself at liberty to insert in this limited list. This enumeration must not be regarded as an index of the actual vegetation; but, with every reservation for the imperfect observation and the early season, I am not satisfied that the flora of Kennedy Channel indicates a milder climate to the north of our winter harbor. I subjoin my scanty list:—

Ranunculus nivalis...........	In quantities about the mossy slopes of Lafayette Bay.
Papaver nudicaule............	Well advanced and recognisable.
Hesperis pallasii..............	Found in Lafayette Bay; the silique recognised by Mr. Durand.
Draba............................	Two forms, (one probably alpina,) associated with recognisable lychnis and cerastium.
Saxifraga oppositifolia......	Beginning to show itself.
" flagellaris.........	This latter in dried state.
Oxyria digynus	In quantities adequate for food.
Salix uva ursi............... " arctica................	} Seen dried and budding along the channel.

If we add to these three grasses, poa, alopecurus, and festuca, with the usual Arctic cryptogams, we have, except in the anomalous case of Hesperis, no plants not common to Lower Smith's Straits and Green's Channel.

Note 51, p. 308.

These remarks will be expanded elsewhere. The presence of marine shells (*Saxicava* and *Astarte*) on the upper terrace-levels about Dallas Bay, and similar facts noticed by Sir Edward Belcher and the Barrow's Straits observers, leave little room to doubt the conclusion. But I do not cite the elevation of the coast, either as deduced from the Esquimaux habitations or otherwise, except as it illustrates changes in the relations which the water and ice once bore to each other. I do not connect it with the question of an open sea.

Note 52, p. 309.

This sledge-runner was of wood and bone together, with holes perforated for the seal-skin lashings used by the natives to scarf their work. It affords unmistakable evidence either of a current-drift and occasional open water from the sound, or of the former presence of natives to the north,—this latter implying competent hunting-resources.

Note 53, p. 309.

A popular analysis of these conditions may be seen in Professor Forbes's recent work on the glaciers of Norway. We cannot refer this open water to any analogous causes with those which explain the other polynias on this estuary. Davis Straits, off Cape Walsingham, where the channel narrows to one hundred and twenty miles, and Smith's Straits, which between Capes Isabella and Ohlsen have a breadth of only thirty-six, are at those points clogged with immense fields of ice, extending in the earlier season from shore to shore and arresting the passage of the drift from above. It is easy to explain the occurrence of polynia below these two barriers,—the North Water of the whalers and the upper water which I met in my unsuccessful effort to reach Beechy Island. But between Capes Barrow and Jackson, where Kennedy Channel is contracted to thirty-five miles across, and where the ices from above, if there were such, ought to be arrested as in the other two cases, we found this open water; while below it, in Peabody Bay, where analogies would suggest the probability of another polynia, we found a densely-impacted solid mass. I do not see how, independently of direct observation, this state of facts could be explained without supposing an iceless area to the farther North.

How far this may extend,—whether it does or does not communicate with a Polar basin,—we are without facts to determine. I would say, however, as a cautionary check to some theories in connection with such an open basin, that the influence of rapid tides and currents in destroying ice by abrasion can hardly be realized by those who have not witnessed their action. It is not uncommon to see such tidal sluices remain open in the midst of winter. Such, indeed, are the polynia of the Russians, the stromhols of the Greenland Danes, and the familiar "open holes" of the whalers.

Note 54, p. 322.

I regret that, after a careful study of the work of my predecessor, Captain Inglefield, I am unable to make his landmarks on the E. coast of Greenland correspond with my own. The few short hours spent by the "Isabel" on Smith's Straits, and the many difficulties which we know to be attendant upon a hurried survey, readily account for discrepancies of bearing and position. A sketch inserted by Captain Inglefield, in his narrative at page 70, locates Cape Frederick VII. as the first headland to the N. of the second indentation, which, according to my survey, should be "Force Bay." But the absence of Pekiutlik, (Littleton Island,) which is unmistakably prominent as a feature of the coast, embarrasses me. My sketches of this coast are in detail.

Note 55, p. 336.

The entire coast between Whale Sound and Cape Alexander is studded with small glaciers. Some of these are of Saussure's second order,—mere troughs upon the flanks of the coast-ridge; but, for the most part, they are connected with interior *mers de glace*, and are urged forward in their descent by the glacial accumulations of large areas. The *mer de glace* which occupies the central plateau of Northumberland is completely isolated and washed by the sea, and is necessarily dependent for its increments upon the atmospheric precipitation of a very limited surface; yet it sustains in its discharge no less than seven glaciers,—perhaps more,—one of which is half a mile in diameter by two hundred feet in depth. It is a startling instance of the redundance of Arctic ice-growth.

NOTE 56, p. 430.

This propensity of the bear—in fact, of all predatory animals—is alluded to by Scoresby and others. It was curiously shown in the March journey of 1854, when a woollen shirt of Mr. McGary's was actually torn to shreds and twisted into coils.

The subjoined are given as aids to physical inquiry on the part of future travellers:—

Directions to Sites of Rensselaer Harbor.

1. The observatory was placed upon the northernmost of the rocky group of islets that formed our harbor. It is seventy-six English feet from the highest and northernmost salient point of this island, in a direction S. 14° E., or in one with said point and the S.E. projection of the southernmost islet of the group.

2. A natural face of gneiss rock formed the western wall of the observatory. A crevice in this rock has been filled with melted lead, in the centre of which is a copper bolt. Eight feet from this bolt, and in the direction indicated by the crevice, stood the magnetometer. This direction is given in case of local disturbance from the nature of the surrounding rocks.

3. On the highest point of the island mentioned in paragraph 1 is a deeply-chiselled arrow-mark filled with lead. This is twenty-nine feet above the mean tidal plane of our winter quarters for the years 1853–54. The arrow points to a mark on a rocky face denoting the lowest tide of the season: both of these are referred by sextant to known points.

4. In an enlarged crack five feet due west of above arrow is a glass jar containing documents. (See p. 345.)

5. A cairn calls attention to these marks: nothing is placed within it.

NOTE.—The author is not responsible for the accuracy of the sketches on pages 291 and 300, the rough original sketches having been modified by the artist.

END OF VOL. I.